Critically Impaired
End of Life Decisior

Decisions to withdraw or withhold life-sustaining treatment are contentious and offer difficult moral dilemmas to both medical practitioners and the judiciary. This issue is exacerbated when the patient is unable to exercise autonomy and is entirely dependent on the will of others.

This book focuses on the legal and ethical complexities surrounding end of life decisions for critically impaired and extremely premature infants. Neera Bhatia explores arbitrary decisions to withdraw or withhold life-sustaining treatment from critically impaired infants and addresses the controversial question: Which lives are too expensive to treat? Bringing to bear such key issues as clinical guidance, public awareness and resource allocation, the book provides a rational approach to end of life decision making, where decisions to withdraw or withhold treatment may trump other competing interests.

The book will be of great interest and use to scholars and students of bioethics and medical law, and medical practitioners.

Neera Bhatia is a Lecturer at the Deakin University School of Law, Australia.

Biomedical Law and Ethics Library

Series Editor: Sheila A. M. McLean

Scientific and clinical advances, social and political developments and the impact of healthcare on our lives raise profound ethical and legal questions. Medical law and ethics have become central to our understanding of these problems, and are important tools for the analysis and resolution of problems – real or imagined.

In this series, scholars at the forefront of biomedical law and ethics contribute to the debates in this area, with accessible, thought-provoking, and sometimes controversial, ideas. Each book in the series develops an independent hypothesis and argues cogently for a particular position. One of the major contributions of this series is the extent to which both law and ethics are utilised in the content of the books, and the shape of the series itself.

The books in this series are analytical, with a key target audience of lawyers, doctors, nurses and the intelligent lay public.

Available titles:

Human Fertilisation and Embryology
Reproducing regulation
Kirsty Horsey and Hazel Biggs

Intention and Causation in Medical Non-killing
The impact of criminal law concepts on euthanasia and assisted suicide
Glenys Williams

Impairment and Disability
Law and Ethics at the Beginning and End of Life
Sheila McLean and Laura Williamson

Bioethics and the Humanities
Attitudes and Perceptions
Robin Downie and Jane Macnaughton

Defending the Genetic Supermarket
The law and ethics of selecting the next generation
Colin Gavagham

The Harm Paradox
Tort law and the unwanted child in an era of choice
Nicolette Priaulx

Assisted Dying
Reflections on the Need for Law Reform
Sheila McLean

Medicine, Malpractice and Misapprehensions
V.H. Harpwood

Euthanasia, Ethics and the Law
From the conflict to compromise
Richard Huxtable

The Best Interests of the Child in Healthcare
Sarah Elliston

Values in Medicine
What are we really doing to patients?
Donald Evans

Autonomy, Consent and the Law
Sheila A.M. McLean

Healthcare Research Ethics and Law
Regulation, review and responsibility
Hazel Biggs

The Body in Bioethics
Alastair V. Campbell

Genomic Negligence
An interest in autonomy as the basis for novel negligence claims
generated by genetic technology
Victoria Chico

Health Professionals and Trust
The cure for healthcare law and policy
Mark Henaghan

Medical Ethics in China
A transcultural interpretation
Jing-Bao Nie

Law, Ethics and Compromise at the Limits of Life
To treat or not to treat?
Richard Huxtable

Regulating Pre-Implantation Genetic Diagnosis
A comparative and theoretical analysis
Sheila A.M McLean and Sarah Elliston

Bioethics
Methods, theories, domains
Marcus Düwell

Human Population Genetic Research in Developing Countries
The Issue of Group Protection
Yue Wang

Coercive Care
Rights, law and policy
Bernadette McSherry and Ian Freckelton

Saviour Siblings
A relational approach to the welfare of the child in selective reproduction
Michelle Taylor-Sands

Human Population Genetic Research in Developing Countries
The issue of group protection
Yue Wang

Stem Cell Research and the Collaborative Regulation of Innovation
Sarah Devaney

Critically Impaired Infants and End of Life Decision Making
Resource Allocation and Difficult Decisions
Neera Bhatia

Forthcoming titles include:

The Jurisprudence of Pregnancy
Concepts of conflict, persons and property
Mary Neal

Regulating Risk
Values in health research governance
Shawn Harmon

The Umbilical Cord Blood Controversies in Medical Law
Karen Devine

The Legitimacy of Medical Treatment
What Role for the Medical Exception?
Sara Fovargue and Alexandra Mullock

Revisiting Landmark Cases in Medical Law
Shaun D. Pattinson

Revisiting the Regulation of Human Fertilisation and Embryology
Kirsty Horsey

The Ethical and Legal Consequences of Posthumous Reproduction
Lewis Browne

Pioneering Healthcare Law
Essays in Honour of Margaret Brazier
Catherine Stanton, Sarah Devaney, Anne-Marree Farrell and Alexandra Mullock

Birth, Harm and the Role of Distributive Justice
Burdens, Blessings, Need and Desert
Alasdair Maclean

About the Series Editor
Professor Sheila McLean is International Bar Association Professor of Law and Ethics in Medicine and Director of the Institute of Law and Ethics in Medicine at the University of Glasgow.

Critically Impaired Infants and End of Life Decision Making

Resource Allocation and Difficult Decisions

Neera Bhatia

Routledge
Taylor & Francis Group

LONDON AND NEW YORK

First published 2015
by Routledge

2 Park Square, Milton Park, Abingdon, Oxon OX14 4RN
711 Third Avenue, New York, NY 10017, USA

Routledge is an imprint of the Taylor & Francis Group, an informa business

First issued in paperback 2017

British Library Cataloguing in Publication Data
A catalogue record for this book is available from the British Library

Library of Congress Cataloging-in-Publication Data
Bhatia, Neera, author.
   Critically impaired infants and end of life decision making : resource
   allocation and difficult decisions / Neera Bhatia.
      pages cm.—(Biomedical law and ethics library)
   Based on author's thesis (doctoral - Deakin University, School of Law
   (Australia), 2014), under the title: Medico-legal decision making for
   incapacitated neonates.
   Includes bibliographical references and index.
   ISBN 978-1-138-82848-3 (hbk)—ISBN 978-1-315-73838-3 (ebk)
   1. Neonatal intensive care—Law and legislation—Australia.   2. Neonatal
   intensive care—Law and legislation—Great Britain.   3. Terminal care—Law
   and legislation—Australia.   4. Terminal care—Law and legislation—Great
   Britain.   5. Neonatal intensive care—Decision making.   6. Terminal
   care—Decision making.   I. Title.
   K4367.P43B48 2015
   344.4104'1970832—dc23   2014046581

ISBN: 978-1-138-82848-3 (hbk)
ISBN: 978-1-138-70477-0 (pbk)

Typeset in Baskerville
by Keystroke, Station Road, Codsall, Wolverhampton

For my parents
Harmesh and Leila

Contents

Acknowledgements   xv
List of abbreviations   xvii
Table of cases   xix
Table of statutes   xxi
Table of legislative instruments   xxiii

1 Introduction   1

1.1   Medicine, technology and the law   1
1.2   Concepts of life and death and the law   2
1.3   Individual autonomy   3
1.4   The importance of end of life decision making for extremely premature and critically impaired infants   4
1.5   Historical development of neonatology   6
1.6   The need to discuss the allocation of finite healthcare resources and infants   7
1.7   Purpose and structure of the book   8
1.8   Conclusion   10
1.9   References   10

2 The effectiveness of the best interests principle   13

2.1   Sanctity of life perspectives   13
     Judeo-Christian tradition   13
     Greco-Roman principles and the Hippocratic Oath   15
     Declaration of Geneva   17
2.2   The best interests principle and the concept of futility   19
2.3   Early case law involving infants from the UK   21
2.4   Legal and ethical challenges in the English seminal case of Airedale NHS Trust v Bland   26
     Sanctity of life   27
     Substituted judgment test   28
     Reliance on the medical profession   29
     Acts and omissions   32
     Does withdrawal of nutrition and hydration amount to starving to death?   34

2.5 *Selected UK cases involving impaired infants 36*

2.6 *The turn of the millennium:* Re A (conjoined twins) *41*

2.7 *Recent decisions: balance sheet of burdens and benefits 45*

2.8 *Early Australian cases involving impaired infants 54*

2.9 Re Marion *and the best interests principle in Australia 57*

2.10 Re Marion (No 2), *the best interests principle and the* Family Law Rules 2004 *60*

2.11 *Recent cases involving impaired infants 61*

2.12 *The effectiveness of the best interests principle 66*

2.13 *Conclusion 67*

2.14 *References 67*

3 Non-uniformity in clinical guidelines   73

3.1 *The threshold of viability 73*

3.2 *The very nature of clinical guidelines 75*

3.3 *Clinical guidelines: United Kingdom 75*

3.4 *Royal College of Paediatrics and Child Health:* Withholding or Withdrawing Life Sustaining Treatment in Children: A Framework for Practice *76*

3.5 *British Medical Association:* Withholding and Withdrawing Life-prolonging Medical Treatment: Guidance for Decision Making *79*

3.6 *General Medical Council:* Treatment and Care Towards the End of Life: Good Practice in Decision Making *81*

3.7 *The UK EPICure studies 82*
EPICure Study 1: 1995 82
EPICure Study 2: 2006 83

3.8 *British Association of Perinatal Medicine:* Management of Babies Born Extremely Preterm at Less Than 26 Weeks of Gestation: A Framework for Clinical Practice at the Time of Birth *85*

3.9 *Nuffield Council on Bioethics:* Critical Care Decisions in Fetal and Neonatal Medicine: Ethical Issues, *2006: a missed opportunity for the UK? 86*

3.10 *Clinical guidelines Australia: the Royal Australasian College of Physicians: Paediatrics and Child Health Division:* Decision Making at the End of Life in Infants, Children and Adolescents *(2008) 89*

3.11 *Australian guidelines: each hospital to its own 91*

3.12 *Perinatal care at the borderlines of viability: a consensus statement based on New South Wales and Australian Capital Territory consensus workshop (2005): another missed opportunity? 92*

3.13 *Academic discussion in this area 95*

3.14 *The need for uniform guidelines 97*

3.15 *Conclusion 98*

3.15 *References 99*

4   The role, impact and importance of key caregivers and decision makers   102

4.1   *Parents: conflicting interests and views 104*
       The influence of media, development of medical
          science and technology 105
       Religious and cultural beliefs 108
       The common denominator: hope 109
       Parental ethnicity 110
       Infants' pain and suffering 113
       The 'dying process' 114
       Disability: perceptions and realities 116
       Relationships of trust and confidence with the medical team 118
       Do parents carry guilt and the burden of responsibility
          in decision making? 120
       Parents as decision makers: fact or fiction?   124

4.2   *Doctors: conflicting interests and views 126*
       Religious beliefs and cross-country attitudes 127
       Doctors' perceptions of death, disability and
          decision making 129
       Different parents, different treatment: are parents treated
          differently by doctors? 132
       Are pre-term infants treated differently to other patients? 133
       The framing effect 134
       The roster lottery 136
       Should doctors be considered as functionaries? 137

4.3   *The judiciary: over-reliance on medical opinion 140*

4.4   *Conclusion 143*

4.5   *References 144*

5   Theories of distributive justice: healthcare and resource allocation for extremely premature and critically impaired infants   150

5.1   *Ethical considerations in medical decision making for impaired infants 150*
       Autonomy 150
       Beneficence 151
       Non-maleficence 151
       Justice (distributive) 151

5.2   *Theories of distributive justice: extremely premature and critically
          impaired infants and resource allocation 152*
       Consequentialist theory: utilitarianism and extremely
          premature and critically impaired infants 153
       Deontology: rights theory and extremely premature
          and critically impaired infants 155

Egalitarian theory and extremely premature and critically
impaired infants 157

5.3   *Three theories, one conclusion: resource allocation should be
a cardinal consideration in end of life decision making for extremely
premature and critically impaired infants 158*

5.4   *Conclusion 159*

5.5   *References 159*

**6   Resource allocation: an objective approach in
end of life decision making for extremely
premature and critically impaired infants**   161

6.1   *Cost versus benefit 162*

6.2   *Quality adjusted life years (QALY) 165*

6.3   *QALY and impaired infants 166*

6.4   *The efficacy of the neonatal intensive care unit (NICU) 169*
Insights from the Unites States 169
Australian and UK NICUs 172

6.5   *The profitability of the NICU 174*

6.6   *Health economics beyond the NICU 176*
Impact on the wider family 179
Opportunity cost 180

6.7   *Australian and UK economic budget pressures 183*

6.8   *The National Disability Insurance Scheme (NDIS) Act in Australia 185*

6.9   *Technology: doing more harm than good? 189*

6.10 *Determining the price and value of life: a common practice? 193*
Road death tolls 193
Triage/emergency room categories 194
The Australian Pharmaceutical Benefits Scheme (PBS) 195

6.11 *The role of the judiciary in resource allocation discussion 196*

6.12 *Conclusion 199*

6.13 *References 200*

7   Other observations and concluding remarks   207

7.1   *An insight from the Netherlands and Belgium: Groningen Protocol:
permissible neonatal euthanasia and beyond 207*

7.2   *Prevention rather than cure 209*

7.3   *Increases in educational awareness and reduction of poverty 210*

7.4   *Prenatal advanced directive 211*

7.5   *Parliamentary intervention 212*

7.6   *Concluding remarks 213*

7.7   *References 216*

Index   218

Acknowledgements

This book began its life as a doctoral thesis, and I thank Deakin University School of Law for the opportunity some years ago to relocate to Australia and initially pursue my PhD, which later transitioned to a lectureship within the school. I am grateful to my colleagues and friends within the school for their continued support.

In particular, I am indebted to my supervisor, Dean and Head of School, Professor Mirko Bagaric, for his continued guidance, encouragement and valuable feedback from the doctoral thesis process through to this book.

Finally, I thank my family, who, although thousands of miles away in the UK, have never allowed me to feel their absence. I thank them for their continued support and belief in me.

Parts of this book have drawn from previously published work. They have been reprinted by permission from the relevant publishers. I acknowledge permission to use the following papers and I thank the editors and publishers for permission to use the materials.

Parts of Chapter 2 of this book have previously been published in the article 'Best interests of neonates: time for a fundamental re-think' was first published by Thomson Reuters in the *Journal of Law and Medicine* (2013) 20 JLM 852. For all subscription inquiries, please phone, from Australia: 1300 304 195, from overseas: +61 2 8587 7980 or online at www.thomsonreuters.com.au/catalogue. The official PDF version of this article can also be purchased separately from Thomson Reuters.

Parts of Chapter 3 have been previously published with kind permission from Springer Science + Business Media: *Journal of Bioethical Inquiry*, 'Deficiencies and missed opportunities to formulate clinical guidelines in Australia for withholding or withdrawing life-sustaining treatment in severely disabled and impaired infants' 10.1007/s11673-014-9572-x (2014), Neera Bhatia and James Tibballs.

Any errors in the book are, of course, mine alone.

List of abbreviations

ACT	Australian Capital Territory
BAPM	British Association of Perinatal Medicine
BMA	British Medical Association
CEMACH	Confidential Enquiry into Maternal and Child Health
ELBW	extremely low birth weight
GDP	gross domestic product
IQ	intelligence quotient
IVF	in-vitro fertility
LST	life-sustaining treatment
NCOB	Nuffield Council on Bioethics
NDIS	National Disability Insurance Scheme
NHS	National Health Service
NICE	National Institute of Clinical Excellence
NICU	neonatal intensive care unit
NSW	New South Wales
PDA	patent ductus arteriosus
PVS	permanent vegetative state
QALY	quality adjusted life years
QoL	quality of life
RACP	Royal Australasian College of Physicians
RCOG	Royal College of Obstetricians and Gynaecologists
RCPCH	Royal College of Paediatrics and Child Health
TAC	Transport Accident Commission
UK	United Kingdom

Table of cases

Australia

Baby D (No 2) [2011] Fam CA 176, 61–2, 63, 73
Baby M (Victorian State Coroner's Office, Record of Investigation into Death, Case No 3149/89, 29 October 1991), 6, 51–5
Department of Health and Community Services v JWB and SMB (1992) 175 CLR 218, 57, 140
Northridge v Central Sydney Area Health Authority (2000) 50 NSWLR 549, 57
Mabo v Queensland (No 2) (1992) 175 CLR 1, 196
Re BWV; Ex parte Gardner (2003) 7 VR 487,
Re F: F v F (Unreported, Supreme Court of Victoria, Vincent, J, 2 July 1986), 54–5
Re Marion (1990) 14 Fam LR 427, 20, 57–9
Re Marion (No 2) see Secretary, Department of Health and Community Services v JWB and SMB
Re MC [2003] QGAAT 13, 57
Secretary, Department of Health and Community Services v JWB and SMB (1992) 175 CLR 218, 20, 57, 60–1, 140
TS & TD v Sydney Children's Hospital [2012] NSWSC 1609, 8, 63–66, 73, 121

European Court of Human Rights

Glass v United Kingdom [2004] ECHR 103 (9 March 2004), 45

New Zealand

Auckland Area Health Board v Attorney General [1993] NZLR 235, 57

United Kingdom

A National Health Service v D [2000] 2 FLR 677, 141
Airedale NHS Trust v Bland [1993] AC 789, 2, 25, 26–36, 98, 199
An NHS Trust v MB [2006] EWHC 507 (Fam) (15 March 2006), 50–3

An NHS Trust v OT [2009] EWCA Civ 409 (14 May 2009), 45–6

Bolam v Friern Hospital Management Committee [1957] 1 WLR 582, 29–30, 79, 98, 141, 194

Daborn v Bath Tramways Motor Co Pty Ltd v Smithey [1946] 2 All ER 333, 194

Dudley v Stephens (1884) 14 QBD 273, 44

F v West Berkshire Health Authority [1989] All ER 545, 20

NHS Trust v Baby X [2012] EWHC 2188 (Fam) (30 July 2012), 53

Portsmouth Hospital NHS Trust v Wyatt [2004] EWCA 2247 (Fam) (17 October 2004), 47–8, 49

R v Arthur (1981) 12 BMLR 1, 21–3, 24, 55, 82, 123, 125

R v Bournewood Community and Mental Health NHS Trust; Ex parte L [1998] All ER 289, 44

R v Cambridge Health Authority; Ex parte B [1995] 2 All ER 129, 197

R v Central Birmingham Health Authority; Ex parte Collier (Unreported, 6 January 1988), 197

R v Central Birmingham Health Authority; Ex parte Walker (1987) 3 BMLR 32, 197

R v Howe [1987] 1 AC 417, 44

Re A (children) (conjoined twins: surgical separation) [2000] 4 All ER 961, 41–4, 48

Re A (male sterilisation) [2000] 1 FLR 549, 49–50

Re B (a minor) (wardship: medical treatment) [1990] 3 All ER (CA) 927, 23–4, 55

Re Baby RB (a child) [2009] EWHC 3269 (Fam) (10 November 2009), 46–7

Re C (a minor) (1997) 40 BMLR 31 (Fam Div), 41, 98

Re C (a minor) (wardship: medical treatment) [1989] 2 All ER 782, 2, 36–7, 48, 64

Re J (a minor) (medical treatment) [1992] 2 FCR 73, 20

Re J (a minor) (wardship: medical treatment) [1990] 3 All ER 930, 37–9, 78, 187

Re J (a minor) (wardship: medical treatment) [1992] 4 All ER 614, 40

Re L (medical treatment: benefit) [2004] EWHC 2713 (Fam), 50

Re R (a minor) (wardship: medical treatment) [1991] 4 All ER 177, 3

United States of America

Schloendorff v New York Hospital (1914) 211 NY 125, 3

Table of statutes

Australia

Charter of Human Rights and Responsibilities Act 2006 (Vic)
s 9, 2, 17
Family Law Act 1975 (Cth)
s 4, 62
s 61B, 20
s 64B(2)(i), 62
s 67ZC, 58
Family Law Rules 2004, 60–6
Medical Treatment Act 1988 (Vic), 34
National Disability Insurance Scheme Act 2013 (Cth), 185, 188
s 22(1), 185
s 23, 185
s 24, 185–6
Powers of Attorney Act 1998 (Qld)
s 103, 189

United Kingdom

Abortion Act 1967, 19
Children Act 1989, 78
s 1, 20
s 3(1), 20
Criminal Code Bill 1897, 44
Human Rights Act 1998, 155
art 2, 2, 156

Table of legislative instruments

European Union

European Convention on Human Rights, 155
art 2, 155
art 5, 155
art 6, 155
art 8, 45

United Nations

United Nations Convention on the Rights of the Child, 2, 78
Universal Declaration of Human Rights, 155

1 Introduction

1.1 Medicine, technology and the law

During their lifespan, most human beings will require the intervention of medicine and possible care. In comparison with other areas of law, medical law profoundly affects people throughout their lives, from the period of pre-conception through to organ donation and the possible withdrawal or withholding of treatment at the end of life.[1]

Medical law is an area of research, practice and, increasingly, litigation. Over the past three decades, it has been the topic of considered and intense academic and legal discussion.[2] During the course of its development, issues that have required medical, ethical and legal debate have become increasingly complex, and topics that were once considered almost science fiction have now become a reality.[3] The rapid advancement of medicine has brought these issues to the fore, correspondingly increasing the public's expectations of medicine, in terms of both the simple treatment and management of illness, and the hope for a complete cure of illness.

Advancements in medical technology and research require a parallel development of the law governing ethics, policies and regulation of medical issues. In Australia and the United Kingdom, matters relating to issues such as human fertilisation and embryology, abortion and human tissue have been legislated. However, there continue to be areas governed under medical law that remain largely unlegislated.[4]

The traditional, conservative foundations of the law and its retrospective nature have observed the development of a widening gulf between the realised and possible achievements of medical science and any corresponding legislation. Put simply, the law has been unable to keep up and, consequently, medical law, while

---

1 Note, 'Developments in the Law: Medical Technology and the Law' (1989–1990) 103 *Harvard Law Review* 1519, 1524.
2 See, especially, Ian Kennedy, *Treat Me Right: Essays in Medical Law and Ethics* (Oxford University Press, 1991) 1–18.
3 One such example of this is the emergence and development of robotic surgery. See, e.g., Hockstein et al., 'A History of Robots: From Science Fiction to Surgical Robotics' (2007) 1(2) *Journal of Robotic Surgery* 113–118.
4 These include issues such as euthanasia and withdrawal or withholding of life-sustaining treatment in both adults and infants.

attempting to accommodate developments in medical science, remains an area with little statutory intervention, dominated largely by case law.

Evidence of this lag can be found in the seminal English case of *Airedale NHS Trust v Bland*, in which Lord Mustill poignantly recognised:

> [T]he law has been left behind by the rapid advances of medical technology. By starting with a clean slate the law would be freed from the piecemeal expedients to which courts throughout the common law world have been driven when trying to fill the gap between old law and new medicine.[5]

1.2 Concepts of life and death and the law

Western society, at least, has observed a shift from divinity to secularity in relation to the contemplation and understanding of concepts of life and death.[6] Once considered to be beyond human control and the preserve of religious leaders, matters of life and death have increasingly become the topic of regular discourse in hospitals and courtrooms as well as in less formal settings, such as talkback radio and internet blogs.[7] Issues surrounding life and death, such as the withdrawal or withholding of life-sustaining treatment, are often discussed in the public arena with individuals and those closely involved and affected by such decisions expressing strong and often divergent opinions.[8]

It is understandable that such issues and the ethical dilemmas they present arouse significant public interest. The finality and irreversibility of life and death decisions, such as the withdrawal or withholding of life-sustaining treatment, are of ultimate importance. It is critical that the law facilitates and guides these decisions in the most appropriate moral and ethical context. While moral, ethical, religious and sociological issues tend to dominate decisions of this kind, individual notions of rights, entitlements and personal autonomy have become a significant feature of western society and, consequently, have also influenced the development of medical ethics and law.

The recognition of a right to life and protection from harm is one of the main ideals in a civilised society, and thus it has the protection of law.[9] As appropriate,

---

5 *Airedale NHS Trust v Bland* [1993] 1 All ER 789. Balcombe LJ made a similar comment in *Re C (a minor) (wardship: medical treatment)* [1989] 2 All ER 782, 789, stating: 'This is a problem of a kind with which, as a result of advances in medical science, the courts in this and other jurisdictions are increasingly being faced.'

6 See, generally, Charles Taylor, *A Secular Age* (Harvard University Press, 2007).

7 See, e.g., Madison Park, 'Death at 25: Blogging the End of Life', *CNN*, 27 April 2010. http://edition.cnn.com/ 2010/HEALTH/04/27/blog.terminal.illness/index.html

8 The role, opinion and views of parents, doctors and the judiciary are discussed in Chapter 4.

9 For example, in the UK: Human Rights Act 1998, art 2: 'Everyone's right to life shall be protected by law. No one shall be deprived of his life intentionally save in the execution of a sentence of a court following his conviction of a crime for which this penalty is provided by law.' See, further, European Convention on Human Rights 1950. In Victoria, Australia, see Charter of Human Rights and Responsibilities Act 2006 s 9: 'Right to life – Every person has the right to life and has the right not to be arbitrarily deprived of life.'

the law will intervene when called upon in life and death situations. However, in many of these instances, the very right demanded is the right to die – a right that is not expressly endorsed by law in Australia or the UK.

Both medical practitioners and the judiciary are placed in a difficult moral dilemma when deciding the legal permissibility of decisions to withdraw or withhold medical treatment essential to maintaining the existence of an incapacitated patient. There are, inevitably, conflicts of opinion in this area, and it is fraught with moral quandaries.

1.3 Individual autonomy

Although the religious and philosophical tenets of western society underpin the principle of sanctity of life, there is no absolute medical obligation to preserve human life at all costs.[10] In matters of life and death, individual autonomy provides a basis for individuals to decide what shall or shall not be done to their person and this autonomy is often a cardinal and determinative principle. The seminal application of this principle can be found in *Schloendorff v New York Hospital*, in which Justice Cardozo famously stated: 'Every human being of adult years and sound mind has the right to determine what shall be done with his body; and a surgeon who performs without the patient's consent commits an assault.'[11]

Individual autonomy is often regarded as being of such importance that in many cases it surpasses competing cardinal virtues, including the sanctity of life, patient welfare, altruistic paternalism and medical best advice and opinion. However, no principle is always paramount and even patient autonomy will sometimes yield to other competing imperatives. Thus, voluntary euthanasia continues to remain illegal in most jurisdictions.[12]

Patient autonomy is an important and empowering principle for competent individuals. Infants cannot express their rights, values or choices. Thus, end of life decision making for this group is probably one of the most profound ethical, legal and medical minefields of our time.

As the model of the western demographic nation-state progresses, topics once considered taboo or intractable are increasingly being discussed and resolved. Life and death decisions concerning critically impaired infants are one issue that impacts families and wider society and requires considered attention.

---

10 An example of the sanctity of life principle can be found in Christianity, where it is recognised and founded on Genesis 9:6: 'Whoever sheds the blood of man, by man shall his blood be shed for God made man in his image.' The sanctity of life principle is considered in greater detail in Chapter 2.
11 *Schloendorff v New York Hospital* (1914) 211 NY 125, 126. In this case, the principle of personal autonomy concerned an adult individual's rights to and freedoms from non-consensual medical intervention. See, also, *Re R (a minor) (wardship: medical treatment)* [1991] 4 All ER 177 CA 183, in which Lord Donaldson stated: 'a doctor is not entitled to treat a patient without the consent of someone who is authorised to give that consent. If he does so, he will be liable in damages for trespass to the person and may be guilty of a criminal assault.'
12 Currently, the jurisdictions that allow lawful voluntary euthanasia include the Netherlands, Belgium, Luxembourg, Switzerland and the US states of Washington and Oregon.

1.4 The importance of end of life decision making for extremely premature and critically impaired infants

This book focuses primarily on decisions to withdraw or withhold life-sustaining treatment from extremely premature infants and those suffering severe disability or debilitating medical conditions.[13] These infants are often referred to as being born at the 'borderline of viability'. This is likely to be the earliest point at which an infant can be delivered alive with a possibility of survival, although most probably with life-sustaining treatment.[14]

For some statistical references, Australia recorded that 8.3% of live births were pre-term in 2011 – that is, infants born before the 37-week gestation period.[15] Of those born in 2011, 6.3% weighed under 2,500 grams.[16] Birth weights of premature infants vary from very low (2,500 grams) to extremely low (under 1,000 grams).[17] In 2011 Australia recorded that 0.9% of infants were born at 20–27-week gestation, a marginally higher percentage than those born at 28–31-week gestation (0.8%).

Figures from the UK highlight similar rates of premature birth: in 2011 7.2% of births were pre-term (born before 37-week gestation).[18] In 2011 1.3% of infants were born at fewer than 24 weeks' gestation.[19] As will be detailed in Chapter 3 onwards, although infants born at such extreme prematurity can now often be saved from death, they rarely avoid life without severe disability.

The information age has engendered public awareness of medical technology. Consequently, parents of extremely premature and critically ill infants are often encouraged by the use of the digital age to request life-sustaining treatment from medical practitioners to attempt to prevent their pre-term infant from death.[20]

---

13 This is generally at 23–25 weeks + 6 days' gestation. See, further, Nuffield Council on Bioethics, 'Background: Extremely Premature Babies. www.nuffieldbioethics.org/neonatal-medicine/neonatal-medicine-background-extremely-premature-babies. Although the primary focus of this book is on extremely premature infants, there is discussion, particularly in Chapters 2 and 4, on withdrawal or withholding of life-sustaining treatment decisions for critically ill infants outside of this remit – infants that are premature and critically impaired.

14 See Kimberley Pfeiffer, 'The Ethics of Caring: Expressing Humanity towards Babies Born at the Borderline of Viability' (2008) 20(02) *Bioethics Research Notes* 21, 21.

15 Z Li, R Zeki, L Hilder and E A Sullivan, 'Australia's Mothers and Babies' (Perinatal Statistics Series No 28, Australian Institute of Health and Welfare, 2011. www.aihw.gov.au/WorkArea/DownloadAsset.aspx?id=60129545698

16 Ibid.

17 Department of Health and Ageing, *Why is it Important?* Australian Government. www.health.gov.au/internet/publications/publishing.nsf/Content/oatsih-hpf-2012-toc~tier1~health-cond~101

18 See Tommy's, *Premature Birth Statistics*. www.tommys.org/page.aspx?pid=387. See, also, Office for National Statistics, *Preterm Births, Data*. www.ons.gov.uk/ons/publications/re-reference-tables.html? edition=tcm%3A77-50818

19 Ibid.

20 Extending this point further, the use of social media also plays a role in informing parents of premature infants. Empirical research published in 2013 found that in 2011 there were 1,497 Facebook groups created for and focusing on premature infants and parents. The largest Facebook groups were in the UK, Australia and North America. See, further, Thoren et al., 'Online Support for Parents of Preterm Infants: A Qualitative and Content Analysis of Facebook 'Preemie' Groups'

Such requests are often made by parents even when the medical prognosis for the premature infant is extremely poor.[21] Lantos and Meadow have described that many parents perceive the neonatal intensive care unit (NICU) as being 'a saviour, a place where miracles will happen and babies are snatched from the jaws of death'.[22] Arguably, this particularly reflects the attitudes of parents with strong religious beliefs who 'wait for such miracles'[23] to occur or those who request the continuation of medical treatment even where doctors consider such treatment to be futile.[24] Where such disagreements cannot be resolved, parents or doctors may seek judicial guidance as to whether treatment can or should be withdrawn.

Undoubtedly, decisions regarding the desirability of treatment in cases concerning critically ill infants are complex, involving multifaceted considerations and competing principles and interests.[25] While there is an abundance of case law on the matter, particularly in the UK, there is a corresponding and notable absence of statutory provision and parliamentary intervention. One of the observations of this book is that decisions to withdraw or withhold life-sustaining treatment from extremely premature and critically ill infants should be governed, or at the very least guided, by a clear and authoritative legislative framework.[26]

Decisions to withdraw or withhold treatment in cases of extremely premature or critically ill infants are fraught with inconsistency and lack of transparency. This is demonstrated in hospital clinical guidelines and case law from the UK, where the courts have been required to consider the withdrawal or withholding of

---

(June 2013) (Online) *Archives of Disease in Childhood: Fetal and Neonatal* 1–5. See also, Miracle Babies Foundation, 'About Us'. www.miraclebabies.org.au

21 Jane Fortin, *Children's Rights and the Developing Law* (Cambridge University Press, 3rd edn, 2009) 376.

22 John D Lantos and William L Meadow, *Neonatal Bioethics: The Moral Challenges of Medical Innovation* (Johns Hopkins University Press, 2006) 5.

23 See, especially, Joe Brierley, Jim Linthicum and Andy A Petros, 'Should Religious Beliefs be Allowed to Stonewall a Secular Approach to Withdrawing and Withholding Treatment in Children?' (30 March 2012) *Journal of Medical Ethics* 100–104. The authors conducted a study about the importance of religion to the family unit in end of life decision making for children in paediatric intensive care. The study was conducted over a three-year period in the UK. The study found that, of the 203 cases reviewed, '11 (65%) involved explicit religious claims that intensive care should not be stopped due to expectation of divine intervention and complete cure together with conviction that overly pessimistic medical predictions were wrong'. The authors concluded: 'While it is vital to support families in such difficult times, we are increasingly concerned that deeply held belief in religion can lead to children being potentially subjected to burdensome care in expectation of "miraculous" intervention.' For the other side of the discussion, see Steve Clarke, 'When they Believe in Miracles' (2013) 39(9) *Journal of Medical Ethics* 573–577; The Week, 'Waiting for a Miracle: Is it Inhumane for Religious Parents to Prolong Treatment of Sick Kids?' *The Week* (Online), 17 August 2012. http://theweek.com/article/index/232122/waiting-for-a-miracle-is-it-inhumane-for-religious-parents-to-prolong-treatment-of-sick-kids#. Similar views are held by parents of premature and critically ill infants. This is considered in Chapter 4.

24 The concepts of futility and quality of life are discussed in greater detail in Chapter 2.

25 As will be considered in Chapter 4, individuals with strong religious beliefs may not face any dilemmas in making treatment decisions, as they are guided by their religious view that all human life is sacred so life-sustaining treatment should not be withdrawn or withheld.

26 Observations and concluding remarks are detailed in Chapter 7. See, also, Loane Skene, 'Legal Issues in Treating Critically Ill Newborn Infants' (1993) 2(3) *Cambridge Quarterly of Healthcare Ethics* 295–308.

life-sustaining treatment. In comparison, in Australia, over the past three decades, there have only been three cases requiring legal intervention, with two of these cases being heard in 2011 and 2012.[27] As medical technology has advanced over the later decades of the twentieth century, the instances in which newborn lives can be saved or extended have greatly increased.[28] Accordingly, the legal and medical professions are facing ever more situations that the inadequate regulatory framework struggles to address.

While adult patients lacking mental capacity may be able to exercise some patient autonomy, infants are entirely dependent on the will of others: principally, doctors, parents and judges.[29] This dependency places infants in an extremely vulnerable position. They are subject to decisions to withdraw or withhold life-sustaining treatment that are often clouded by the subjective beliefs of those closely involved in their care.[30] Currently, there is no clear approach to decisions in this area and clarity is unlikely to be achieved within the existing framework given the difficulty in reconciling factors that are often complicated by subjective social, cultural, religious and ethical beliefs.

1.5 Historical development of neonatology

Paediatric medicine concerns the care and treatment of sick children. Neonatology exists as a branch of paediatrics specific to the treatment of newborns. Specialisation in neonatology includes the treatment of infants[31] with symptoms such as low birth weight, prematurity and congenital malformation. The impetus to provide medical intervention for premature infants – that is, those born before full-term pregnancy – did not commence out of benevolence or a duty to protect.[32] Serious attempts to save very young lives began as a drive to rebuild and regenerate a destroyed population after the Franco-Prussian war during 1870–1871 in Paris.[33] The medical science of neonatology also began to develop in England.[34]

---

27 There have been four cases to date in Australia, one requiring coronial intervention, See, further, *Baby M* (Victorian State Coroner's Office, Record of Investigation into Death, Case No 3149/89, 29 October 1991) VIC. Case law from the UK and Australia is discussed in Chapter 2.
28 See, e.g., Callie Watson, 'With Technological Advances, Most Premature Babies Survive against the Odds', *The Australian* (Online), 4 November 2012. www.theaustralian.com.au/news/most-premature-babies-survive-against-the-odds/story-e6frg6n6-1226510132523
29 Often adult patients may declare their treatment wishes in the form of an advanced directive. However, see Alasdair MacLean, 'Advance Directives and the Rocky Waters of Anticipatory Decision Making' (2008) 16(1) *Medical Law Review* 1–22. MacLean highlights the problematic nature of advance directives; in particular, the author critiques the authority, autonomy and implementation of advice directives.
30 Primarily the treating doctors, parents and judges. Chapter 4 explores the role and impact of these groups.
31 Often referred to as 'neonates' for the first 28 days of life.
32 Today, a full-term pregnancy is calculated at 37–42 weeks' gestation.
33 See, e.g., Russell Viner and Janet Golden, 'Children's Experiences of Illness' in Roger Cooter and John Pickstone (eds), *Companion to Medicine in the Twentieth Century* (Routledge, 2003) 575–601.
34 See, especially, Peter M Dunn, 'The Birth of Perinatal Medicine in the United Kingdom' (2006) 11(6) *Seminars in Fetal and Neonatal Medicine* 386–397.

In western society, providing medical treatment is probably considered to be motivated by preserving or improving quality of life. However, neonatology as a science was formed from practical considerations arising out of the geopolitical patchwork of nineteenth-century Europe, where famines, war and poverty contributed to population loss that required a solution, including the preservation of the existing population. It is generally considered that the first infant incubator was developed by Tarnier, a French obstetrician, in 1880 at the Paris maternity hospital.[35] By the turn of the twentieth century, another French physician, Pierre-Constant Budin, had concluded that the use of the infant incubator was an integral piece of equipment for improving the chances of survival of premature infants.

Over the past half-century, western medicine has witnessed both a widespread increase in public awareness and a corresponding increase in efforts to develop new technologies to improve survival and health outcomes of premature infants. However, despite these efforts, of those infants who are treated and survive, many do so with severe disability.[36]

1.6 The need to discuss the allocation of finite healthcare resources and infants

Decisions to withdraw or withhold life-sustaining treatment from extremely premature and critically ill infants have an emotional and financial impact on many individuals. Parents are those most affected by such decisions However, the broader family circle and wider society may also be profoundly impacted by end of life decisions.

With ageing populations in the UK and Australia, the allocation of scarce public funds is increasingly coming under scrutiny. There is a limited supply of healthcare resources that cannot meet the demands and needs of all patients indefinitely. One group of patients that are heavy consumers of finite healthcare resources are extremely premature and critically ill infants.

Chapter 6 of this book consider the costs associated with keeping extremely premature and severely disabled infants alive. This book suggests that isolating considerations of the initial cost of treating an extremely premature infant for it to 'survive' is flawed. This is because it fails to provide an accurate representation of the true costs involved in the treatment and care necessary for an imperilled infant during its lifetime. Although conceivably benevolent, the explicit costs and implicit costs of keeping severely imperilled infants alive have far-reaching social and familial ramifications. Decisions to save and preserve the lives of impaired infants should not be limited to the immediate financial costs of medical treatment.

---

35 See, especially, Jeffrey P Baker, *The Machine in the Nursery: Incubator Technology and the Origins of Newborn Intensive Care* (Johns Hopkins University Press, 1996) 25–44.
36 See, e.g., Saroj Saigal and Lex W Doyle, 'An Overview of Mortality and Sequelae of Preterm Birth from Infancy to Adulthood' (2008) 371(9608) *The Lancet* 261–269. This is discussed in greater detail in Chapters 3 and 6.

More explicitly, there should be a full appreciation of the cost of disability to the family, requirements for long-term care and the benefits and associated costs of life, not only to the patient but also to society.

Ostensibly, a closer evaluation of the allocation of resources would assist in injecting some objectivity in decision making for impaired infants, the consideration of which would diminish much of the subjectivity, although none of the associated emotion that currently informs end of life decision making, and allow for a more rational approach. There is a need to guide the discussion in this area with greater transparency. It is this need that this book proposes to address, by stimulating further debate and candid dialogue as to whether treating certain impaired lives confers a diminishing benefit against the lifelong costs of their sustenance.

1.7 Purpose and structure of the book

Arguably adults are biologically hardwired to care and respond to the needs of infants – impaired infants perhaps even more so, given their greater vulnerability. It can be no surprise, then, that discussions regarding end of life decision making and allocation of finite healthcare resources, particularly as they apply to these extremely vulnerable patients, strike an emotional chord with most people. For some, this sensitivity is manifested to the extent that discussions of this type are considered not only unnecessary but actually harmful and cruel.

It is important to acknowledge the widely divergent views in this area to clarify the exact purpose and intent of this book, which follows next, as much as what it is not about. This book does not advocate for withdrawal of treatment *en masse*. Rather, the primary aim of this book is to highlight that the current practices in decision making to withdraw or withhold life-sustaining treatment from premature and critically ill infants in the UK, and more recently in Australia, are nebulous and unsatisfactory.[37] More specifically, this book contends that end of life decisions for infants born extremely prematurely should be driven by a more objective, transparent and tangible approach. In this regard this book advances the existing debate and learning in this area. The key points that it attempts to establish are:

1   The law regarding treatment decisions about critically ill infants is obscure and incapable of providing meaningful guidance to those closely involved in the care and decision-making process, namely doctors, parents and the courts.
2   Resource allocation and corresponding quality of life should be important considerations regarding the treatment of impaired infants.
3   Ostensibly, resource allocation does not drive decisions in this area.

---

37   The most recent case in Australia that has required legal intervention is *TS & TD v Sydney Children's Hospital ('Mohammed's case')* [2012] NSWSC 1609. This case is discussed in Chapter 2.

4   *In fact*, resource allocation and quality of life decisions seem to cohere with the outcome of medical and judicial decisions in this area.
5   Resource allocation should be a cardinal consideration regarding the treatment of extremely premature and impaired infants. This would explain and justify existing practices and lead to more sound policies and decisions.

While recognising the existing academic work in this area to date, this book contests existing practices and traditional thinking, and provides recommendations for achieving more consistent and objective outcomes in decision making for extremely premature and critically ill infants.

Predominantly, religious, cultural and subjective beliefs drive decisions and debate in end of life decision making. Although important, they should not overwhelm the debate, and objective medical, social and economic factors should be weightier. The later chapters of this book consider how such objectivity can be established.

This chapter has provided an introduction to the relationship between law, medicine and technology, and increasing public awareness and engagement in discussion about death and dying. It has offered a brief reflection on the historical development of neonatal care and treatment in modern medicine. Additionally, it sets out the purpose and structure of the book.

Chapter 2 provides a detailed critical analysis of selective case judgments involving end of life decisions concerning critically ill infants. It examines the complex nature and relevance of the sanctity of life principle – *that all human life is sacred and requires the utmost care and protection* – in decision making for impaired infants. The chapter also assesses subjectivity and the arbitrary nature of decision making for these infants by evaluating the application and effectiveness of the best interests principle applied by the English and Australian courts and medical practitioners to allow the withdrawal or withholding of life-sustaining treatment from critically ill infants.

In addition, Chapter 2 evaluates medico-legal concepts of futility, quality of life and intolerability, developed and discussed at length by judges in determining infant end of life decisions. A key aspect of this book is examining the current stream of judicial reasoning in this area, establishing a baseline from which the current orthodoxy can be evaluated and critiqued.

Chapter 3 progresses to critique the efficacy and arbitrary nature of various frameworks applied in hospitals in the UK and Australia. This chapter also critically examines the impact and effectiveness of the much publicised Nuffield Council on Bioethics report: *Critical Care Decisions in Foetal and Neonatal Medicine: Ethical Issues*, 2006.[38]

---

38 Nuffield Council on Bioethics, *Critical Care Decisions in Fetal and Neonatal Medicine: Ethical Issues* (Nuffield Council on Bioethics, 2006).

The subjective role, impact and importance of primary caregivers and decision makers – those closely involved in the decision-making process (parents, doctors, judges) – in withdrawing or withholding life-sustaining treatment from critically ill infants is examined in Chapter 4. Further, Chapter 4 explores the competing interests of each group, and how these are evaluated and weighed.

In Chapter 5, the discussion turns to explore and apply theories of distributive justice and resource allocation with regard to critically impaired infants. It considers whether there is a plausible theory of distributive justice that could be applied to decisions to ration limited healthcare.

Chapter 6 moves on to consider the limited financial resources available to treat extremely premature and critically ill infants, particularly those suffering severe disability. Relevant to this discussion are the profound short- and long-term impacts of decisions to keep extremely premature and critically ill infants alive – in particular, life after hospital discharge and the effect this may have on the infant, wider family circle and the greater community. It examines the role that resource allocation should have in informing medical decisions in a more objective and transparent manner.

Chapter 7 provides other observations and considerations that may guide end of life decision making for premature and critically impaired infants. This chapter also provides a summary of the book and concluding remarks.

1.8 Conclusion

Death is an inevitable event for all of us, but this book focuses on life and death decisions for one of the most vulnerable groups of society. Decisions concerning whether critically ill infants live or die should not be circumvented due to those infants' vulnerability. On the contrary, given the long-term ramifications for many individuals involved in such decision making, it is necessary to base such discussion on more objective and pragmatic grounds. The next chapter examines the effectiveness of the best interests principle in end of life decision making for impaired infants.

1.9 References

Airedale NHS Trust v Bland [1993] 1 All ER 789.

Baby M (Victorian State Coroner's Office, Record of Investigation into Death, Case No 3149/89, 29 October 1991) VIC.

Baker, Jeffrey P, *The Machine in the Nursery: Incubator Technology and the Origins of Newborn Intensive Care* (Johns Hopkins University Press, 1996).

Brierley, Joe, Jim Linthicum and Andy A Petros, 'Should Religious Beliefs be Allowed to Stonewall a Secular Approach to Withdrawing and Withholding Treatment in Children?' (30 March 2012) *Journal of Medical Ethics* 100.

Charter of Human Rights and Responsibilities Act 2006.

Clarke, Steve, 'When they Believe in Miracles' (2013) 39(9) *Journal of Medical Ethics* 573–577.

Department of Health and Ageing, *Why is it Important?* Australian Government. www.health.gov.au/internet/publications/publishing.nsf/Content/oatsih-hpf-2012-toc~tier1~health-cond~101

Dunn, Peter M, 'The Birth of Perinatal Medicine in the United Kingdom' (2006) 11(6) *Seminars in Fetal and Neonatal Medicine* 386.

Fortin, Jane, *Children's Rights and the Developing Law* (Cambridge University Press, 3rd edn, 2009).

Hockstein NG, CG Gourin, RA Faust, et al., 'A History of Robots: From Science Fiction to Surgical Robotics' (2007) 1(2) *Journal of Robotic Surgery* 113.

Human Rights Act 1998.

Kennedy, Ian, *Treat Me Right: Essays in Medical Law and Ethics* (Oxford University Press, 1991).

Lantos, John D and William L Meadow, *Neonatal Bioethics: The Moral Challenges of Medical Innovation* (Johns Hopkins University Press, 2006).

Li, Z, R Zeki, L Hilder and E A Sullivan, 'Australia's Mothers and Babies' (Perinatal Statistics Series No 28, Australian Institute of Health and Welfare, 2011. www.aihw.gov.au/WorkArea/DownloadAsset.aspx?id=60129545698

MacLean, Alasdair, 'Advance Directives and the Rocky Waters of Anticipatory Decision Making' (2008) 16(1) *Medical Law Review* 1.

Madison Park, 'Death at 25: Blogging the End of Life', *CNN*, 27 April 2010. http://edition.cnn.com/2010/HEALTH/04/27/blog.terminal.illness/index.html

Miracle Babies Foundation, 'About Us'. www.miraclebabies.org.au

Note, 'Developments in the Law: Medical Technology and the Law' (1989–1990) 103 *Harvard Law Review* 1519.

Nuffield Council on Bioethics, 'Background: Extremely Premature Babies'. www.nuffieldbioethics.org/neonatal-medicine/neonatal-medicine-background-extremely-premature-babies

Nuffield Council on Bioethics, *Critical Care Decisions in Fetal and Neonatal Medicine: Ethical Issues* (Nuffield Council on Bioethics, 2006).

Office for National Statistics, *Preterm Births, Data*. www.ons.gov.uk/ons/publications/re-reference-tables.html?edition=tcm%3A77-50818

Pfeiffer, Kimberley, 'The Ethics of Caring: Expressing Humanity towards Babies Born at the Borderline of Viability' (2008) 20(02) *Bioethics Research Notes* 21.

Re C (a minor) (wardship: medical treatment) [1989] 2 All ER 782.

Re R (a minor) (wardship: medical treatment) [1991] 4 All ER 177.

Saigal, Saroj and Lex W Doyle, 'An Overview of Mortality and Sequelae of Preterm Birth from Infancy to Adulthood' (2008) 371(9608) *The Lancet* 261.

Schloendorff v New York Hospital (1914) 211 NY 125.

Skene, Loane, 'Legal Issues in Treating Critically Ill Newborn Infants' (1993) 2(3) *Cambridge Quarterly of Healthcare Ethics* 295.

Taylor, Charles, *A Secular Age* (Harvard University Press, 2007).

Thoren, Emelie Maria, Boris Metze, Christoph Bührer and Lars Garten, 'Online Support for Parents of Preterm Infants: A Qualitative and Content Analysis of Facebook "Preemie" Groups' (June 2013) (Online) *Archives of Disease in Childhood: Fetal and Neonatal* 1.

Tommy's, *Premature Birth Statistics*. www.tommys.org/page.aspx?pid=387

TS & TD v Sydney Children's Hospital ('Mohammed's case') [2012] NSWSC 1609.

Viner, Russell and Janet Golden, 'Children's Experiences of Illness' in Roger Cooter and John Pickstone (eds), *Companion to Medicine in the Twentieth Century* (Routledge, 2003).

Watson, Callie, 'With Technological Advances, Most Premature Babies Survive against the Odds', *The Australian* (Online), 4 November 2012. www.theaustralian.com.au/news/most-premature-babies-survive-against-the-odds/story-e6frg6n6-1226510132523

The Week, 'Waiting for a Miracle: Is it Inhumane for Religious Parents to Prolong Treatment of Sick Kids?' *The Week* (Online), 17 August 2012. http://theweek.com/article/index/232122/waiting-for-a-miracle-is-it-inhumane-for-religious-parents-to-prolong-treatment-of-sick-kids#

2 The effectiveness of the best interests principle

Chapter 1 provided an overview of the purpose and structure of this book. It included a brief insight into the historical impetus to save pre-term infants, which would in time lead to the development of the NICU. Chapter 1 also discussed the advancement of science and medical technology, and the corresponding need for development of the law in matters of life and death.

This chapter examines the best interests principle as applied by the courts in determining whether to withdraw or withhold treatment from critically ill infants. The focus of this chapter is an analysis of some of the relevant case law and the application of the best interests test.

This leads to a critical evaluation of the function and effectiveness of the best interests principle as it applies to end of life decisions for impaired infants. Additionally, this chapter illustrates the first of several speculative and subjective factors that are currently applied to decisions to withdraw or withhold life-sustaining treatment from critically ill infants.[1]

Before examining the best interests principle and its application in relevant case law from the UK and Australia, this chapter begins by considering the historical and religious orthodoxy underpinning modern-day societal approaches to life and death. The principle of sanctity of life is informed by this view and an understanding of its genesis is necessary to illustrate its gradual attrition over time, and the prevailing notion of the principle of best interests in relation to decisions to withdraw or withhold life-sustaining treatment from impaired infants.

2.1 Sanctity of life perspectives

Judeo-Christian tradition

Distilled, the sanctity of life principle is that human life is a gift from God and is sacred. The doctrine of sanctity of life is most widely associated with the

---

1 Chapters 3 and 4 discuss other subjective and arbitrary factors that currently inform decision making. Chapter 6 argues that resource allocation should be a cardinal consideration in treatment decisions for extremely premature and critically impaired infants, thus injecting a degree of objectivity to end of life decision making.

Judeo-Christian tradition asserting that life is precious and valuable.[2] According to the book of Genesis, God created man in his own image and, as it is gifted, only God may take life.[3] Further, Keown, a leading advocate for the sanctity of life principle, highlights that those in favour of this school of thought believe 'human life is . . . therefore, possessed of an intrinsic dignity which entitles it to protection from unjust attack'.[4]

In his book *History of European Morals*, Lecky provides what some commentators have referred to as a 'classical account' of the sanctity of human life:

> Considered as immortal beings, destined for the extremes of happiness or of misery, and united to one another by a special community of redemption, the first and most manifest duty of the Christian man was to look upon his fellow-men as sacred beings and from this notion grew up the eminently Christian idea of sanctity of human life . . . it was one of the most important services of Christianity that besides quickening greatly our benevolent affections it definitely and dogmatically asserted the sinfulness of all destruction of human life as a matter of amusement, or of simple convenience, and thereby formed a new standard higher than any which then existed in the world.[5]

More recently, Amarasekara and Bagaric have discussed the sanctity of life as being one of the highest moral orders over human law, describing it as 'a belief in eternal life allied to sanctity of human life, and a metaphysical value attached to pain and suffering. Underpinning these is an assertion of the primacy of Divine, Eternal or Natural Law over human law.'[6] The idea of living by virtue of 'guiding principles' or an 'acceptable moral system'[7] can be found in many biblical texts, in particular the Book of Exodus and the Ten Commandments. Perhaps the most acknowledged commandment in society today and the most relevant to this book is from the King James Bible: Exodus: 20:13 – 'Thou shalt not kill.'

---

2 The importance of the sanctity of life doctrine is also found in eastern religions such as Hinduism and the religious scriptures of the Bhagawat Gita. See, e.g., O P Dwivedi, 'Satyagraha for Conservation: Awakening the Spirit of Hinduism' in J Ronald Engel and Joan Gibb Engel (eds), *Ethics of Environment and Development: Global Challenge, International Response* (University of Arizona Press, 1990) 203–207. Also, see Cameron Stewart, 'The Sanctity of Life in Law: Comparisons between Jewish, Catholic, Islamic and Common Law Approaches' in Peter Radan, Denise Meyerson, Rosalind F Croucher (eds), *Law and Religion: God, the State and the Common Law* (Routledge Studies in Religion, Volume 9, 2004) 249–273.

3 Book of Genesis: 1:26 and 1:27. Robert L Barry suggests that it is immoral for an individual to take the life of another, as it 'deprived God of a possession which is rightly His'. See, further, Robert L Barry, *The Sanctity of Human Life and its Protection* (University Press of America, 2002) 19.

4 John Keown, *Euthanasia, Ethics and Public Policy: An Argument Against Legislation* (Cambridge University Press, 2002) 40.

5 Quoted in Helga Kuhse, *The Sanctity-of-Life Doctrine in Medicine* (Oxford University Press, 1987) 17.

6 Kumar Amarasekara and Mirko Bagaric, *Euthanasia, Morality and the Law* (Peter Lang Publishing, 2002) 130.

7 Jonathan Glover, *Causing Death and Saving Lives* (Pelican Books, 1977) 39. See, also, the influential text by Jean Jacques Rousseau, *The Social Contract* (Hafner Publishing Company, 1947) (first published 1762).

The ideal that human life is sacrosanct and of the greatest importance is 'emotionally appealing'[8] and, intuitively, probably the easiest approach to take in matters of life and death. In this regard, Brazier asserts: 'to most people who are not philosophers the answer is simple. There is a deep and embedded instinct that taking human life is wrong. Life is a most precious possession. All other possessions, all potential joys, depend upon its continued existence.'[9]

The primacy of this principle has diluted over time in line with evolving social and political thought, and is enforced today with less rigidity than previously. In a western modern secular society, the rigid application of these principles distilled from religious philosophies and traditions is limited and it is arguable that it does not have the same support that it may once have enjoyed.

For many, to live a life in accordance with this most fundamental principle of the sanctity of life is both honourable and practical. This is reflected in the laws governing our societies. Even if most individuals do not conform to the biblical moral code for reasons of virtue or belief, they will still adhere to the legal code for reasons of community and identity. In addition to the religious philosophies regarding the sanctity of life, some of the longest-standing and most influential philosophies of Greek medicine derive from Hippocrates.

Greco-Roman principles and the Hippocratic Oath

Ancient Greek philosophers and texts played an important role in the birth of medical ethics. Both Aristotle and Plato placed importance on the principle of life, believing that the body and soul were one unit, with the soul ultimately being the 'life principle' of the body.[10] The Hippocratic Oath is the most well-known Greek medical text and is thought to have established the principles of medical ethics, obligations and responsibilities bestowed on medical practitioners. It was written by the Greek physician Hippocrates of Kos, an archetypal figure of western civilisation, circa fourth and fifth century BCE.[11] Many believe Hippocrates to be the father of medicine, who rejected notions of superstition, legend and myths, laying the foundations of medicine as a science guided by ethics and professionalism.[12]

---

8 Sheila McLean, *Old Law, New Medicine: Medical Ethics and Human Rights* (Pandora, 1999) 116.
9 Margaret Brazier, *Medicine, Patients and the Law* (Penguin Books, 3rd edn, 2003) 44.
10 See the major treatise by Aristotle, in particular, Aristotle (English translation by A L Peck), *On the Generation of Animals* (W Heinemann, 1943); Aristotle (Translated by Richard Cresswell), *On the History of Animals* (Henry G Bohn, 1862); Aristotle (Translated by Hugh Lawson-Tancred), *De Anima (On the Soul)* (Penguin, 1986); Aristotle (Translated by J A K Thomson), *The Nicomachean Ethics* (Penguin, 1955) and Aristotle (Translated by T A Sinclair), *The Politics* (Penguin, 1981). Plato touched on this issue when discussing suicide in *Crito* and *Phaedo*. See Plato (Translated by Benjamin Jowett) *Crito* (Forgotten Books, 2008) and Plato (Translated by David Gallop) *Phaedo* (Oxford University Press, 1993). Other works by Plato also provide some discussion of honouring the soul. In particular, *The Laws* (Book V) and Part XI of *The Republic*. See, also, Steven H Miles, *The Hippocratic Oath and the Ethics of Medicine* (Oxford University Press, 2004).
11 Thomas Alured Faunce, *Pilgrims in Medicine: Conscience, Legalism and Human Rights* (Koninklijke Brill NV, 2005) 125.
12 Some scholars believe that Pythagoreans wrote the Hippocratic Oath.

However, in his book *Pilgrims in Medicine*, Faunce, sceptical of the way in which Hippocrates is often revered, asserted:

> The Hippocratic Oath is often portrayed as a course of culture-neutral professional virtues and foundational ethical principles. Its espousal of medical duties not to do harm (non-maleficence).[13]

Faunce further stated:

> To enter houses only for the good of patients (beneficence), to practise within the bounds of competence and to respect a patient's confidences, even after they are dead, show an egalitarian respect for human dignity remarkable, though not necessarily unique for its time.[14]

A translated version of the Oath from the *National Library of Medicine* reads:[15]

> I swear by Apollo the physician, and Asclepius, and Hygieia and Panacea and all the gods and goddesses as my witnesses, that, according to my ability and judgement, I will keep this Oath and this contract.
>
> To hold him who taught me this art equally dear to me as my parents, to be a partner in life with him, and to fulfil his needs when required; to look upon his offspring as equals to my own siblings, and to teach them this art, if they shall wish to learn it, without fee or contract; and that by the set rules, lectures, and every other mode of instruction, I will impart a knowledge of the art to my own sons, and those of my teachers, and to students bound by this contract and having sworn this Oath to the law of medicine, but to no others.
>
> I will use those dietary regimens which will benefit my patients according to my greatest ability and judgement, and I will do no harm or injustice to them.
>
> I will not give a lethal drug to anyone if I am asked, nor will I advise such a plan; and similarly I will not give a woman a pessary to cause an abortion.
>
> In purity and according to divine law will I carry out my life and my art.
>
> I will not use the knife, even upon those suffering from stones, but I will leave this to those who are trained in this craft.
>
> Into whatever homes I go, I will enter them for the benefit of the sick, avoiding any voluntary act of impropriety or corruption, including the seduction of women or men, whether they are free men or slaves.
>
> Whatever I see or hear in the lives of my patients, whether in connection with my professional practice or not, which ought not to be spoken of outside, I will keep secret, as considering all such things to be private.

---

13 Alured Faunce, above, n 11, 121
14 Ibid.
15 Translation by Michael North, National Library of Medicine, History of Medicine Division, *Greek Medicine*. www.nlm.nih.gov/hmd/greek/greek_oath.html

So long as I maintain this Oath faithfully and without corruption, may it be granted to me to partake of life fully and the practice of my art, gaining the respect of all men for all time. However, should I transgress this Oath and violate it, may the opposite be my fate.

Although the Hippocratic Oath may be considered as an aspirational body of principles, it has evolved significantly from its founding principles to the current medical declaration taken by practitioners. Brazier highlights:

Its first premise is that the doctor owes loyalty to his teachers and his brethren. Obligations to exercise skill for the benefit of patients' health come second. Abortion, direct euthanasia and abetting suicide are prohibited. Improper sexual relations with patients are banned. Confidentiality in all dealings with patients is imposed.[16]

While the principle of patient confidentiality remains as rigid today as when the Oath was first written, other elements are now outdated, reflecting society's current mores. For example, in Australia and the UK, the practice of abortion is no longer prohibited, doctors pay for their tuition at medical school and, although prohibited in law, euthanasia is widely supported.[17]

The current-day declaration made by medical practitioners has evolved to incorporate contemporary values and changes in societal attitude. Central features of this renewed oath focus on the principles of respect for human life, honour, nobility and dignity. These principles do not necessarily translate to the absolute preservation of human life. The modern-day declaration taken by many medical practitioners is considered next.

Declaration of Geneva

As a consequence of the atrocities committed by doctors in Germany during the Second World War,[18] the World Medical Association recommended global medical ethical guidelines, on which the Declaration of Geneva was founded in 1948.[19] The Declaration emphasises equality, dignity and human rights.

The explicit prohibition of euthanasia and abortion in the Hippocratic Oath is not found in the Declaration. The most recently amended version of the

---

16 Brazier, above, n 9, 36.
17 See, also, G Iacovelli, 'The Evolution of the Hippocratic Oath' (1989) 1(1) *Medicina nei Secoli* 39–48.
18 The Nuremburg Trials: The Doctor Trials, held at the Palace of Justice in Nuremburg, Germany, began on 9 December 1946. The trial documented the medical experiments and torture that individuals were subjected to during the Second World War. See, further, George J Annas and Michael A Grodin, *The Nazi Doctors and the Nuremberg Code: Human Rights in Human Experimentation* (Oxford University Press, 1992); Michael Robert Marrus, 'The Nuremberg Doctors Trial in Historical Context' (1999) 73(1) *Bulletin of the History of Medicine* 106–123.
19 The United Nations was founded post-Second World War. In addition to the Declaration of Geneva, the United Nations General Assembly adopted the *Universal Declaration of Human Rights*. See, e.g., Mann et al., 'Health and Human Rights' (1994) 1(1) *Health and Human Rights* 6–23.

Declaration was adopted at the 173rd WMA Council Session, Divonne-les-Bains, France, in May 2006.[20] It is taken at the time of being admitted as a member of the medical profession, and states:

I solemnly pledge to consecrate my life to the service of humanity.
I will give to my teachers the respect and gratitude that is their due.
I will practise my profession with conscience and dignity.
The health of my patient will be my first consideration.
I will respect the secrets that are confided in me, even after the patient has died.
I will maintain, by all the means in my power, the honour and the noble traditions
    of the medical profession.
My colleagues will be my sisters and brothers.
I will not permit considerations of age, disease or disability, creed, ethnic origin,
    gender, nationality, political affiliation, race, sexual orientation, social
    standing or any other factor to intervene between my duty and my patient.
I will maintain the utmost respect for human life.
I will not use my medical knowledge to violate human rights and civil liberties,
    even under threat.
I make these promises solemnly, freely and upon my honour.

Today, modified versions of the Declaration of Geneva are used by many medical schools for students to declare their professional and ethical commitment to the practice of medicine.[21]

This chapter began by examining the genesis and historical, philosophical and theological foundations of the sanctity of life principle – that all human life is sacred.[22] Thus far, it has been noted that the Hippocratic Oath taken by medical practitioners has undergone modification and the most current declaration taken by medical practitioners focuses on respect for human life, which does not impose an absolute obligation to preserve human life at all costs. The gradual erosion of the sanctity of life principle and its staunch application in law is illustrated in the case law examined later in this chapter.

---

20 World Medical Association, *WMA Declaration of Geneva*. www.wma.net/en/30publications/ 10 policies/g1
21 A study conducted across several university medical faculties in Australia and New Zealand between 2000 and 2001 found that varying versions of the Hippocratic Oath and the Declaration of Geneva were used at graduating and declaration ceremonies. See, further, Paul M McNeill and Bruce S Dowton, 'Declarations Made by Graduating Medical Students in Australia and New Zealand' (2002) 176(3) *Medical Journal of Australia* 123–127.
22 John Keown has highlighted three competing interests that the law should consider when making end of life decisions. These are 'vitalism, sanctity of life and quality of life'. Kewon argues that the sanctity of life principle is a 'middle way' between two extremes, these extremes being a vitalist approach – 'that regardless of pain, suffering, or expense that life-prolonging treatment entails, it must be administered because human life must be preserved at all costs' – and a quality of life approach – 'accepting that certain lives are of no benefit and may lawfully be terminated by omission'. See, especially, John Keown, 'The Incompetent Patient: Sanctity of Life, Quality of Life and Vitalism' in Michael Parker and Donna Dickenson (eds), *The Cambridge Medical Ethics Workbook* (Cambridge University Press, 2001) 27–32.

This shift away from the sanctity of life principle in law has been noted by eminent academics. Keown asserts that 'the western world is undergoing a legal revolution' and 'respect for life's inviolability has been eroded increasingly by efforts to promote largely unbridled individual autonomy and the notion that some human lives, those which pass a certain "Quality" threshold, merit protection'.[23] In contrast, Huxtable asserts a more progressive view about the erosion of the sanctity of life principle, referring to its 'survival' and application in English case law,[24] stating:

> English law therefore continues to promote the sanctity of life in the face of competent requests to have life ended. Quite how long that final barrier will stand remains to be seen, since the logic of autonomy and quality of life might ultimately necessitate dismantling.[25]

The 'dismantling' of the sanctity of life principle is demonstrated by the development and application of the best interests principle in law. Decisions to lawfully withdraw or withhold life-sustaining treatment from incapacitated patients illustrate that end of life decision making does not always equate to a preservation of life. This chapter focuses on the first of several factors that are currently of central importance when making decisions to withdraw or withhold life-sustaining treatment from premature and critically ill infants: that is, the effectiveness of the best interests principle.

2.2 The best interests principle and the concept of futility

As noted in Chapter 1, unlike competent patients, infants cannot express their wishes or choices in relation to medical treatment, articulate their individual autonomy or consent to or refuse treatment. Therefore, all decisions for impaired infants are (at least at first instance) made by their parents.

As Skene notes, 'the parents of a baby or a young infant are legally entitled to decide what medical treatment their child will – or will not – have, provided that they act in the child's best interests'.[26] Under the protection of the law in Australia,

---

23 John Keown, 'The Legal Revolution: From Sanctity of Life to Quality of Life and Autonomy' (1997–1998) 14(2) *Journal of Contemporary Health Law and Policy* 253–285. Keown provides an example of the erosion of the sanctity of life principle in law by the introduction of the Abortion Act 1967 in the UK, whereby abortion 'was transformed from a serious criminal offence to a minor medical procedure, commonly performed for reasons of social convenience rather than medical necessity'. Richard Huxtable provides the further example of the decriminalisation of suicide in the UK to highlight the erosion of the sanctity of life principle. See Richard Huxtable, 'D(en)ying Life: The Sanctity of Life Doctrine in English Law' (2002) 14(3) *Retfoerd* 60–81.
24 Richard Huxtable, 'D(en)ying Life: The Sanctity of Life Doctrine in English Law' (2002) 14(3) *Retfoerd* 60, 60.
25 Ibid 79.
26 Loane Skene, *Law and Medical Practice: Rights, Duties, Claims and Defences* (Lexis Nexis Butterworths, 3rd edn, 2008) 120.

under s. 61B of the Family Law Act 1975, parental responsibly includes, 'all duties, powers, responsibilities and authority which, by law, parents have in relation to children'.[27]

Under English jurisdiction, parental responsibility is defined under s. 3 (1) of the Children's Act 1989 as, 'all the rights, duties, powers, responsibilities and authority which by law a parent of a child has in relation to the child and his property'.[28]

However, where parents disagree with either the discontinuation or continuation of medical treatment recommended by medical practitioners, the court has inherent power and *parens patriae* jurisdiction to make orders and determinations with the child's welfare as its paramount consideration.[29] As the 'parent of the nation', it is settled law that the courts' 'prime and paramount consideration must be the best interests of the child'.[30] In both English and Australian legislation, there is no specific definition of 'best interests'.[31] Such interests are simply to be the prime and paramount 'consideration' of the courts in making decisions for children.[32] This assertion is supported by Eekelaar:

> [T]he heavily subjective nature of the power granted to the judges means that, so long as he or she does not claim to be applying it as a conclusive rule of law, a judge can consider almost any factor which could possibly have a bearing on a child's welfare and assign to it any weight he or she chooses.[33]

However, even with the lack of any normative basis on which the best interests principle can be established, it remains the benchmark for deciding life and death decisions for impaired infants.[34] The best interests principle is so powerful that it

27 Section 61B Family Law Act 1975 (Cth).
28 Section 3(1) Children Act 1989.
29 The *parens patriae* is also an inherent jurisdiction of Australian Supreme Courts. For an extensive discussion of parental power in decision making for children and the parens patriae jurisdiction, see *Re Marion* (1990) 14 Fam LR 427 at first instance and then the High Court of Australia judgment, *Department of Health and Community Services v JWB and SMB (Marion's case)* (1992) 175 CLR 218. See, also, J Seymour, 'Parens Patriae and Wardship Powers: Their Nature and Origins' (1994) 14(2) *Oxford Journal of Legal Studies* 159–188. The paramount consideration of the child's welfare is governed under s. 1 of the Children Act 1989 in the UK.
30 *Re J (a minor) (medical treatment)* [1992] 4 All ER 614.
31 However, Nicholson CJ detailed factors that should be considered when determining whether a medical procedure/treatment was in the 'best interests' of an intellectually disabled teenager in *Re Marion (No 2)* (1992) 175 CLR 218. This is discussed in greater detail later in the chapter.
32 Archard extends this point further, arguing that the use of the indefinite and definite articles 'a' and 'the', in addition to the use of 'prime and paramount', allows for several interpretations of the best interests principle. Further, the use of 'consideration' allows for other factors to be considered, as opposed to a definite and authoritative assertion as to the child's best interests. See, especially, D W Archard, 'Children's Rights' in E N Zalta et al. (eds), *Stanford Encyclopaedia of Philosophy* (Winter 2002). http://plato.stanford.edu/archives/win2002/entries/rights-children
33 J Eekelaar, *Regulating Divorce* (Clarendon Press, 1991) 248.
34 The best interests principle is also applied to cases of incapacitated and incompetent adult and adolescent patients. In the seminal English case of *F v West Berkshire Health Authority* [1989] All ER 545, it was decided that a sterilisation of a mentally disabled but sexually active patient was in her best interests.

can, at times, overwhelm competing principles such as patient autonomy and even the right to life.[35] Despite its important status and the number of decisions in which it has been applied, the criteria by which it is informed remain surprisingly unclear.

While determining whether the continuation of life-sustaining treatment is in the best interests of a patient, medical practitioners and the courts also consider the concept of futility. In doing so, the courts, overwhelmingly with the endorsement of medical opinion, prescribe that further treatment will provide no benefit or improvement to the patient's health status or prognosis. Arguably, the concept of futility is as inexplicit and ambiguous as the best interests principle. Given that both concepts are overwhelming co-dependent and the application of the terms remain a central issue in end of life decision making, there is a compelling need to improve the clarity and objectivity of these concepts.[36]

The best interests principle and the concept of futile treatment have been discussed, endorsed and applied in both English and Australian jurisdictions. Most cases requiring legal intervention have occurred in the UK; the number of decisions from the UK compared with Australia is disproportionate, even allowing for its sizeable population advantage. The reason for this is unclear. Nevertheless, the analysis commences with a consideration of the case law from the UK.

2.3 Early case law involving infants from the UK

During the early 1980s, the issue of withholding or withdrawing treatment from severely disabled infants began to gain the awareness of the courts and the public in the UK. The British cases of Baby John Pearson and Baby Alexandra led to greater public awareness of the medical dilemmas concerning infants. Doctors also became more cautious and aware of their actions being subject to scrutiny.

The case of *R v Arthur* concerned a reported criminal prosecution in relation to a doctor withholding care from an infant.[37] John Pearson was born with Down syndrome in June 1980 to Molly Pearson in Derby General Hospital.[38] His parents did not want him to survive. Baby Pearson's mother is reported to have told nurses, 'I don't want it, duck.'[39] The treating physician, Dr Arthur, instructed

---

35 This point is illustrated throughout this chapter in cases that have required legal intervention, where parents consider that life-sustaining treatment should be continued, contrary to medical opinion. However, it has been noted that, given the infinite range of typically tragic medical conditions that can afflict individuals, it is understandable that the best interests test can never be expressed with absolute rigidity to form a precise rule. For a discussion of the distinction between rules and principle, see Ronald Dworkin, *Taking Rights Seriously* (Harvard University Press, 4th edn, 1977) 22–28, 76–77.

36 Stewart asserts that there have been several failed attempts to define and elucidate the concept of futility by an objective standard. See, e.g., Cameron Stewart, 'A Defence of the Requirement to Seek Consent to Withhold and Withdraw Futile Treatments' (2012) 196(6) *Medical Journal of Australia*, 406, 406.

37 *R v Arthur* (1981) 12 BMLR 1.

38 Helga Kuhse and Peter Singer, *Should the Baby Live?* (Oxford University Press, 1985) 1.

39 Ibid 2. 'Duck' is a term of endearment used in some parts of the UK.

the nurses to give 'nursing care only', which included a strong painkiller called dyhydrocodeine (DF 188) in four-hourly intervals as required.

However, although Baby Pearson was born with many of the common features of Down syndrome – slanting eyes, a flattened nose, a large tongue and a broad head – he did not have any of the other more severe abnormities that can afflict people with the chromosomal defect, such as heart defects or intestinal blockages.[40] He was capable of taking nourishment, by means of food and water. However, he was taken into a separate room and given only water and the drug DF 188. By the first evening of 'letting nature takes its course', John was 'going grey'.[41] He died three days later.

Dr Arthur had provided 'nursing care only' and had previously allowed other unwanted newborns to die with only the awareness of their parents and the hospital staff. However, in this case, one of the hospital staff informed an anti-abortion organisation called Life, which then reported the case to the police. Dr Arthur was later arrested and charged with murder, owing to having given Baby Pearson unnecessary and inappropriate drugs, in addition to allowing him to be starved to death. This was not a case of withdrawing or withholding medical treatment, but of withholding basic nourishment.[42]

The case was heard before Justice Farquharson and a jury at Leicester Crown Court in November 1981. The prosecution relied on evidence of the pathologist, Dr Usher, who alleged that the cause of death was lung poisoning by the DF 118 prescribed by Dr Arthur. In addition, Dr Usher claimed that, in an 'uncomplicated' case of Down syndrome such as that of Baby Pearson, the use of DF 118 was unnecessary.

However, doubt was later cast on Dr Usher's reasoning and evidence by the defence. Professor Emery stated that Baby Pearson had been suffering other defects before birth that may have caused his death. Moreover, several other medical physicians and colleagues considered Dr Arthur's course of action as being 'normal medical practice'.[43]

The evidence put forward by the defence led to the charge of murder being reduced to attempted murder, in a trial in which neither Dr Arthur nor Baby Pearson's parents gave evidence. During his interview with the police, Dr Arthur claimed his main intention in prescribing DF 118 was to alleviate any suffering the infant may have endured.[44] After two hours of deliberation,

---

40 Ibid.
41 Peter Singer, *Rethinking Life and Death* (Text Publishing, 1994) 121.
42 Sarah Elliston, *The Best Interests of the Child in Healthcare* (Routledge Cavendish, 2007) 155.
43 Kuhse and Singer, above, n 38, 123.
44 This is contrary to the view that providing excessive medication or withdrawing or withholding life-sustaining treatment that intentionally causes the death of an infant amounts to murder. Considering the decision in *R v Arthur*, Kuhse argues that there are instances and distinctions that should be drawn between killing and letting die. The author asserts that there may be cases in which it is morally permissible to intentionally allowing an infant to die, such as when the infant is suffering excessive pain. See, especially, Helga Kuhse, 'A Modern Myth. That Letting Die is Not the Intentional Causation of Death: Some Reflections on the Trial and Acquittal of Dr Leonard Arthur' (1984) 1(1) *Journal of Applied Philosophy* 21–38.

the jury returned to the dock, acquitting Dr Arthur. Justice Farquharson stated to the jury:

> The case really revolves round the question of what is the duty of the doctor when prescribing treatment for a severely handicapped child suffering from a handicap of an irrevocable nature where parents do not wish the child to survive.[45]

Kennedy interpreted Justice Farquharson's words as establishing a criterion justifying ending the life of an infant in the instance 'where the child is irreversibly disabled and . . . rejected by its parents'.[46]

Arguably, the decision in *R v Arthur* was flawed. The courts are not bound by the decisions or choices of either parents or medical practitioners. The judge placed heavy emphasis on the medical opinion presented by several expert witnesses. In his summing up before the jury, the judge stated: 'I imagine you will think long and hard before concluding that doctors, of the eminence we have heard . . . have evolved standards that amount to committing a crime.'[47] In subsequent decisions made by the courts, discussed later in this book, judges vehemently declare that the wishes of parents and medical opinion, although given consideration, are not determinative in decision making.

Considering that in this decision an infant was allowed to die because of the circumstances of his uncomplicated Down syndrome, it would be understandable to assume that another case in the same year, heard before the same judicial system, would lead to a similar result. In *Re B (a minor) (wardship: medical treatment)*,[48] the court was asked to decide on surgical treatment for an infant suffering an intestinal obstruction and who had Down syndrome.

Known as 'Baby Alexandra', her parents refused to authorise the surgery on the grounds that it was for either God or nature to decide the fate of their daughter. The Court of Appeal declared that the best interests of the infant were served by allowing treatment. In a brief judgment of three pages, it was concluded that life, in this case, trumped death, medical and public opinion at the time.[49]

Templeman LJ stated:

> It devolves on this court in this particular instance to decide whether the life of this child is demonstrably going to be so awful that in effect the child must be condemned to die or whether the life of this child is still so imponderable that it would be wrong for her to be condemned to die . . . Faced with that

---

45 *R v Arthur* (1981) 12 BMLR 1, 5.
46 Ian Kennedy, *Treat Me Right* (Oxford University Press, 1988) 155.
47 *R v Arthur* (1981) 12 BMLR 1, 22.
48 *Re B (a minor) (wardship: medical treatment)* [1990] 3 All ER (CA) 927.
49 Janet Read and Luke Clements, 'Demonstrably Awful: The Right to Life and the Selective Non-Treatment of Disabled Babies and Young Children' (2004) 31(4) *Journal of Law and Society* 482, 486.

choice, I have no doubt that it is the duty of this court to decide that the child must live.[50]

However, it is apparent further in the judgment that his lordship allowed for contrary applications of the principle of best interests in the future by stating: 'there may be cases . . . of severe proved damage where the future is so certain and where the life of the child is so bound of pain and suffering that the court might be driven to a different conclusion.'[51]

Unlike in the case of Baby Alexandra, John Pearson's withdrawal of treatment and subsequent death was judged to be in his best interests, as Justice Farquharson deemed an irreversible disability and parental rejection as a permissible reason to end his life. The inconsistency in the decisions made by the courts in these early cases, both of which involved infants afflicted by Down syndrome, is noteworthy.

The decision in *R v Arthur*, in which the court determined to allow an infant with uncomplicated Down syndrome rejected by his parents to die, is illustrative of the non-application or the erosion of the sanctity of life principle. However in *Re B* (on appeal), Justice Templeman found no evidence that, even with an intestinal blockage, Baby Alexandra's 'quality of life' would be hindered or would be any worse than any other child with Down syndrome. As Gunn and Smith succinctly state:

> On the facts as they appeared to Dr Arthur at the time of his decision and, indeed, up to the time of the child's death, John Pearson's circumstances were, if anything, better than Baby B's. If those responsible for Baby B owed a duty to keep her alive, there must have been at least an equal duty on those responsible for John Pearson.[52]

In *Re B*, the attitude of David Plank, Director of Social Services, was very different from that of the doctors: 'we decided that clearly it was right that the baby should have the operation because the baby was an independent person and had a right to life . . . she was a child first and had Down syndrome second.'[53]

Robertson considered the need for a uniform, authoritative decision-making process in end of life decisions in 1981, soon after the Pearson case, stating:

> The criteria cannot be whatever doctors and families decide . . . rather they should be developed by an authoritative body that is representative of the

---

50 *Re B (A Minor) (wardship: medical treatment)* [1990] 3 All ER (CA) 927, 929.
51 Ibid.
52 M J Gunn and J C Smith, 'Arthur's Case and the Right to Life of a Down's Syndrome Child' (1985) (Nov) *Criminal Law Review* 705, 709.
53 Read and Clements, above, n 49, 501.

community as a whole, such as legislature, a national commission or some publicly constituted body that reflects a wide range of societal views.[54]

Robertson's suggestion of a 'community caucus' is commendable, although deserving of some caution. As already noted in this chapter, societal views, values and perceptions continually evolve, as demonstrated by the widespread public acceptance of both the parental and medical decisions taken in the Pearson case in 1981. At the time of Dr Arthur's acquittal, a contemporary British newspaper reported that women rejoiced, 'Thank God'. This societal attitude was further evidenced in a separate poll conducted by the BBC of 2,000 adults, which reflected widespread support for Dr Arthur, with 86% of British citizens stating that a doctor should not be found guilty of murder if, with the agreement of the parents, a severely handicapped baby dies.[55]

It is very likely that a case such as that of Baby Pearson would be decided differently today.[56] Most cases concerning critically ill infants heard by the courts in more recent times have involved parental objections to life-sustaining treatment being withdrawn or withheld. As will be considered later in this chapter, more recent case decisions are far removed from that of Baby John Pearson, in which the treatment decision was based on his condition and parental rejection.

Three decades after the incongruous decisions in the cases discussed above, the arbitrary nature with which end of life decisions are made remains an issue in need of reform, as illustrated in later case decisions.

Post-*R v Arthur* and *Re B*, end of life decision making by means of withdrawal or withholding life-sustaining treatment was subject to significant legal consideration and scrutiny in the seminal English case, *Airedale National Health Service Trust v Bland*,[57] which concerned the withdrawal and withholding of life-sustaining treatment from an incapacitated adult.

54 John A Robertson, 'Substantive Criteria and Procedures in Withholding Care from Defective Newborns' in Stuart F Spicker, Joseph M Healy and H Tristram Engelhardt (eds), *The Law–Medicine Relation: A Philosophical Exploration* (Reidel Publishing Company, 1981) 217, 223.

55 Kuhse and Singer, above, n 38, 10. For further reading of the newspaper article reporting women rejoicing see, 'Women Cry "Thank God" as Dr Arthur is Cleared', *The Times* (UK), 6 November 1981.

56 A study conducted in Canada in the early 1990s found a significant change in medical practitioner attitudes towards the withdrawal or withholding of treatment for infants born with Down syndrome. Compared with a similar study conducted in 1975, the study found: 'Positive changes in physicians' attitudes during the past 15 years have been influenced by parent advocacy groups, court decisions, and studies showing that the ultimate intellectual and social skills of Down syndrome children are greater than was previously believed. The most prominent variable associated with attitudes was the physician's age: the older the physician, the more likely he or she would be non-supportive of active treatment on behalf of the Down syndrome individual.' See, especially, Robert H A Haslam and Ruth Milner, 'The Physician and Down Syndrome: Are Attitudes Changing?' (1992) 7(3) *Journal of Child Neurology*, 304–331. A similar societal shift in attitude has been evidenced in the UK; see, e.g., Polly Curtis, 'Down's Syndrome Changing Attitudes', *The Guardian* (Online) 1 September 2007. www.theguardian.com/stage/2007/sep/01/theatre3

57 *Airedale NHS Trust v Bland* [1993] AC 789.

Although the focus of this book is on decisions to withdraw or withhold life-sustaining treatment from premature and critically impaired infants, it is prudent to examine the application of the best interests principle in the seminal case of *Bland*. Chiefly, the case provided an important legal platform compelling the courts to explore the legal and ethical role of the best interests principle and its employment in decisions to allow for the lawful withdrawal or withholding of life-sustaining treatment.

2.4 Legal and ethical challenges in the English seminal case of *Airedale NHS Trust v Bland*

The concept of best interests was considered at length in the case of *Airedale National Health Service Trust v Bland*.[58] The legal judgments focused on whether it was in the best interests of a patient in a permanent vegetative state to die.[59] Anthony Bland was a victim of the Hillsborough football disaster on 15 April 1989. From this, he was left with motor reflexes, but showed no indication of significant cognitive function and was being kept alive via artificial life-sustaining machinery. After he had remained in the same mental and physical state for three and a half years, his family and the medical professionals responsible for his care sought a declaration that no civil or criminal liability would result in discontinuing life-sustaining treatment.

Bland was the first case in which the English courts were required to consider the lawful discontinuation of life-sustaining treatment concerning an adult patient. In *Bland*, the court decided in favour of discontinuing artificial hydration and nutrition. However, reaching this decision was not an easy or comfortable decision for their honours to make. Both the Court of Appeal and the House of Lords were confronted with what Miola refers to as 'a blank canvass and recognition that the questions put to them were intrinsically moral and ethical'.[60]

Sir Bingham's description at the Court of Appeal of Anthony Bland's physical condition provides a useful starting point for this discussion:

> Mr Bland lies in bed in the Airedale General Hospital, his eyes open, his mind vacant, his limbs crooked and taut. He cannot swallow, and so cannot be spoon-fed without a high risk that food will be inhaled into the lung. He is fed by means of a tube, threaded through the nose and down into the

58 Ibid.
59 The origins of the term PVS are discussed by Sir Stephen Brown in *Airedale NHS Trust v Bland* [1993] AC 789, 797. The term 'permanent vegetative state' was devised by Professor Bryan Jennet of Glasgow and Professor Plum of New York. For a discussion about the terminology and understanding of the term PVS, see, e.g., C J Borthwick and R Crossley, 'Permanent Vegetative State: Usefulness and Limits of a Prognostic Definition' (2004) 19(4) *Journal of Neuro Rehabilitation* 381–389.
60 Jose Miola, *Medical Ethics and Medical Law: A Symbiotic Relationship* (Hart Publishing, 2007) 154.

stomach, through which liquefied food is mechanically pumped. His bowels are evacuated by enema. His bladder is drained by catheter.[61]

One of the grounds on which Airedale NHS Trust sought a declaration to discontinue medical treatment lawfully in *Bland* was 'for the sole purpose of enabling Mr Bland to end his life and die peacefully with the greatest dignity and the least of pain, suffering and distress'.[62]

The issue that confronted each of the judges in *Bland* was how to reach their concurring conclusions. Their honours sought to argue that it was lawful to discontinue treatment, but without explicitly advocating that inevitable death was in his best interests. Each of the judges took his own novel route to come to the same conclusions. The judgments by their Honours in Bland are illustrative of the legal and ethical challenge between the sanctity of life principle and the competing concept of patient autonomy.

Sanctity of life

Judges at the Court of Appeal and the House of Lords discussed the sanctity of life principle at some length. McGee has described the decision in *Bland* to allow treatment to be withheld as 'inexorably leading towards the deterioration of the sanctity of life principle'.[63]

Hoffman LJ's judgment in the Court of Appeal began by discussing the importance of the sanctity of life principle and the intrinsic value of human life:

> Our belief in the sanctity of life explains why we think it is almost always wrong to cause the death of another human being, even one who is terminally ill or so disabled that we think that if we were in his position we would rather be dead.[64]

However, his Honour swiftly progressed to highlight the contrast between the sanctity of life principle and the competing doctrine of patient autonomy, stating:

> Take, for example, the sanctity of life and the right to self-determination. We all believe in them and yet we cannot always have them both. The patient who refuses medical treatment which is necessary to save his life is exercising his right to self-determination. But allowing him, in effect, to choose to die, is something which many people will believe offends the principle of the sanctity of life.[65]

---

61 *Airedale NHS Trust v Bland* [1993] AC 789, 807.
62 Ibid 807–808.
63 Andrew McGee, 'Finding a Way Through the Ethical and Legal Maze: Withdrawal of Medical Treatment and Euthanasia' (2005) 13(3) *Medical Law Review* 357, 384.
64 *Airedale NHS Trust v Bland* [1993] AC 789, 826.
65 Ibid 826–827.

Only a few paragraphs later, in his judgment, Hoffman LJ asserted that between the two conflicting principles there might be a requirement for a 'painful compromise to be made'.[66]

Lord Keith in the House of Lords was more robust in his approach, stating:

> The principle [of sanctity of life] is not an absolute one. It does not compel a medical practitioner on pain of criminal sanctions to treat a patient, who will die if he does not, contrary to the express wishes of the patient. It does not authorise forcible feeding of prisoners on hunger strike. It does not compel the temporary keeping alive of patients who are terminally ill where to do so would merely prolong their suffering.[67]

Substituted judgment test

The substituted judgment test often applied under American jurisdiction focuses on the treatment options that the incapacitated patient *would have* opted for based on the values or views or lifestyle choices of the patient while still having capacity.[68]

Their Honours considered the test in *Bland* and the court assessed that further treatment would simply prolong Anthony Bland's 'futile' existence. As such, his existence was measured against his prior life as a youthful and energetic adolescent. This was illustrated by Lord Browne-Wilkinson, who stated: 'the withdrawal of food and Anthony Bland's subsequent death would be for his benefit, and attach importance to impalpable factors such as personal dignity and the way Anthony Bland would wish to be remembered.'[69] As his father succinctly stated: 'he certainly wouldn't want to be left like that.'[70] Lord Goff considered the substituted judgment test, stating:

> I wish however to refer at this stage to the approach adopted in most American courts under which this courts seeks, in a case in which the patient is incapacitated from expressing any view on the question whether life-prolonging treatment should be withheld in the relevant circumstance, to determine what decision the patient himself would have made had he been

---

66 Ibid 827.
67 Ibid 859.
68 McQueen and Walsh argue that the substituted judgment test is flawed as it 'focuses disproportionately on the person's statements rather than on the person's overall best interests'. See, especially, Moira M McQueen and James L Walsh, 'The House of Lords and the Discontinuation of Artificial Nutrition and Hydration: An Ethical Analysis of the Tony Bland Case' (1991–1994) 35 *Catholic Lawyer* 363, 368. The substituted judgment test is a contrast to the best interests test, which takes a more paternalistic role in deciding what is 'best' for the patient. The origins of the substituted judgment test can be found in the nineteenth-century 'Lunacy Law', whereby 'Lord Eldon crafted the legal fiction of doing that which it is probable the lunatic himself would have done'. See, especially, Louise Harmon, 'Falling Off the Vine: Legal Fictions and the Doctrine of the Substituted Judgment' (1990) 100(1) *Yale Law Journal* 1, 1.
69 *Airedale NHS Trust v Bland* [1993] AC 789, 879–880.
70 Ibid 807.

able to do so. This is called the substituted judgment test, and it generally involves a detailed inquiry into the patient's views and preferences.[71]

While ultimately rejected as an applicable test for decision making in *Bland*, at the Court of Appeal, Lord Hoffman affirmed a view similar to the substituted judgment test, stating, 'we should try our honest best to do what we think he would have chosen'.[72] However, unlike in cases involving incapacitated adults, the best interests principle when applied to infants is not distracted by comparisons of the life and capacities that the patient enjoyed prior to the illness or injury that now afflicts them.

The court in *Bland* favoured and applied the best interests principle as the cornerstone in deciding to withdraw or withhold life-sustaining treatment. Although not as subjective as the substituted judgment test, the application of the best interests principle in decisions to withdraw or withhold life-sustaining treatment raises others concerns, which are discussed below and considered later in this chapter.

Reliance on the medical profession

Lord Keith reached his conclusion by applying the test laid down in *Bolam v Friern Hospital Management Committee*,[73] which states that a doctor has a duty to act in the best interests of patients as understood by a 'responsible body' of medical opinion. In relying on this test, Lord Keith abjured himself of any moral responsibility to reach a decision in *Bland*: 'a medical practitioner is under no duty to continue to treat such a patient where a large body of informed and responsible medical opinion is to the effect that no benefit at all would be conferred by continuance.'[74]

Lord Goff was seemingly more forthright about the role of doctors. He also relied on the *Bolam* test and the ethics committee of the British Medical Association (BMA) in stating: 'he [the doctor] will be acting with the benefit of guidance from a responsible and competent body of relevant professional opinion.'[75]

Like Lord Keith, Lord Goff was unwilling to commit to a more independent position on the matter of lawful withdrawal of treatment:

> The truth is that, in the course of their work, doctors frequently have to make decisions which may affect the continued survival of their patients, and are in reality far more experienced in matters of this kind than judges. It is nevertheless the function of the judges to state the legal principles upon which the lawfulness of the actions of doctors depend; but in the end the

71 Ibid 871.
72 Ibid 829–830.
73 *Bolam v Friern Hospital Management Committee* [1957] 1 WLR 582.
74 *Airedale NHS Trust v Bland* [1993] AC 789, 858–859.
75 Ibid 871.

decisions to be made in individual cases must rest with the doctors themselves.[76]

In effect, Lord Goff considered that it was the role of doctors to make end of life decisions and that the courts and judges were required to endorse the conduct of medical practitioners.

That two of the presiding judges arrived at their conclusions for best interests via the application of the *Bolam* test demonstrates its limitations. As a test, it has not been formulated and hypothesised in a wholly independent and informed manner.[77] Stewart reinforces this view, arguing that the *Bolam* test 'places the assessment of best interests solely within the sphere of medical competence'.[78] Stone, in the *New Law Journal*, raised similar arguments:

> The reliance on the *Bolam* test of medical negligence to determine whether it is in the patient's best interests to be allowed to die is scarcely an ideal approach where it is the continued existence of the patient rather than the conduct of the doctor which is to be assessed. 'Best interests' is a nebulous concept at the best of times.[79]

Lord Browne-Wilkinson did not show the same deference to the medical profession, highlighting that there might be instances in which a doctor, in deciding to withdraw life-prolonging treatment, 'may well be influenced by his own attitude to the sanctity of human life'.[80] However, Lord Goff considered that, for this potential offence and the attendant consequences, a 'change of medical practitioner' would provide the necessary resolution.[81]

Although the courts have the jurisdiction to override medical practitioners, judges rarely do so. Lord Browne-Wilkinson's wording conveys the impression that the courts feel inconvenienced in having to make decisions regarding areas in which, 'in the past, doctors exercised their own discretion in accordance with medical ethics'.[82] In the area of prolonging life, doctors 'took the responsibility of deciding whether the perpetuation of life was pointless'.[83]

---

76 Ibid.
77 Right Honourable Lord Woolf argues that the courts should not interfere with medical decision making unless the courts are justified in doing so. Lord Woolf refers to the court's role being that of a 'regulatory body' rather than a decision-making body. See, especially, Right Honourable Lord Woolf, 'Are the Courts Excessively Deferential to the Medical Profession?' (2001) 9(1) *Medical Law Review* 1–16. This book contends that this view is flawed and end of life decision making should be governed by an authoritative body.
78 Cameron Stewart, 'Legal Constructions of Life and Death in the Common Law' (2002) 2(Summer) *Oxford University Commonwealth Law Journal* 67, 86.
79 Julie Stone, 'Withholding Life-Sustaining Treatment' (1995) 145(6686) *New Law Journal* 354, 354.
80 *Airedale NHS Trust v Bland* [1993] AC 789, 884. Empirical research has found that medical practitioners are influenced in end of life decision making based by their personal values and beliefs. The role and impact of key caregivers and decision makers is discussed in Chapter 4.
81 *Airedale NHS Trust v Bland* [1993] AC 789, 874.
82 Ibid 880.
83 Ibid.

It is clear that Lord Browne-Wilkinson's preference in *Bland* was for doctors to make life and death decisions and for the courts not to be troubled or confronted by such. Previously, doctors were given wide latitude to make difficult decisions behind closed doors; they assumed control and sole responsibility, and were seldom challenged. While not overtly criticising this shift away from the infallibility of doctors, Lord Browne-Wilkinson acknowledged the reason behind the increasing incidence of intervention by the courts:

> [T]here are now present amongst the medical and nursing staff of hospitals those who genuinely believe in the sanctity of human life, no matter what the quality of that life, and report doctors who take such decisions to the authorities with a view to prosecution for a criminal offence.[84]

Arguably, reliance on the medical profession to make end of life decisions allows for less discomfort, debate or discussion by the courts, and does not force the courts to have to consider end of life decision making with the need to formulate any unified principles in this area.

Any association between the discontinuation of treatment and euthanasia was explicitly denied by Lord Lowry: 'I reject the idea, which is implicit in the appellant's argument, that informed medical opinion is these respects is merely a disguise for a philosophy which, if accepted, would legalise euthanasia.'[85] Lord Browne-Wilkinson was also vigorous in attempting to prevent the terms 'death' and 'best interests' being coined together, by asserting;

> [T]he critical decision to be made is whether it is in the best interests of Anthony Bland to continue the invasive medical care involved in artificial feeding. That question is not the same as, 'Is it in Anthony Bland's best interests that he should die?'[86]

Ensuring that the onus for 'responsibility and accountability' remained with the medical profession, and perhaps revealing some of the discomfort discussed above, Lord Browne-Wilkinson commented:

> [I]t follows that the legal question in this case is not whether the court thinks it is in the best interests of Anthony Bland to continue to receive intrusive medical care but whether the responsible doctor has reached a reasonable and bona fide belief that it is not.[87]

Lord Mustill seemed to believe that Anthony Bland had no best interests at all, stating: 'the distressing truth which must not be shirked is that the proposed

84 Ibid.
85 Ibid 876.
86 Ibid 884.
87 Ibid.

conduct is not in the best interests of Anthony Bland, for he has no best interests of any kind.'[88] While a bold statement, it was not helpful in responding to the immediate matter at hand: that is, whether it was in his best interests to have life-sustaining treatment withdrawn or withheld.

Unlike his learned friend Lord Browne-Wilkinson, Lord Mustill did not show the same blind confidence in the medical profession in determining life and death decisions. Lord Mustill considered the role of the courts and the law in decision making with caution, and acknowledged the difficulties facing judges in determining the best interests of the patient:

> But when the intellectual part of the task is complete and the decision maker has to choose the factors which he will take into account, attach relevant weights to them and then strike a balance the judge is no better equipped, though no worse, than anyone else.[89]

In line with the contention of this book, Lord Mustill did not consider doctors to be those 'best equipped' to make such decisions – a welcome change to the general tenor of the judgment.[90]

Acts and omissions

The courts in *Bland* were required to differentiate between the 'act' of withdrawing life-prolonging treatment or merely 'omitting' to provide it. The distinction between the two was of significant importance to the court because without resort to this distinction the court would have effectively legalised euthanasia. As discussed earlier in this chapter, in the 1980s judgment in *R v Arthur*, the courts underlined the importance of distinguishing between 'letting die' by means of omission or 'killing' by an act. This issue continued to confront the courts over a decade later in *Bland*.

Lord Goff addressed this complexity:

> So to act is to cross the Rubicon which runs between on the one hand the care of the living patient and on the other hand euthanasia – actively causing his death to avoid or to end his suffering. Euthanasia is not lawful at common law.[91]

Subsequent comments reflected an appreciation of the complexities of the distinction between acts and omissions:

> It is true that the drawing of this distinction may lead to a charge of hypocrisy; because it can be asked why, if the doctor, by discontinuing treatment is

88 Ibid 897.
89 Ibid 887.
90 The role, impact and function that the medical profession should have in end of life decision making is discussed in greater detail in Chapter 4.
91 *Airedale NHS Trust v Bland* [1993] AC 789, 865.

entitled in consequence to let his patient die, it should not be lawful to put him of out his misery straight away, in a more humane manner, by lethal injection, rather than let him linger on in pain until he dies. But the law does not feel able to authorise euthanasia, even in circumstances such as these.[92]

His Honour was concerned about the possible repercussions and the potential for unintended consequences, as 'once euthanasia is recognised as lawful in these circumstances, it is difficult to see any logical basis for excluding it in others'.[93]

In the Court of Appeal, Lord Hoffman also considered the infamous 'lethal injection' scenario. In opposition to the judges in the House of Lords, who thought the use of an injection would be 'more humane' than any suffering caused by the withdrawal of nutrition and hydration for an extended period of time, he asserted: 'I must start by considering why most of us would be appalled if he was given a lethal injection. It is, I think, connected with our view that the sanctity of life entails its inviolability by an outsider.'[94] However, he went on to say: 'on the other hand, we recognise that, one way or another, life must come to an end.'[95]

Lord Hoffman's view is aptly defined by Kuhse's novel term, 'qualified sanctity of life', which affirms:

> It is absolutely prohibited either intentionally to kill a patient or intentionally to let a patient die, and to base decisions relating to the prolongation or shortening of human life on considerations of its quality or kind; it is, however, sometimes permissible to refrain from preventing death.[96]

Lord Browne-Wilkinson considered that the objective of lawfully allowing the patient to die would alleviate the family's suffering,[97] while still acknowledging the difficulties in reconciling the difference between a positive act to end Anthony Bland's life and a mere omission to preserve it:

> [T]he conclusion I have reached will appear to some as almost irrational. How can it be lawful to allow a patient to die slowly though painlessly, over a

92 Ibid.
93 Ibid.
94 Ibid 831.
95 Ibid.
96 Kuhse, above, n 5, 23. See also, Helga Kuhse, 'Debate: Extraordinary Means and the Sanctity of Life' (1981) 7(2) *Journal of Medical Ethics* 74–82.
97 In *Bland*, Lord Browne-Wilkinson considered that allowing treatment to be withdrawn from Anthony Bland would perhaps ease some of the distress his family experienced with his prolonged PVS state. However, Amareskara and Bagaric promote that in cases of active euthanasia, a slow dying process allows for 'a last minute change of mind . . . [that is not possible] in the case of active euthanasia and we can be more certain of the patient's commitment to the decision to die'. See Amarasekara and Bagaric, above, n 6, 98.

period of weeks from lack of food but unlawful to produce his immediate death by a lethal injection, thereby saving his family from yet another ordeal to add to the tragedy that has already struck them?[98]

Lord Mustill concurred:

Unlike the conscious patient he [Bland] does not know what is happening to his body, and cannot be affronted by it; he does not know of his family's continuing sorrow. By ending his life the doctors will not relieve him of a burden become intolerable, for others carry the burden and he has none.[99]

In dealing with the distinction between acts and omissions, the judges were required to consider the manner in which Anthony Bland's life could be brought to an end. The issue raised some discomfort, as it did not concern the withdrawal of medical treatment but the withdrawal of hydration and nutrition.[100]

Does withdrawal of nutrition and hydration amount to starving to death?

Lord Keith began by considering that artificial feeding amounted to medical treatment and care. He considered nourishment to be a form of 'medical technique' because of the way it was administered.[101]

Lord Goff extended the point, addressing the concept of futility of treatment: 'When such treatment has no therapeutic purpose of any kind, as where it is futile because the patient is unconscious and there is no prospect of any improvement in his condition.'[102] Further, 'in a case such as the present, it is the futility of the treatment which justifies its termination';[103] it is 'no longer in his best interests'[104] for such treatment to continue. He concluded that, to 'terminate' such futile treatment, continuation of artificial feeding would have to cease. He did not understate the ethical and highly emotive nature of the discontinuation, stating:

---

98 *Airedale NHS Trust v Bland* [1993] AC 789, 885.
99 Ibid 897.
100 It should be noted that in some jurisdictions, such as that in New South Wales in Australia, omissions may still give rise to culpability. For discussion about withdrawal of feeding tubes (artificial nutrition and hydration) in Victoria, Australia, see the landmark decision in Re BMV: Ex parte Gardner (2003) 7 VR 487, in which Justice Morris of the Supreme Court of Victoria ruled that the appointed guardian in the case had authority under the Victorian Medical Treatment Act 1988 to refuse artificial nutrition and hydration via percutaneous endoscopic gastrostomy (PEG) from a 69-year-old unconscious female patient with advanced-stage dementia. See, e.g., Michael A Ashby and Danuta Mendelson, 'Gardner; re BWV: Victorian Supreme Court Makes Landmark Australian Ruling on Tube Feeding' (2004) 181(8) *Medical Journal of Australia* 442–445.
101 *Airedale NHS Trust v Bland* [1993] AC 789, 858.
102 Ibid 869.
103 Ibid.
104 Ibid 867.

[I]t can be said that the patient will as a result starve to death; and this may bring before our eyes the vision of an ordinary person slowly dying of hunger, and suffering all the pain and distress associated with such a death. But here it is clear from the evidence that no such pain or distress will be suffered by Anthony, who can feel nothing at all.[105]

The medical perspective on the withdrawal or withholding of artificial feeding was discussed in the international medical journal *The Lancet* in the early 1990s, where Ahronheim and Gasner commented:

The use of the word 'starvation' is especially provocative when applied to clinical consequences of withholding or withdrawing artificial feeding . . . such images disturb our well-fed society but . . . are irrelevant to discussions of feeding patients who are hopelessly ill.[106]

Not surprisingly, as the majority of judges in *Bland* relied heavily on medical opinion to justify their decisions to allow Anthony Bland to die, Lord Hoffman made reference to the American coined terms 'sloganism and emotional symbolism':

I do not think one should make light of these deeply intuitive feelings, which derive, as I have said, from a principle of kindness which is a badge of our humanity. But like the principle of the sanctity of life, they cease to provide true guidance in the extreme case.[107]

A recent Victorian pilot study found that the provision of proper palliative care facilitates a natural body response, reporting that 'terminal dehydration is seen as part of the homeostatic process involving an adaptive physiological response when the dying body goes into multi-system failure'.[108] Arguably, responsible doctors would contend that they are simply facilitating this adaptive physiological response and allowing nature to take its course while managing the pain. They may dispute they are hastening the process, and it is likely they would have the support of the courts in this regard.

---

105 Ibid 870.
106 Judith C Ahronheim and M Rose Gasner, 'The Sloganism of Starvation' (1990) 335(8684) *The Lancet* 278, 278. Similar terminology was inaccurately applied in the case of Maria Korp in Victoria, Australia, in 2005. Maria Korp was reported missing in February 2005 and found alive but in a state of post-coma unresponsiveness four days after her disappearance. Victorian public advocate Julian Gardner authorised the withdrawal of artificial hydration and nutrition and for palliative care to be implemented. The case aroused much controversy and publicity, and the withdrawal of tube feeding was sensationalised by the press media as 'starving her to death'. See, especially, Julian Gardner, 'Dilemmas in End-of-life Care: The Maria Korp Case' in Simon Barraclough and Heather Garner (eds), *Analysing Health Policy: A Problem Orientated Approach* (Elsevier, 2008) 166–176.
107 *Airedale NHS Trust v Bland* [1993] AC 789, 832.
108 Pamela Van der Riet, Denise Brooks and Michael Ashby, 'Nutrition and Hydration at the End of Life: Pilot Study of a Palliative Care Experience' 2006 14(2) *Journal of Law and Medicine* 182, 185.

The judges in *Bland* wrestled with semantics to allow doctors to withdraw nutrition and hydration lawfully, renaming it as the withdrawal of medical treatment that no longer served Anthony Bland's best interests, and was thus futile. Arguably, one of the issues of contention in *Bland* was the application of the doctrine of causation. All parties concerned with Bland's care (including the family's Catholic priest) agreed that continuation of treatment was not in his best interests. The central issue was whether discontinuation amounted to an act or an omission, and the court considered this to be an omission rather than an act.

Given the time, energy and painstaking efforts spent wrestling with the phraseology of what essentially amounted to euthanasia, the courts would have been better served by dealing directly with the life and death issues that confronted them. This reluctance to be seen as sanctioning any form of euthanasia has compelled recent judgments to invoke obscure and sometimes indefensible principles, standards and criteria, which are explored and illustrated in the case judgments discussed below. Having discussed many of the key issues that the court was required to consider in *Bland*, the next section of this chapter explores the relevant case law and manner in which judges apply the best interests principle to cases of impaired infants.

2.5 Selected UK cases involving impaired infants

The case law considered in this section is critiqued sequentially for ease of understanding the evolution and development of judicial thought regarding the best interests principle and its application in end of life decisions concerning premature and critically ill infants.

The following cases examine the courts' application of the best interests principle to allow the lawful withdrawal or withholding of life-sustaining treatment. The cases also highlight the recurring reluctance of the courts to oppose medical opinion in making end of life decisions.

The case of *Re C (a minor) (wardship: medical treatment)*,[109] concerned an infant suffering from congenital hydrocephalus, a blockage of cerebral spinal fluid to the brain and brain malformation. The infant was diagnosed as severely and irreversibly brain damaged. The local authority sought a declaration from the court to determine 'what treatment should be given in the best interests of C if, as sooner or later was inevitable, she suffered some infection or illness over and above the handicaps from which she was already suffering'.[110]

The medical practitioner responsible for the care of the infant recommended that the objective of treatment should be to ease her suffering and pain rather than to prolong her life. In order for such an objective to be met, medical practitioners stated it was unnecessary to provide antibiotics, intravenous infusions or nasogastric feeding mechanisms.

---

109   *Re C (a minor) (wardship: medical treatment)* [1989] 2 All ER 782.
110   Ibid 784.

Interestingly, in the Court of Appeal judgment, Lord Donaldson MR was required to clarify what he referred to as a 'misleading phrase' in Justice Ward's initial judgment. In the first instance, in concluding that the hospital authority could lawfully withhold further treatment, Justice Ward had stated: 'I direct that leave be given to the hospital authorities to treat the ward to die, to die with the greatest dignity and the least of pain, suffering and distress.'[111]

Referring to Justice Ward's initial 'failure to express himself with his usual felicity',[112] Lord Donaldson MR was quick to 'revise' the sentence in the judgment to: 'I direct that leave be given to the hospital authorities to treat the ward in such a way that she may *end her life* and die peacefully with the greatest dignity and the least of pain, suffering and distress.'[113] This illustrates a rare occasion in which the court was originally overly frank in its judgment. However, the higher court was quick to turn the statement in question away from anything bordering the controversial.

Another leading case illustrating the preparedness of courts to equate best interests with probable death was *Re J (a minor) (wardship: medical treatment)*.[114] In this case, Baby J was born prematurely at 27 weeks' gestation and, due to a shortage of oxygen and impaired blood supply, received severe brain damage. The infant subsequently suffered recurring convulsions and periods during which he stopped breathing, and on various occasions the infant was placed on ventilation. However, he was diagnosed as neither dying nor near the point of death, although the prognosis was made that he would develop spastic quadriplegia.

The medical practitioners sought the approval of the court to ensure that in the event the infant suffered another collapse and stopped breathing, a mechanical ventilator should not aid him. Again, the courts agreed with the doctors declaring that it would be lawful for doctors not to provide mechanical ventilation that was 'intrusive and painful and palliative care could be offered'.[115] The decision in *Re J* is important and influential to later decisions in that, although Baby J would never lead a 'normal' life in the sense of seeing and hearing, the baby was neither dying nor likely to die if given the appropriate medical treatment and support.

In the Court of Appeal, Lord Donaldson MR discussed the likely prognosis:

It is debatable whether he will ever be able to sit up or to hold his head upright. J appears to be blind, although there is a possibility that some degree of sight may return. He is likely to be deaf. He may be able to make sounds which reflect his mood, but he is unlikely ever to be able to speak, even to the extent of saying 'Mum' or 'Dad'. It is highly unlikely that he will develop even limited intellectual abilities. Most unfortunately of all, there is a likelihood that he will be able to feel pain to the same extent as a normal

---

111 Ibid 787.
112 Ibid.
113 Ibid.
114 *Re J (a minor) (wardship: medical treatment)* [1990] 3 All ER 930.
115 Skene, above, n 26, 351.

baby, because pain is a very basic response. It is possible that he may achieve the ability to smile and to cry.[116]

Balcombe LJ explained the medical procedures that the infant would be subjected to:

> He would have to be fed by a nasogastric tube or intravenously; the latter method would probably be the safer. Drips have to be re-sited from time to time. Constant blood sampling is necessary to ensure that the oxygen levels are neither too high nor too low. External cardiac massage may be necessary with the injection of drugs directly into the heart. There are no half measures to intensive support and the evidence was that there is a risk that these procedures may cause significant distress to J. who is thought to feel pinpricks and other forms of pain.[117]

The fact that the infant was not dying but that he would be subject to invasive medical treatments, and, more importantly, would suffer pain, created a greater dilemma for the judges in the appeal court. The prognosis and decision by the court to allow the lawful withdrawal of future ventilation is illustrative of the dilution of the sanctity of life principle. Although the judges were reluctant to declare overtly that the principle was redundant, this was evident in the significant contradictions by their Honours in the case.

Lord Donaldson MR referred to an established point of law when he stated: 'We know that the instinct and desire for survival is very strong. We all believe in and assert the sanctity of human life.'[118] Taylor LJ also acknowledged the doctrine of the sanctity of life: 'The court's high respect for the sanctity of human life imposes a strong presumption in favour of taking all steps capable of preserving it, save in exceptional circumstances.'[119] Further:

> As a corollary to the second principle, it cannot be too strongly emphasised that the court never sanctions steps to terminate life. That would be unlawful. There is no question of approving, even in a case of the most horrendous disability, a course aimed at terminating life or accelerating death.[120]

It would appear that Taylor LJ had firmly accepted the fundamental stance of the law concerning life and death issues, and may have opposed the decision to allow the infant to die in any future instances of breathing difficulties. However, he then progressed: 'The court is concerned only with the circumstances in which steps should not be taken to prolong life.'[121]

---

116 *Re J (a minor) (wardship: medical treatment)* [1990] 3 All ER 930, 933.
117 Ibid 940.
118 Ibid 938.
119 Ibid at 943.
120 Ibid.
121 Ibid.

This is a considerable *volte-face* from his previous acknowledgment of the doctrine of the sanctity of life, made within the same paragraph of his judgment. That such a cardinal principle or ideal can be defeated based on such a fine distinction as the difference between accelerating death and not prolonging life demonstrates a lack of real commitment to it in the first place.[122]

It is apparent from the judgments in *Re J* that each of the judges in turn attempted to justify the prevention of further ventilation based on the infant's future quality of life. The judges in *Re J* adopted a patently paternalistic approach, by providing that the prevention of further treatment would provide some form of 'salvation' for the infant from a life that the judges and medical practitioners considered 'intolerable'. Arguably, the courts found it necessary to employ such benevolent terms to mask the reality that best interests probably equates to death. Where the withdrawal or withholding of life-sustaining treatment is in the best interests of a critically ill infant, such discussion should be guided by greater transparency and based on clearer criteria.

Taylor LJ's statement is illustrative of this benevolence:

> Despite the court's inability to compare a life afflicted by the most severe disability with death, the unknown, I am of the view that there must be extreme cases in which the court is entitled to say: The life which this treatment would prolong would be so cruel as to be intolerable.[123]

In *Re J*, the courts seemingly applied a deemed autonomy role that if Baby J were able to express his own free will and patient autonomy, he would have reached the same decision as the judges and medical practitioners.

Further, Taylor LJ asserted:

> At what point in the scale of disability and suffering ought the court to hold that the best interests of the child do not require further endurance to be imposed by positive treatment to prolong its life? I consider the correct approach is for the court to judge the quality of life the child would have to endure if given the treatment and decide whether in all the circumstances such a life would be so afflicted as to be intolerable to that child. I say 'to that child' because the test should not be whether the life would be tolerable to the decider. The test must be whether the child in question, if capable of exercising sound judgement, would consider the life tolerable.[124]

---

122 Several commentators have considered the distinction between not prolonging life and accelerating death as a 'legal fiction'. See, generally, Len Doyal, 'Dignity in Dying Should Include the Legalization of Non-Voluntary Euthanasia' (2006) 1(2) *Journal of Clinical Ethics* 65–67. For further discussion of the illusory nature of the acts and omissions doctrine, see Amarasekara and Bagaric, above, n 6.

123 *Re J (a minor) (wardship: medical treatment)* [1990] 3 All ER 930, 944.

124 Ibid 945.

The Court of Appeal judgment illustrates a position of deemed autonomy taken by the judges:

> [W]here a ward of court suffered from physical disabilities so grave that from his point of view be so intolerable if he were to continue living that he would choose to die if he were in a position to make a sound judgement, the court could direct that treatment without which death would ensue from natural causes need not be given to the ward to prolong his life, even though he was neither on the point nor dying.[125]

Thus, the judges in the appeal court rejected the outright primacy of sanctity of life in favour of appreciating the 'quality' of life that the impaired infant would be subject to, to establish what would be in his best interests.[126]

However, there is no reference within the judgments in *Re J* of how the 'quality' of a disabled infant's life is to be measured. There is a strong presumption in favour of withdrawing treatment when the patient's life will be 'intolerable' or considerably 'awful', but a lack of precision is evident in defining what should be considered as a life that lacks substantial 'quality'.

This provides another example of the ineffectiveness of the best interests principle and the additional concepts that have been introduced by the courts to allow the lawful withdrawal or withholding of life-sustaining treatment. This book does not contend that life must be preserved at all costs; however, life and death decisions should be made with greater transparency and tangibility, rather than continuing to be based on subjective and undefined concepts.

The imprecision and ambiguity evident in the judgments regarding the 'quality of life' argument is considered by Gostin:

> It is difficult to argue with the premise underlying the 'quality of life' position, for there must come a point for most of us where life is so devoid of meaning and contentment that it is not worth living. As a philosophic position, its weakness is that the factors that would justify forsaking continued life are seldom, if ever, specified. If one accepts that continued life is not in the infant's interests, then those who make this decision must be clear about the criteria adopted. Yet the basis for identifying and measuring those interests under a 'quality of life' standard is unclear.[127]

---

125 Ibid 931.
126 See, also, *Re J (a minor) (wardship: medical treatment)* [1992] 4 All ER 614, concerning a 16-month-old infant who, because of a fall, had sustained severe brain damage and was left mentally and physically disabled.
127 Larry Gostin, 'A Moment in Human Development: Legal Protection, Ethical Standards and Social Policy on the Selective Non-Treatment of Handicapped Neonates' (1985) 11 *American Journal of Law and Medicine* 31, 40.

Subsequently, in *Re C (a minor)*,[128] the court was again faced with a case concerning a 16-month-old child suffering from spinal muscular atrophy. She had been placed on ventilation to support her breathing. Her doctor concluded that it would not be in her best interests to continue indefinite ventilation. Further, as it was highly probable that the infant would suffer a further respiratory relapse, it would not be in her best interests to be re-ventilated. The hospital sought a declaration to withdraw ventilation. The infant's parents were prepared to allow the withdrawal of ventilation to see whether their infant could breathe independently. However, they wished the ventilation to be reinstated in the event of further breathing difficulties. The declaration was granted. Sir Stephen Brown concluded:

> I believe that in this case I should assent to the course, which is proposed by the Hospital Trust. I do so with a feeling of grave solemnity because I realise that the parents themselves will be greatly disappointed. It is a sad feature of this matter that there is, in fact, no hope for C, and what has to be considered is her best interests to prevent her from suffering as would be inevitable if this course were not to be taken.[129]

From the case law examined thus far, it is evinced that often the courts consider the withdrawal or withholding of life-sustaining treatment to be in the best interests of premature or critically ill infants.

The decisions in the cases discussed so far establish the strong judicial belief in medical practitioners' autonomy to decide the best interests of an incapacitated infant. Montgomery asserts that 'important moral judgements are being clothed with the mystique of professional expertise and appropriated by medicine from their proper place as social and political problems'.[130] Seemingly, end of life decisions that equate to certain death founded on the best interests principle are not publicly expressed as such and should instead be understood as judicial reasoning cloaked by clinical opinion.

The next section of this chapter continues the critique of case law and its application of the best interests principle and the introduction of further concepts applied by the courts to allow for the lawful withdrawal or withholding of life-sustaining treatment from impaired infants. The cases examined below once again illustrate that the outcomes of legal decisions are nearly always consistent with the opinion of medical practitioners.

2.6 The turn of the millennium: *Re A (conjoined twins)*

At the turn of the millennium, the case of *Re A (children) (conjoined twins: surgical separation)*[131] made news around the world. It concerned conjoined twins, Mary

---

128 *Re C (a minor)* (1997) 40 BMLR 31 (Fam Div).
129 Ibid 38.
130 Jonathan Montgomery, 'Time for a Paradigm Shift Medical Law in Transition' (2000) 53(1) *Current Legal Problems* 363, 363.
131 *Re A (children) (conjoined twins: surgical separation)* [2000] 4 All ER 961.

and Jodie, joined at the lower abdomen. It was predicted that Jodie's circulatory system would collapse within a matter of weeks under the strain of supporting herself and Mary.

In light of medical testimony, the High Court ordered the twins to be separated against the wishes of their devout Catholic parents and the Archbishop of Westminster, Cormac Murphy-O'Connor. Mary and Jodie's parents believed that the twins were a gift from God and that their fate and best interests should remain in God's hands. However, religion or morals were given no consideration when the matter went before Ward LJ, who stated: 'This court is a court of law, not of morals, and our task has been to find, and our duty is then to apply, the relevant principles of law to the situation before us, a situation which is quite unique.'[132]

Bound under s. 1 (1) Children Act 1989, which provides that the 'welfare of the child shall be the court's paramount consideration', in addition to the competing best interests of the twins, the court's task was undoubtedly complex.

The court acknowledged that, if it acted in the best interests of Mary, then Jodie would also die after an estimated six months. If the court acted in the best interests of Jodie, then Mary would die immediately. After much deliberation and legal debate the Court of Appeal authorised the separation of the twins. Ward LJ discussed the competing interests of the twins, stating:

> The reality here – harsh as it is to state it, and unnatural as it is that it should be happening – is that Mary is killing Jodie. That is the effect of the incontrovertible medical evidence and it is common ground in the case. Mary uses Jodie's heart and lungs to receive and use Jodie's oxygenated blood. This will cause Jodie's heart to fail and cause Jodie's death as surely as a slow drip of poison. How can it be just that Jodie should be required to tolerate that state of affairs?[133]

Referring to Keown's assertion about the sanctity of life, Ward LJ emphasised: 'Human life is created in the image of God and therefore possessed of an intrinsic dignity, which entitled it to be protected from unjust attack.'[134] However, he then concluded:

> Mary may have a right to life, but she has little right to be alive. She is alive because and only because, to put it bluntly, but nonetheless accurately, she sucks the lifeblood of Jodie and she sucks the lifeblood out of Jodie. She will survive only so long as Jodie survives. Jodie will not survive long because constitutionally she will not be able to cope. Mary's parasitic living will be the cause of Jodie's ceasing to live.[135]

---

132 Ibid 969.
133 Ibid 1016.
134 Ibid 999.
135 Ibid 1010.

Ward LJ considered: 'The sanctity of life doctrine does, however, acknowledge that it may be proper to withdraw or withhold treatment . . . the question is whether treatment is worthwhile not the patient's life.'[136] Here, the judge attempted the impossible, to marry the sanctity of life principle and the concept of futile treatment. As discussed earlier in this chapter, the religious and philosophical underpinnings of the sanctity of life principle are that all life is sacred; decisions to withdraw or withhold futile treatment, even when an infant is not dying, do not protect or save all life.

Ward LJ continued by applying the 'substituted judgment' approach that was rejected in *Bland*: 'If Jodie could speak, she would surely protest, "Stop it, Mary, you're killing me". Mary would have no answer to that.'[137]

The Court of Appeal concluded that it would be in the best interests of the twins to give Jodie a chance of survival, even at the cost of another life. Ward LJ attempted to justify the separation as a form of self-defence: 'The reality here, harsh as it is to state it and unnatural as it is that it should be happening, is that Mary is killing Jodie.'[138]

Justice Ward also made reference to the American term 'unjust aggressor', in which he drew an analogy to a six-year-old boy on a shooting spree in a school playground. Although in law that six-year-old is innocent, it is lawful to kill that child in self-defence.[139] However, in arguing that the same situation applied in this case, Justice Ward was incorrect. Mary was not deliberately trying to harm Jodie and the harm that Jodie suffered was through no choice of Mary's. Both twins were 'harmed' by genetic malformation, a sad state that neither of them had chosen.

In this case, the Court of Appeal again demonstrated reverence to the medical profession, and Ward LJ appeared to confer a quasi-judicial role on them:

> Faced as they are with an apparently irreconcilable conflict, the doctors should be in no different position from that in which the court itself was placed in the performance of its duty to give paramount consideration to the welfare of each child. The doctors must be given the same freedom of choice as the court has given itself and the doctors must make the choice along the same lines as the court has done.[140]

Their Lordships referred to texts including Aristotle and Cicero,[141] to justify in law killing one twin to allow the other to live. However, these texts did not supply the answer; instead, the judgment in *Bland* was used, in which the House of Lords found the doctor's withholding or withdrawing of treatment lawful in cases of certain death. As considered earlier in this chapter, a person who omits to act is

136 Ibid 1000.
137 Ibid.
138 Ibid 1016.
139 Ibid 1017.
140 Ibid 1016.
141 Ibid 1041.

said to let the patient die of a pre-existing illness or injury, whereas a person who acts is deemed to have killed the patient.

In *Bland*, life-sustaining treatment in the form of artificial nutrition and hydration was withdrawn, and the doctor's conduct was held to be an omission. The judgments by Lord Browne-Wilkinson and Lord Mustill highlighted that both judges doubted the morally and intellectually dubious distinction between acts and omissions. The decision in *Bland* was significant as far as accepting as lawful conduct with an aim or objective resulting in death. In so doing, the House of Lords shifted the boundary between what is and what is not murder.

By contrast, the Court of Appeal in *Re A (children) (conjoined twins: surgical separation)* cannot be accused of hiding behind the act or omission, killing or letting die dichotomy. The judges acknowledged that any procedure to separate the twins would be a positive act, leaving the judges in a quandary as to how the treating doctors would not be guilty of a charge of murder. Thus, in addition to futility, quality of life, intolerability and best interests, the judges introduced legal terms applied in criminal and family law to justify killing Mary to keep Jodie alive.

Ward LJ preferred to base his decision on a balancing exercise between Mary's right to life and the breach of duty to save Jodie's life. Justice Walker sought to distinguish Mary's death as a foreseen consequence as opposed to an intended killing. Further, the court resurrected the much debated doctrine of necessity, to justify the separation in law.

Justice Brooke based the justification of the lawfulness of the separation on the doctrine of necessity, which has been inapplicable in previous murder cases, and is not available as a defence to homicide.[142] A striking aspect of this judgment was his reference to a quote by Sir James Stephen, who acted as one of the commissioners on the Criminal Code Bill 1897, stating:

> Compulsion by necessity is one of the curiosities of the law, and so far as I am aware is a subject on which the law of England is so vague that, if cases raising the question should ever occur, the Judges would practically be able to lay down any rule which they considered expedient.[143]

The courts acknowledged that a defence of necessity is not a firm legal principle, and that it can be readily applied wherever the law deems fit. In this instance, it was applied to the lawful separation of conjoined twins that would result in the death of one of them.[144] The next section of this chapter considers recent judicial reasoning and case law from the UK.

142 *R v Bournewood Community and Mental Health NHS Trust ex parte L* [1998] 3 All ER 289; *Dudley v Stephens* (1884) 14 QBD. 273; *R v Howe* [1987] 1 AC 417.

143 *Re A (children) (conjoined twins: surgical separation)* [2000] 4 All ER 961, 1036.

144 The principle of necessity has been applied to other areas such as abortion and emergency treatment. Some commentators suggest that the principle of necessity is a tenable consideration in end of life decision making. Magnusson supports the application of the defence of necessity and the principle of double jeopardy in *Re A (children) (conjoined twins: surgical separation)* and in

2.7 Recent decisions: balance sheet of burdens and benefits

As has been noted thus far and will be further highlighted in this section, the courts overwhelmingly defer to medical opinion in decisions to withdraw or withhold life-sustaining treatment from impaired infants. Although the case of *Glass v United Kingdom*[145] did not concern an impaired infant, but a child, the decision is of particular interest given its rarity.

The case concerned a severely disabled child, David, who required round-the-clock care. After an operation to alleviate a respiratory obstruction, he suffered postoperative complications that included infections and the assistance of a ventilator. The treating doctors were of the medical opinion that further treatment would not be in his best interests. However, members of his family, particularly his mother, disagreed with the medical practitioners. His mother was of the belief that the doctors, with the assistance of morphine and Do not resuscitate orders (DNR) would mean that her son would 'be helped on his way'[146] and effectively be euthanised.

In this case, the European Court of Human Rights held that there had been a violation of Article 8 of the European Convention on Human Rights: right to respect for private and family life. The decision is important in providing some weight to parental wishes in treatment decisions. While most cases concerning end of life decisions for impaired infants and children override the wishes of parents in favour of medical opinion, in this case greater weight was given to the wishes of the child's mother.[147] However, the triumph of parental wishes over medical opinion must be celebrated with some caution. As Jackson has noted, 'the breach of Article 8 in the *Glass* case would have been prevented if the doctors had made a timely application to the court'. Further, it was noted: 'It is clearly possible, perhaps even probable, that the court would have granted the declaration authorizing non-treatment of this severely disabled child.'[148]

The case of *An NHS Trust v OT*[149] went before the courts in 2009. Baby OT had a rare metabolic disorder and suffered brain damage and respiratory problems. His parents went to the High Court to prevent doctors from stopping treatment. When this proved unsuccessful, the parents appealed against the decision of the doctors and the High Court that it was in OT's best interests for

general palliative care. See, especially, Roger S Magnusson, 'The Devil's Choice: Re-Thinking Law, Ethics, and Symptom Relief in Palliative Care' (2006) 34(4) *Journal of Law, Medicine and Ethics* 559–569.
145 *Glass v United Kingdom* [2004] ECHR 103 (9 March 2004).
146 Ibid [12].
147 See, especially, Richard Huxtable and Karen Forbes, '*Glass v United Kingdom*: Maternal Instinct v Medical Opinion' (2004) 16(3) *Child and Family Law Quarterly* 339–354. The role and influence of parental wishes and opinions is discussed in greater detail in Chapter 4.
148 Emily Jackson, *Medical Law: Texts, Cases and Materials* (Oxford University Press, 2006) 979.
149 *NHS Trust v OT* [2009] EWCA Civ 409 (14 May 2009).

treatment to be stopped. However, Justice Ward and Justice Wilson did not overturn the decision. OT's parents noted:

> That was the real argument between us and the doctors – they think his life is intolerable and that his disability is such that his life has little purpose; but we, along with some of the nurses, believed that he experiences pleasure and that he has long periods where he was relaxed and pain free.[150]

Also in 2009, Justice McFarlane in the Royal Courts of Justice was required to consider the case of *Re: Baby RB (a child)*.[151] Born on 10 October 2008, RB suffered from a rare genetic disorder, congenital myasthenic syndrome. Justice McFarlane described RB as:

> profoundly disabled by a defect which prevents the effective transmission of messages from his brain and nerves to his muscles. It affects every aspect of his physical life. Apart from being able to make small movements of his lower arms and hands, he has little control over his limbs. His face is incapable of expression and his eyelids hang low and are not often open. A tube through which air passes to his lungs passes through one nostril and a feeding tube in the other nostril. His need for breathe [sic] is now such that, unless the machine delivers air one every three seconds, his body will go into crisis and decline.[152]

By the age of 13 months, medical practitioners were of the opinion that ventilation should be stopped and that RB should be allowed to die. A doctor caring for Baby RB, referred to as Doctor F, stated that Baby RB was 'living on a knife edge'.[153]

The infant's parents could not agree as to what was in his best interests. RB's mother agreed with medical opinion and supported the application to withdraw ventilation from RB. However, the infant's father believed strongly that a surgical procedure should be performed to create space in his airway for him to breathe without ventilation and he should be allowed to be cared for at home. The views of Baby RB's father were supported by Professor Kirkham, a neurologist at Southampton Hospital, who considered that 'a cure' for Baby RB's medical condition could possibly be found in the 'foreseeable future', thus allowing him to operate a mechanical wheelchair in later years.[154]

---

150 'Couple's Distress at Baby Ruling', *BBC News*, 21 March 2009. http://news.bbc.co.uk/2/hi/uk_news/ 7956450.stm. This case again illustrates the reliance placed on medical opinion by the courts. The tensions that arise between medical teams and parents are discussed further in Chapter 4.

151 *Re Baby RB (A Child)* [2009] EWHC 3269 (Fam) (10 November 2009).

152 Ibid [2].

153 Elizabeth Day, 'Baby RB: Heartbreak in Court 50 as Life of a One-year-old Hangs in the Balance', *The Guardian* (Online), 8 November 2009. www.guardian.co.uk/society/2009/nov/08/baby-rb-court-case

154 Ibid.

At the beginning of the hearing, Baby RB's father set out his extensive knowledge of his son's condition and needs, and had recorded a video showing Baby RB playing with a rattle and banging a drum, activities that practitioners had stated RB would not be able to enjoy.[155]

Throughout the hearing, evidence was provided by leading experts regarding RB's condition, future development and treatment options. Justice McFarlane was satisfied with the majority medical evidence provided, stating he had 'total confidence' that both parents and the medical team 'had done all that they possibly could have to make RB's life as viable, comfortable and enjoyable as it could be'.[156] Arguably, the judge had already decided it was in RB's best interests that ventilation be stopped.

Presumably, with some relief to the court, within a week of the hearing commencing, RB's father returned having changed his mind, and agreed that ventilation should be discontinued in his son's best interests.[157] Justice McFarlane stated, 'I suspect that the father and I have travelled a similar path down the evidential road and have now reached the same conclusion.'[158]

Again, demonstrating the courts deference to medical opinion, with particular gratitude for Professor B's opinion, and referring to Professor B as an 'independent voice' discussing the 'burdens and benefits' of RB's life in the future,[159] the court adopted a balance sheet approach, measuring RB's life in terms of burdens, benefits, futility and worthwhileness.

Thus far, it has been illustrated that, in addition to the nebulous concept of best interests, the courts have, over time, introduced other subjective and indefinable concepts to allow the lawful discontinuation of life-sustaining treatment. Terms such as 'worthwhileness', 'futility' and 'burdens and benefits of treatment' are subjective, and all individuals closely involved in the care and decision-making process may measure their importance differently.[160]

The deficiencies of this approach are further illustrated in the 2004 case of *Portsmouth Hospital NHS Trust v Wyatt*,[161] which made global headlines. The case concerned Charlotte Wyatt and was the first to consider withdrawal or withholding of treatment from a minor in an open court, without the anonymity of the parties'

155　Ibid.
156　*Re Baby RB (A Child)* [2009] EWHC 3269 (Fam) (10 November 2009) [8].
157　Cameron Stewart, 'Withdrawal of Treatment from a Newborn with Congenital Myasthenic Syndrome' (2010) 7(1) *Journal of Bioethical Inquiry* 3, 3.
158　*Re Baby RB (A Child)* [2009] EWHC 3269 (Fam) (10 November 2009) [9].
159　Ibid.
160　By way of example, John Keown suggests that the central issue is not whether the patient's life is 'worthwhile', but rather whether treatment would be 'worthwhile'. See, especially, John Keown, 'Restoring Moral and Intellectual Shape to the Law after Bland' (1997) 113(3) *Law Quarterly Review* 481. Further, both Harris and Freeman separately state that the most important factor is a 'worthwhile' life, and the secondary factor must be whether 'treatment is worthwhile' to allow the patient to enjoy a particular quality of life. See, especially, Michael Freeman, 'Whose Life is it Anyway?' (2001) 9 *Medical Law Review* 259–280; John Harris, 'Human Beings, Persons and Conjoined Twins: An Ethical Analysis of the Judgment in Re A' (2001) 9(3) *Medical Law Review* 221, 225.
161　*Portsmouth Hospital NHS Trust v Wyatt* [2004] EWCA 2247 (Fam) (7 October 2004).

names.[162] This approach was taken at the request of her parents, who believed that transparency in the decision-making process was important.

Although the transparency was welcomed from a societal and community point of view, from a legal viewpoint the court's decision to allow doctors to discontinue treatment lawfully was not revolutionary. Predictably, the courts placed considerable weight and reliance on medical opinion.

Charlotte was born prematurely and suffered considerable disabilities, including poor kidney function, difficulty breathing and brain damage. At the time the case went before the law, Charlotte was 11 months of age and her chances of survival for another 12 months were estimated at 5%. The medical opinion of those caring for her was that, in the event of respiratory failure, it was not in her best interests to continue to survive on mechanical ventilation.

However, Charlotte's parents strongly maintained that it was their duty to preserve her life and that it was not her time to die. Considering medical opinion and evidence that Charlotte experienced pain and possibly little or no pleasure, Justice Hedley concluded that, in the event that Charlotte needed 'invasive treatment' that would be 'intolerable', the medical team could withhold the use of mechanical ventilation.

This declaration was made for a six-month period. However, after six months, Charlotte's parents returned to the court, contending that she was no longer considered terminally ill and that the declaration should be removed. Justice Hedley did not remove the declaration and continued to rely on the medical opinion that Charlotte's health had not improved. Justice Hedley boldly began his judgment in the High Court stating: 'On the basis of the unanimous medical evidence in this case, the issue in all probability is not whether this baby should live or die but how and when she should die.'[163]

Similar to in *Re A (conjoined twins)*, in which Ward LJ began his judgment stating that 'this court is a court of law, not of morals',[164] Justice Hedley began:

> What is the role of the court in all this? Any civilised society must have the means by which intractable disputes, whether between the state and the citizen or between citizens themselves are to be resolved. That is the purpose of the courts and the system of civil and family justice in this country. This kind of dispute is to be resolved by a Judge of the Family Division and whilst the judge will be more aware than anyone of his own limitations in deciding as profound an issue as this, decision there simply has to be. It may well be that an external decision is in the end a better solution than the stark alternatives of medical or parental veto.[165]

162 In *Re C (a minor) (wardship: medical treatment)* [1989] 2 All ER 782, 783. In this case, Lord Donaldson MR addressed the issue of an injunction to protect the parents as well as local and health authorities from harassment because of the sensitive nature of the case.

163 *Portsmouth Hospital NHS Trust v Wyatt* [2004] EWCA 2247 (Fam) (7 October 2004) [1].

164 *Re A (children) (conjoined twins: surgical separation)* [2000] 4 All ER 961, 969.

165 *Portsmouth Hospital NHS Trust v Wyatt* [2004] EWCA 2247 (Fam) (7 October 2004) [4].

However, such profound statements about the authority and impartiality of the courts could be deemed redundant, given that judges habitually defer to medical opinion to reach their final decisions.

The judge considered the burdens and benefits of treatment, and concluded that three things would benefit Charlotte and presumably be in her best interests: comfort and little pain, as much time as possible in the presence of her parents, and that she meets her end surrounded by the love and affection of those around her.[166] After 'deriving considerable assistance'[167] from the judgment of Lord Donaldson MR in the first *Re J* case of the 1990s, Justice Hedley found:

> Helpful though these passages are, it is in my view essential that the concept of 'intolerable to that child' should not be seen as a gloss on, much less a supplementary test to, best interests. It is a valuable guide in the search for best interests in this kind of case.[168]

Although Justice Hedley found passages from the judgment of *Re J* to be of some benefit, it was not the most relevant authority on the matter of best interests. Instead, the judgment of Thorpe LJ in *Re A (male sterilisation)*,[169] concerning an adult male patient lacking capacity, was preferred:

> There can be no doubt in my mind that the evaluation of best interests is akin to a welfare appraisal. . . . Pending the enactment of a checklist or other statutory direction it seems to me that the first instance judge with the responsibility to make an evaluation of the best interests of a claimant lacking capacity should draw up a balance sheet.[170]

Interestingly, the 'balance sheet' to weigh up the benefits and burdens of treatment considered by Thorpe LJ in *Re A* was endorsed and applied by the Court of Appeal in *Wyatt*. Justice Wall's concluding comments on the best interests test are particularly pertinent:

> In our judgment, the intellectual milestones for the judge in a case such as the present are, therefore, simple, although the ultimate decision will frequently be extremely difficult. The judge must decide what is in the child's best interests.[171]

The 'intellectual milestones' referred to by Justice Wall are by no means revolutionary. They are simply an amalgam of key statements made by judges in

---

166 Ibid [38].
167 Ibid [24].
168 Ibid.
169 *Re A (male sterilisation)* [2000] 1 FLR 549.
170 *Portsmouth Hospital NHS Trust v Wyatt* [2004] EWCA 2247 (Fam) (7 October 2004) [26].
171 Ibid [87].

previous decisions to withdraw or withhold life-sustaining treatment. Milestones were considered at paragraph 87 of the judgment:

> In making that decision, the welfare of the child is paramount, and the judge must look at the question from the assumed point of view of the patient *(Re J)*. There is a strong presumption in favour of a course of action which will prolong life, but that presumption is not irrebuttable *(Re J)*. The term 'best interests' encompasses medical, emotional, and all other welfare issues *(Re A)*. The court must conduct a balancing exercise in which all the relevant factors are weighed *(Re J)* and a helpful way of undertaking this exercise is to draw up a balance sheet *(Re A)*.[172]

Justice Wall failed to provide any detail or elaboration of the 'milestones' in *Wyatt*. Arguably, this was a lost opportunity to clarify the vague nature of the best interests test and end of life decision making for critically ill patients. By expanding on these milestones, the best interests test could have been injected with further structure and precision.

The *Wyatt* case was followed by *Re L (medical treatment: benefit)*,[173] which concerned Baby Luke, who was born with Edwards syndrome, a chromosome abnormality that has an average two-month life expectancy. Luke suffered serious cardiac problems and had experienced several cardiac arrests that required resuscitation. While the doctors caring for Luke believed it to be in his best interests not to resuscitate him in the event of another cardiac arrest, his mother disagreed and wanted treatment continued. Dame Butler-Sloss ruled in favour of the medical team, and Luke died soon after the case was concluded in the High Court. Dame Butler-Sloss followed previous authority, stating that the preservation of life is most favourable, 'but not where treatment would be futile'.[174]

As has been evinced, it is uncommon for a judge to rule against medical opinion. However, in the case of *An NHS Trust v MB*,[175] Justice Holman held that the discontinuation of medical treatment was not in the infant's best interests. Born on 25 August 2004, Baby M appeared 'normal'. However, at seven weeks, he was diagnosed with type 1 spinal muscular atrophy (the most severe) and had since remained hospitalised. At the time of the judgment, M was 18 months old. Justice Holman described M's condition as:

> degenerative and progressive, i.e. it can only get worse. It may in some sufferers reach a plateau, but it cannot get better. It affects the voluntary muscles (but not the involuntary muscles such as those of the heart) which become progressively weaker and may ultimately cease to work at all.[176]

172 Ibid.
173 *Re L (medical treatment: benefit)* [2004] EWHC 2713 (Fam).
174 Jane Fortin, *Children's Rights and the Developing Law* (Cambridge University Press, 3rd edn, 2009) 379.
175 *An NHS Trust v MB* [2006] EWHC 507 (Fam) (15 March 2006).
176 Ibid [5].

In addition, M suffered epilepsy, could not breathe unassisted and was fed via a gastrostomy tube. The medical opinion of his treating doctors was:

> [Q]uality of life for M is now so low and that the burdens of living are now so great that it is unethical (the word 'cruel' has been used) to continue artificially to keep him alive, and that his endo-tracheal tube should be withdrawn. By the use of sedatives, he could have a peaceful, pain free and dignified death, but he would die almost immediately, probably within a few minutes.[177]

His parents disagreed and sought support from the courts. His mother asserted that he showed marked cognitive function:

> M does indeed show pain or distress by frowns and by tears. She says that he similarly displays pleasure to her by his eyebrows going up slightly rather than going down, and she can see the merest movement upwards of the side of his lips as if he is trying to smile. She says that his eyes fix on her and will follow her until, because he cannot move his head, he cannot see her any more. She says that when his brother and sister are there, which they very frequently are, he shows recognition of them and his eyebrows and corner of his mouth will move slightly upwards. If she touches his thumb it will move. She is convinced that he sees, hears and takes in certain TV and DVD programmes and music on CDs.[178]

Justice Holman considered the concepts of 'quality of life' and 'burdens and benefits' that have become regular legal discourse. After considering the medical evidence, Justice Holman decided that M should continue on ventilation, as he demonstrated cognitive function and was able to interact and bond with his family.

His Honour disagreed with the treating doctor's opinion that Baby M's quality of life was 'so low that the burdens of living are now so great that it is unethical to keep him alive'.[179] The judge applied a linear approach based on his cognitive abilities:

> M is not unconscious, still less in a permanent vegetative state. He is conscious. He is awake most or all of the day, and then sleeps at night. It is probable, and must certainly be assumed, that he continues to see and to hear and to feel touch; to have an awareness of his surroundings and in particular of the people who are most close to him, his family; and to have the normal thoughts and thought processes of a small child of 18 months . . . But people talk to him and stories are read to him; he is shown TV and DVDs and music is

177 Ibid [10].
178 Ibid [43].
179 Ibid [10].

played to him on CDs; and it must be assumed that he processes all these sights and sounds in his mind like any other child of his age and gains pleasure from them.[180]

The decision in this case represented an important change in tenor to previous judgments. However, as illustrated in the case law examined thus far, Justice Hoffman failed to critique or examine the effectiveness or efficiency of the best interests principle, stating: 'The law around this topic is now well established and tolerably clear.'[181] Justice Holman ambitiously created 'ten propositions', which he believed did not require the 'need for copious reference to authority'.[182] These 'propositions' were in no way novel and were largely based on the 'intellectual milestones' laid down in *Wyatt*, which, as noted earlier, were a montage of parts of previous judgments.[183] This case provided the court with another opportunity to consider a normative basis on which the best interests principle could have been established but the court failed to take that opportunity.

Nevertheless, some of the propositions merit consideration, in particular in highlighting the court's attempt to provide some substance and clearer context to defining 'best interests'. Proposition four stated that withdrawal or withholding of life-sustaining treatment decisions 'must be decided by the application of an objective approach or test'.[184] However, this objectivity was contradicted by proposition five:

> Best interests are used in the widest sense and include every kind of consideration capable of impacting on the decision. These include, non-exhaustively, medical, emotional, sensory (pleasure, pain and suffering) and instinctive (the human instinct to survive) considerations.[185]

Proposition five is simply a rephrased version of part of Justice Wall's vague intellectual milestone of 'medical, emotional, and all other welfare issues' from the *Wyatt* case. In conclusion, Justice Holman decided that, although not immediately, in the event that Baby M required invasive treatment, the doctors did not have to provide resuscitation and that Baby M would, therefore, die naturally. It would appear that the judge in this case did not allow himself to become embroiled in medical opinion and academic debate regarding quality of life issues, as is evident in his closing paragraph:

> Every day some parents somewhere, in consultation with doctors, have to make agonising decisions about the best interests of children with severe

---

180 Ibid.
181 Ibid [16].
182 Ibid.
183 See proposition 6–8 at [16].
184 Ibid.
185 Ibid.

SMA or similar disorders. I hope that this judgment and decision will neither deter doctors from commencing ventilation when they consider it should be tried; nor lead any parent who has taken or may take, on the advice of doctors, the agonising decision not to start, or to discontinue, ventilation, to feel that their decision was mistaken.[186]

The final case to be examined in this section is that of *NHS Trust v Baby X and others*.[187] Baby X was born a healthy child in 2011, but later suffered an accident at home that led to irreversible brain damage. The treating consultant described Baby X's condition as being comatose, showing no interaction with his parents or carers. He did not recognise touch, voice or his surroundings. Both the treating physicians and other hospital staff concluded that artificial ventilation was no longer in Baby X's best interests. Further, continuing treatment with no signs of improvement was futile.

The case for withdrawal of treatment was heard before Justice Hedley. Both parents opposed the medical opinion with which they were presented. They believed that their son should be given every possible chance of improvement, and their faith prevented them from giving consent to withdraw treatment that would inevitably lead to Baby X's death.

Justice Hedley's judgment was brief at eight pages. In a forthright fashion, he stated: 'The question in this case is whether a baby known as *X* should be removed from a ventilator and made the subject only of palliative care.'[188]

In the judgment, the 'balance sheet' approach of burdens and benefits was again highlighted. However, this was not considered worthy of any real discussion: 'given the enormity and chronicity of the brain damage suffered in this case, the conventional list of burdens and benefits is not very extensive.'[189]

Justice Hedley suggested that caring and nurturing for their infant was in itself a burden on Baby X's parents: 'They come from a faith tradition in which the obligations of parenthood are clear: they are to give lifelong care to X whatever in fact the burden upon them doing so may be.'[190]

Untypically, the minority medical opinion of Professor Vloeberghs was that greater weight should be given to the views and opinions of the parents.[191] This was a considerable change from previous cases, considering that, as previously argued, most decisions concerning neonatal withdrawal of treatment are substantially guided and influenced by medical opinion.[192]

However, while Justice Hedley concluded that it would be lawful for the medical team to withdraw ventilation and provide palliative care for Baby X, as in previous

---

186 Ibid [109].
187 *NHS Trust v Baby X and others* [2012] EWHC 2188 (Fam) (30 July 2012).
188 Ibid [1].
189 Ibid [20].
190 Ibid [16].
191 Ibid [21].
192 This is discussed in Chapter 4.

judgments already considered, his Honour also stated: 'In those circumstances issues surrounding death must be faced now in a way that otherwise would be quite unwarranted.'[193] This ensures the decision is not considered euthanasia, which the English courts fervently avoid.

In concluding this section, the trend of judicial decisions demonstrates that the courts place great weight on medical opinion, and justify decisions to allow the lawful withdrawal or withholding of life-sustaining treatment by applying nebulous terms such as intolerability, futility and a balance sheet of benefits and burdens. In some cases, the courts have decided that inevitable death equates with best interests, even in cases in which the infant is not dying but is severely disabled due to physical and/or mental trauma. This book argues that where such decisions are made, they should be guided by greater transparency and objectivity; decisions should not continue to be made under the guise of a sense of benevolence by applying the ill-defined best interests principle. The case law that has been examined thus far has derived from the UK. The next section of this chapter turns to consider the comparatively few but nevertheless important cases concerning critically ill infants from Australia.

2.8 Early Australian cases involving impaired infants

The Australian approach to the withdrawal or withholding of treatment from patients is similar to that of the UK and often follows decisions from English cases. However, in the first case to be considered, Justice Vincent in the Victorian Supreme Court effected a radical departure from the line of English legal thought in his dismissal of the concept of 'quality of life'.

Re F: F v F[194] concerned an infant suffering spina bifida. The father sought an application from the court, alleging that the infant was being deprived of food for it to starve to death. An order was made that the infant be fed until a thorough examination of the case could take place. Unlike in a majority of cases, no medical evidence was brought before the court, nor did the hospital attend the hearing. The issue before Justice Vincent was the application from the child's father that the child was being denied 'sustenance'. The judge simply ordered that the 'hospital take reasonable and necessary steps to pursue good medical practice'.[195]

The order made by Justice Vincent in this case was vague and ambiguous in light of there being no medical evidence about the infant's prognosis and only the allegation that the infant was being 'starved'. His Honour was extremely cautious not to make a decision that could have compounding consequences for any future cases. As such, Justice Vincent arguably 'sat on the fence' in this case:

[N]o parent, no doctor, no court, has any power to determine that the life of any child, however disabled that child may be, will be deliberately taken away

---

193 Ibid [26].
194 *Re F: F v F* (Unreported, Supreme Court of Victoria, Vincent J, 2 July 1986).
195 Ibid 20.

from it . . . [the law] does not permit decisions to be made concerning the quality of life, nor does it enable any assessment to be made as to the value of any human being.[196]

Justice Vincent's decision and judgment in this case is strikingly different from that of the judges in the UK some five years earlier. For example, in *Re B*,[197] Lord Templeman found:

[A]t the end of the day it devolves on this court in this particular instance to decide whether the life of the child is demonstrably going to be so awful that in effect the child must be condemned to die, or whether the life of this child is still so imponderable that it would be wrong for her to be condemned to die.[198]

Returning to Justice Vincent's statement, it is questionable as to who has the 'power' to make such decisions, if not the law, parents or doctors. Ultimately, his Honour ordered the medical team to 'take necessary and reasonable steps' and to 'pursue good medical practice', which could include ensuring that a patient does not suffer pain or discomfort, by means of withdrawal or withholding of treatment.

Some years later, the case of *Baby M* in Victoria was considered in a coronial inquest.[199] In this example, the medical team worked in conjunction with the parents of a severely ill infant. Some of the facts of this case, and the situation in which the doctors and the parents of Baby M found themselves, mirror the 1981 English case of *R v Arthur*. In the case of *Baby M*, recently identified as being named Allison,[200] she was born on 14 July 1989 with serious abnormalities, including wasting of the muscles, inability to walk, incontinence and no sexual function.[201]

Allison's parents were devout Catholics who sought regular advice from Roman Catholic spiritual advisors. However, they agreed with the opinion of the medical team that invasive treatment or surgery should not be administered. Baby M was given pain relief and an open crib, dying some 12 days after the decision was made. Baby M's great-aunt informed a right-to-life organisation of this matter, which then informed the police. It was alleged that the doctors, in conjunction with Baby M's parents, had decided to allow her to die due to her quality of life being considered so poor that it was not worthy of preservation.[202]

---

196 Ibid 9.
197 *Re B (a minor) (wardship: medical treatment)* [1990] 3 All ER (CA) 927.
198 Ibid 929.
199 *Baby M* (Victorian State Coroner's Office, Record of Investigation into Death, Case No 3149/89, 29 October 1991) VIC.
200 Kate Hagan, 'Doctors Tread Ethical Minefield, 21 Years On', *The Age* (Victoria), 14 August 2010, 4.
201 Helga Kuhse, 'A Report from Australia: Quality of Life and the Death of Baby M' (1992) 6(3) *Bioethics* 233, 234.
202 Ibid 235.

The central issue considered by the doctors and the coroner in this case surrounded Baby M's quality of life. Where the pattern in English case law has insisted on giving the utmost regard and preference to medical opinion, it would seem that in this case, the coroner, Wendy Wilmoth, took on the role of an impartial adjudicator. Albeit in contradiction to Lord Donaldson's judgment in *Re J* and, it would seem, outside the remit of her duties as coroner, she stated:

> This gives recognition to the role of quality of life considerations, and recognises the lack of absolutes in life, whilst still upholding principle . . . that no parent or court can judge the quality of a person's life to be so low as not to be deserving of continuance.[203]

The two treating doctors in this case, Drs Loughman and McDougall, discussed their decision to withdraw treatment publicly in a newspaper article in 2010.[204] Dr McDougall reported having 'wrestled with the decision for years' and remained concerned about the 'impact on Allison's family'. However, he felt he had 'closure at last' after her parents sought a reunion with the doctors in 2008.[205]

At the time of the coronial report, the treating doctors were provided with considerable support and solace by virtue of the final coroner's report, which stated that the decisions made by the parties involved were 'reasonable and appropriate'.[206] The coroner found:

> The decisions made by Baby M's doctors and parents, and the careful steps taken to ensure these decisions were legally, ethically and morally sound, have been tested and found entirely reasonable and appropriate. The community's interest is best served by . . . leaving the decision-making with doctors and their respective advisers, conscientiously determining the best course for their child.[207]

Until 2011, no other cases in Australia concerning withdrawal or withholding of treatment from critically impaired infants have required legal or coronial intervention.[208] Although a significantly smaller number of cases have gone before Australian courts as compared with the UK, there is healthy academic debate and an exceptional body of literature in the field of end of life decision making for incapacitated patients in Australia.[209] A landmark case that considered the best interests principle and medical treatment concerning minors in Australia is

203 Ibid 242.
204 Hagan, above, n 200, 4.
205 Ibid.
206 Skene, above, n 26, 353.
207 Hagan, above, n 200, 4.
208 A possible explanation for this may be the smaller population of individuals in Australia compared with the UK.
209 Faunce and Stewart assert that 'the discussion about what Australian courts would do has been largely confined to legal academia'. See, further, Thomas A Faunce and Cameron Stewart, 'The Messiha and Schiavo Cases: Third-party Ethical and Legal Interventions in Futile Care Disputes'

Marion's case. It remains a leading authority in this area and the discussion now turns to its details.

2.9 *Re Marion* and the best interests principle in Australia

The case of *Re Marion* concerned the non-therapeutic sterilisation of an intellectually disabled teenager, known under the pseudonym of Marion.[210] At first instance the case went before Nicholson CJ, Strauss and McCall JJ of the Family Court of Australia in 1990. It was noted that:

> The applicants were the parents of a 13-year-old daughter who was mentally and physically disabled. The parents sought authorisation, as a matter of caution, for the performance of sterilisation procedure on the child. The respondent was the Northern Territory Department of Health and Community Services; the Human Rights and Equal Opportunities Commission was granted leave to intervene and the Commonwealth Attorney-General was invited by the court to intervene.[211]

In support of their application for the authorisation of the sterilisation procedure, Marion's parents pointed out that:

> [A]s the child was incapable of caring for herself physically and/or properly understanding the nature and implications of sexuality, pregnancy and motherhood, it was in the best interests of the child to undergo hysterectomy and ovariectomy to prevent pregnancy; to prevent menstruation and menstrual bleeding with consequent psychological and behavioural problems; and to stabilise and prevent hormonal fluxes with consequential stress and behavioural problems.[212]

Some of the key issues that the Family Court were required to consider were whether Marion's parents could lawfully authorise the sterilisation without court authorisation and, if not, whether the Family Court had the jurisdiction to do so.

(2005) 183(5) *Medical Journal of Australia* 261, 261. Willmott, White and Cooper also acknowledge that 'traditionally, decisions in Australia to withhold or withdraw life-sustaining medical treatment have not been brought before the courts'. See, Lindy Willmott, Ben White and Donna Cooper, 'Interveners or Interferers: Intervention in Decisions to Withhold and Withdraw Life-Sustaining Medical Treatment' (2005) 27(4) *Sydney Law Review* 597, 621. The authors note that there has been a 'small but steady stream' of cases involving incapacitated adult patients. See, especially, *Northridge v Central Sydney Area Health Authority* (2000) 50 NSWLR 549; *Re BWV* [2003] VSC 173; *Re MC* [2003] QGAAT 13; *Slaveski v Austin Health* [2010] VSC 493; New Zealand case of *Auckland Area Health Board v Attorney General* [1993] NZLR 235.

210 *Re Marion* (1990)14 Fam LR 427. When the case went before the High Court of Australia it was cited as *Department of Health and Community Services v JWB and SMB (Marion's case)* (1992) 175 CLR 218.

211 *Re Marion* (1990) 14 Fam LR 427.

212 *Re Marion (No 2)* (1992) 175 CLR 218.

In light of the legal repercussions of providing medical treatment to a patient without his/her consent and the possibility of charges of battery and assault, it was imperative to determine who could consent to the medical treatment in *Marion's case*. The High Court of Australia determined that the Family Court does have the 'welfare' jurisdictional power to determine such matters.[213] Further, the High Court also concluded that the scope of the Family Court's power extended to issues outside the scope of parental responsibility, thus allowing the court to override decisions made by parents with regard to the child's welfare. Ultimately, the Family Court must act in the 'best interests' of the child.

Another important point was determined in *Marion's case*: that parental responsibility and decision making on behalf of children is limited by the category of medical procedure and the competence of the child. In particular, the High Court established that parents do not have authority to make medical treatment decisions for their children that are very serious and have irreversible consequences.[214]

The determinations made by the High Court in *Marion's case* are important in that they provide the Family Court with greater clarity as to its scope and jurisdictional power in cases that concern medical treatment decisions and children. The case also opened up the legal discussion on the best interests principle. Justice Brennan's minority judgment in the High Court is of particular consideration, in which he critiqued the best interests principle. His Honour raised some compelling points that largely align with the central tenants of this book, namely that the best interests principle is nebulous and is shrouded by the subjectivity of caregivers and decision makers. Brennan J noted:

> [I]t must be remembered that, in the absence of legal rules or a hierarchy of values, the best interest approach depends upon the value system of the decision-maker. Absent any rule or guideline that approach simply creates an examinable discretion in the repository of the power.[215]

Some of the competing and subjective interests of decision makers and care givers that Brennan J discussed in *Marion's case* resonate with the contention of this book, and are apparent in end of life decision making in respect of premature and critically impaired infants. His Honour highlighted:

> The anxious goodwill of the repository of the power – whether parents, guardians or courts – can generally be assumed, but there are too many

---

213 See s. 67ZC of the Family Law Act 1975 (Cth).
214 Such as a hysterectomy. The High Court considered in detail both therapeutic and non-therapeutic treatments. Further, the High Court concluded that a sterilisation was a 'step of last resort'. Brennan J stated: 'It is true that the phrase "best interests of the child" is imprecise, but no more than the "welfare of the child" and many other concepts with which courts must grapple. As we have shown, it is confined by the notion of "step of last resort".' *Secretary, Department of Health and Community Services v JWB and SMB (Marion's case)* [1991–1992] 175 CLR, 259.
215 *Secretary, Department of Health and Community Services v JWB and SMB (Marion's case)* (1992) 175 CLR 218, 271.

factors which tend to distort a dispassionate and accurate assessment of the true interests of the child. There are some powerful if unarticulated influences affecting, albeit in good faith, the presentation of information on which a decision as to the best interests of the child is to be made and the making of that decision. I mention some of those influences: the interests of those who bear the burden of caring for the child, the interests of those who will be involved in the sterilization if it proceeds, the scarcity of public resources.[216]

Brennan J quoted the following powerful passage from an article by Professor Ian Kennedy, which undoubtedly aligns with his views on the vagueness of the best interests principle:

> The best interests formula may be beloved of family lawyers but a moment's reflection will indicate that although it is said to be a test, indeed *the* legal test for deciding matters relating to children, it is not really a test at all. Instead, it is a somewhat crude conclusion of social policy. It allows lawyers and courts to persuade themselves and others that theirs is a principled approach to law. Meanwhile, they engage in what to others is clearly a form of 'ad hocery'.[217]

Professor Kennedy's persuasive assertion continued with:

> The best interests approach of family law allows the courts to atomize the law, to claim that each case depends on its own facts. The court can then respond intuitively to each case while seeking to legitimate its conclusion by asserting that it is derived from the general principle contained in the best interests formula. In fact, of course, there is no general principle other than the empty rhetoric of best interests; or rather, there is some principle (or principles) but the court is not telling. Obviously the court must be following *some* principles, otherwise a toss of a coin could decide cases. But these principles, which serve as pointers to what amounts to the best interests, are not articulated by the court.[218]

---

216 Ibid 272. Resource Allocation and the role of the judiciary is discussed in greater detail in Chapter 6. For further critical examination of the High Court decision in *Re Marion*, see, especially, Natasha Cica, 'Sterilising the Intellectually Disabled: The Approach of the High Court of Australia in *Department of Health v. J.W.B. and S.M.B.*' (1993) 1 (3) *Medical Law Review* 186–231.

217 *Secretary, Department of Health and Community Services v JWB and SMB (Marion's case)* (1992) 175 CLR, 218, 271. For the entire paper, see Ian Kennedy, 'Patients, Doctors and Human Rights' in Robert Blackburn and John Taylor (eds), *Human Rights for the 1990s: Legal, Political and Ethical Issues* (Mansell, 1991).

218 *Secretary, Department of Health and Community Services v JWB and SMB (Marion's case)* (1992) 175 CLR 218, 271.

2.10 *Re Marion (No 2)*, the best interests principle and the *Family Law Rules 2004*

Following the determinations of the High Court, *Marion's case* went back to Nicholson CJ of the Family Court to consider the originating application for authorisation for the sterilisation of Marion. The case was cited as *Re Marion (No 2)*, in which the Family Court confirmed that the sterilisation could be authorised as a 'step of last resort'.[219] In light of Brennan J's critical evaluation of the best interests principle, of particular magnitude is Nicholson CJ's judgment in *Re Marion (No 2)*. His Honour discussed a number of factors that should be considered when deciding whether the medical treatment/procedure was in Marion's best interests. Nicholson CJ noted the relevant factors as to the proposed procedure or treatment and to any alternative procedure or treatment:[220]

1   the particular condition of the child which requires the procedure or treatment
2   the nature of the procedure or treatment proposed
3   the reasons for which it is the proposed that the procedure treatment be carried out
4   the alternative courses of treatment that are available in relation to that condition
5   the desirability of and effect of authorising the procedure or treatment proposed rather than the available alternatives
6   the physical effects on the child and the psychological and social implications for the child of:

   • authorising the proposed procure or treatment
   • not authorising the proposed procure or treatment

7   the nature and degree of any risk to the child of:

   • authorising the proposed procure or treatment
   • not authorising the proposed procure or treatment

8   with the views (if any) expressed by:

   • the guardian(s) of the child
   • a person who is entitled to the custody of the child
   • a person who is responsible for the daily care and control of the child
   • the child.

His Honour then proceeded to discuss each of the factors in relation to Marion's sterilisation. Arguably, Nicholson CJ's list of factors are encouraging in providing more guidance in decision making and the application of the best

---

219 *Re Marion (No 2)* (1992) 175 CLR 218.
220 Ibid 351–352.

interests principle than the arbitrary, raw formulation from the English cases examined earlier.

The considerations that Nicholson CJ laid down in *Re Marion (No 2)* are of considerable importance in that they can provide guidance in determining whether treatment withdrawal of withholding of life-sustaining treatment is in the best interests of premature and critically impaired infants also. To date, the factors set out by Nicholson CJ are probably the closest formula in determining the best interests principle with some objectivity. This is further supported by the Family Law Rules 2004, in particular Rule 4.09 of the Family Law Rules, which echo the factors listed by Nicholson CJ, thus essentially codifying the list of factors from *Re Marion (No 2)* into regulation. The judicial impact and importance of the legal discussions in *Marion's case* still resonate with the courts today. This is evinced in the courts' considerable referral to the landmark in matters relating to parental responsibility and scope of parental power in the recent case of *Baby D (No 2)*.[221]

Returning to treatment decisions concerning critically ill infants in Australia, within a space of two years following a 20-year hiatus, two cases reached the Australian courts. These recent cases may herald a change in the Australian legal landscape, with future cases potentially requiring judicial intervention or sanction. Although it is too early to predict what decisions and reasoning the Australian courts will make in future cases, an examination of the application of the best interests principle in Australian cases involving infants continues below.

2.11 Recent cases involving impaired infants

In 2011 the Australian courts were required to consider the case of *Baby D (No 2)*,[222] a twin born at 27 weeks in Melbourne. Neither twin was born suffering physical or intellectual abnormalities. However, Baby D was the weaker, with her sibling making a strong and full recovery and no longer requiring ventilation.

Baby D continued to have breathing difficulties and, due to the insertion of breathing equipment, began to suffer with airway inflammation. Her treating doctors, with the use of steroids, removed the tubes, assisting her to breathe. However, her respiratory problems remained. Due to a lack of oxygen for a period of 35 minutes during an emergency resuscitation, Baby D suffered brain damage. Her brain stem, which controls basic function, was undamaged, and she could respond to touch and feel; however, she also felt pain and distress. Although the tube remained in place to ensure her airways were open, she breathed independently and did not require such intensive care. After five months in this state, both her doctors and her parents began to consider removal of the tube. However, they were uncertain as to the best course of action should Baby D suffer similar distress in the future.

---

221 See, especially, *Baby D (No 2)* [2011] Fam CA 176 at paragraphs 173–174 and 186–233.
222 *Baby D (No 2)* [2011] Fam CA 176. See, also, Ian Kerridge, Michael Lowe and Cameron Stewart, *Ethics and Law for Health Professions* (Federation Press, 4th edn, 2013) 602.

With such uncertainty, the medical team referred to the hospital ethics committee to consider whether palliative care, in the form of pain relief and sedation, would be more appropriate if Baby D suffered respiratory distress in the future. The committee believed that the question required legal resolution, and as such directed Baby D's parents to seek advice from the courts. Stewart highlighted that the key issue requiring consideration by the courts was whether the parents could consent to the removal of the tube and whether such removal and palliative care were in Baby D's best interests.[223]

Under the Family Court's jurisdiction, Justice Young considered this issue. He referred extensively to the decision and judicial discussion in *Marion's case*, which, as discussed earlier, related specifically to parental consent to issue of medical treatment. Justice Young determined that the decision to extubate Baby D fell within the remit of parental responsibility under ss. 4 and 64B(2)(i) of the federal Family Law Act 1975, which state that any person fulfilling a parenting role has the responsibility to make decisions on any aspect of care, welfare or development of the child; thus Baby D's parents could lawfully consent to the procedure. Unfortunately, Baby D had since died.

This legal decision is important, ultimately allowing parents to make end of life treatment decisions for their sick infants without requiring court intervention. Justice Young accepted the opinions of the medical experts but declined to make any assessment of the nature of best interests, which has been the subject of criticism.[224] The doctors involved had deposed that their recommendation to withdraw and withhold treatment on Baby D had been based on elements of the three classical components of best interests. Justice Young stated:

> The consensus amongst all of the very experienced and qualified medical practitioners . . . is that any future life for Baby D must, with certainty, be seen to be one that is, at the least, very burdensome and futile with no expectation of any enjoyment of life and without sight and any meaningful brain capacity.[225]

However, laying the parental responsibility aspect aside, the decision in Baby D in 2011 was not ground-breaking – it had not posed any particularly challenging ethical or legal dilemma for the court. It simply affirmed that where parents and doctors are in agreement about the withdrawal or withholding of life-sustaining treatment the courts are reluctant to intervene.

The case attracted considerable attention among members of the public, who seemed surprised that parents were able to make such decisions on behalf of their

223 Cameron Stewart, 'Withdrawal of Treatment from Newborns in Australia: *Baby D (No 2)* [2011] Fam CA 176', *Journal of Bioethical Inquiry* (2011) 8<DOI 10.1007/s11673-011-9321-3> 227, 228.
224 See, especially, M Williams, J Chesterman and P Grano, 'Challenging Australia's "Closed" Model of Neonatal Care: The Need for Reform following *Re Baby D (No 2)*' (2012) 19(4) *Journal of Law and Medicine* 835–853.
225 *Baby D (No 2)* [2011] Fam CA 176, [149].

children. It also garnered criticism from members of the Office of the Public Advocate with regards to such decisions being made without judicial exploration of the best interests of the child and claiming that such decisions are often made by parents and clinicians without external oversight.[226]

The final case examined in this section is the case of *TS & TD v Sydney Children's Hospital ('Mohammed's case')*.[227] The case of *Baby D (No 2)* notwithstanding, *Mohammed's case* was the first in which the Australian courts had to consider the withdrawal or withholding of life-sustaining treatment with a similar gravity to that with which the English courts have been tasked over the past three decades.

Mohammed's parents sought a court order to compel the hospital to 'mechanically ventilate Mohammed and not to leave him breathing either naturally, or else only with oxygen being delivered to him, as at present, by the non-invasive method of CPAP'.[228] Mohammed was born in March 2012 with mosaic trisomy 21, commonly known as Down syndrome. Shortly after birth, he was also diagnosed with a cardiac defect, medically known as patent ductus arteriosus (PDA). At two and a half months of age, he was admitted to hospital and, 'with the exception of two day visits home, and one overnight visit', had not left the hospital since.[229] The prognosis for sufferers of PDA, which chiefly involves the collection of lactic acid in the body, includes:

> nausea, vomiting, severe breathing problems, and an abnormal heartbeat. The neurological problems which are a feature of PDA include delayed intellectual development and delayed development of motor skills, such as sitting and walking. Other neurological problems can include intellectual disability, seizures, weak muscle tone or hypotonia, poor coordination, and difficulty walking.[230]

Mohammed suffered with profound developmental delay, seizures, blindness, deafness and cardiac failure, requiring continuous positive airway pressure. In addition, he was unable to move, as he had no control over his muscles, and did not respond to touch, other than pain.[231] Doctors advised against further invasive treatment on the basis that the condition was incurable and mechanical ventilation was not in his best interests.[232]

Justice Garling ruled in favour of the doctors that mechanical ventilation would cause pain and discomfort, would provide only temporary benefit and would not

---

226 M Williams, J Chesterman and P Grano, 'Challenging Australia's "Closed" Model of Neonatal Care: The Need for Reform Following *Re Baby D (No 2)*' (2012) 19(4) *Journal of Law and Medicine* 835–853.
227 *TS & TD v Sydney Children's Hospital ('Mohammed's case')* [2012] NSWSC 1609 [11].
228 See, further, Ian Kerridge, Michael Lowe and Cameron Stewart, *Ethics and Law for Health Professions* (Federation Press, 4th edn, 2013) 602.
229 *TS & TD v Sydney Children's Hospital ('Mohammed's case')* [2012] NSWSC 1609 [25].
230 Ibid [28].
231 Ibid [33–34].
232 Ibid [76].

alleviate his condition. Rather, his best interests were to receive pain relief and palliative care.[233] The judge was careful to consider Mohammed's parents' views that their son was 'a fighter'.[234] His Honour went on to say, 'I entirely accept the genuineness and sincerity of the submissions of Mohammed's parents. I accept that it is their view that Mohammed's best interests are that he be placed on a ventilator.'[235] Justice Garling sought guidance from the English case of *Re C (a minor) (wardship: medical treatment)* and the *Re J* [1990] 3 All ER 930 case discussed earlier in this chapter.

Arguably, as the first Australian case of its kind, it provided a timely opportunity for the court to explore and critically analyse the effectiveness and arbitrary nature of the best interests principle, seemingly driven by the sentiments of the medical team and endorsed by the courts. However, Justice Garling took a conservative stance and followed the judicial reasoning of the English courts, stating:

> Mohammed's life is to be measured in the short term. He should not be subjected to pain and discomfort for the remainder of his life by being placed on mechanical ventilation from which he will not be weaned. It is for these reasons that I agree with the expert opinions of Mohammed's doctors that it would be better for him to be treated by pain relief and palliative care than by the invasive procedure of mechanical ventilation. That is what is in his best interests. This conclusion is sufficient to warrant a rejection of the parents' application.[236]

Justice Garling, following the direction of the English courts and relying heavily on medical opinion, stated:

> [I]t is not the role of the court to interfere in such a professional relationship and to compel action by an unwilling participant which would have the consequence of placing that individual in the position, in good conscience, of choosing between compliance with a court order and compliance with their professional obligations.[237]

Further, Justice Garling's reluctance to make a decision contrary to medical advice was concerning. As he said, 'Regardless of my opinion, I would not have been prepared as a matter of discretion to order them to do something with which they did not agree.'[238] In concluding, Justice Garling stated:

233 For a discussion on palliative care, see Ben White and Lindy Willmott, 'How Should Australia Regulate Voluntary Euthanasia and Assisted Suicide?' (2012) 20(2) *Journal of Law and Medicine* 410, 414.
234 *TS & TD v Sydney Children's Hospital ('Mohammed's case')* [2012] NSWSC [73].
235 Ibid [74].
236 Ibid [90–91].
237 Ibid [93].
238 Ibid [94].

[T]he court's responsibility is to assess what is in Mohammed's best interests and not to allow its judgment to be swayed by sympathy, and the attractive ease of requiring the medical practitioners to provide mechanical ventilation for Mohammed.[239]

Although noting that further treatment would not be in the infant's best interests, his Honour did not consider issues of 'quality of life' at any great length. Justice Garling found that the standard Macquarie Dictionary meaning of 'quality of life' – that enjoyment which can be got from living based on having sufficient physical and mental health to be able to participate in a meaningful way–was inapplicable in the case before him. Applying a somewhat, literal interpretation of the term 'quality of life' as defined by the dictionary, his Honour found:

> [A]s it seems to me, when applying that term to a 9 month old baby who does not yet talk or communicate verbally, and does not physically respond to anything other than painful stimuli, and cannot see or hear, identifying the integers which comprise an assessment of the baby's *'quality of life'* is impossible. Any such assessment necessarily reflects the individual values of the assessor.[240]

Thus, Justice Garling rejected assessment of 'quality of life' as an index of 'best interests'. He found that assessing the infant's 'quality of life' was open to the subjective interpretation of such life by each person assessing his life, stating, 'I have not made any such assessment and I have disregarded as irrelevant any expression of opinion by any of the doctors as to what Mohammed's quality of life is or will be.'[241] However, as noted earlier, seemingly, his Honour did not apply the same level of caution and potential subjectivity to the application of the term 'best interests' – on the basis of medical opinion that being placed on a ventilator was not in his best interests.

Conceivably, it was less confronting for the court to agree with medical opinion, and in doing so conform to English precedent, rather than enter into any robust and explorative debate concerning the nature and effectiveness of the best interests principle. This is disappointing, given that Nicholson CJ discussed factors that should be considered in relation to medical treatment and children in *Marion's case* with such gravitas.

2.12 The effectiveness of the best interests principle

This chapter has examined case law from the UK and Australia in which the central determinant for discontinuation of life-sustaining treatment has been the application of the best interests principle. Overwhelmingly, nebulous concepts

---

239 Ibid [96].
240 Ibid [96].
241 Ibid [70].

such as best interests, futility and a 'balance sheet' of benefit or burdens of treatment determine whether life-sustaining treatment should be withdrawn or withheld from premature infants.[242]

In the case of premature or critically ill infants, who are unable to express their treatment choices, the courts are asked to act and apply the best interests principle – that the courts' 'prime and paramount consideration must be the best interests of the child'. What is truly in the best interests of the infant? Any answer to this question would be too speculative. Courts seemingly use the term 'best interests', which tends to cloak decisions that will result in death for the patient. Arguably, the courts apply best interests to convey a sense of benevolence and to transform into an honourable act what is essentially state-sanctioned taking of a life.

This chapter has highlighted that the best interests test is not sufficiently definable and is ineffective as the central determinant for decisions to withdraw or withhold life-sustaining treatment from critically ill infants. The only clarity that applies in this area is not doctrinal; rather, it is in the outcome of cases. With an inconsequential number of exceptions, the outcome of the best interests tests is that judges make decisions consistent with the weight of medical advice, with this advice being consistent with that choice that will end life most rapidly of the available options.

There are no clear answers to the circumstances in which infants should be permitted to die. Analysis of the case law has demonstrated that many important, often competing, interests are at stake, with no clear reference point against which these should be evaluated. This has resulted in the current situation in which determinations are clouded in obscure and vague principles.

Judges appear to pay lip service to doctrines such as sanctity of life and parental opinion. The emphasis and importance placed on medical advice and opinion suggests that this allows judges to abdicate themselves of any real responsibility for making life and death decisions by simply legitimising medical practitioners' conduct. The legal judgments considered in this chapter highlight the court's reluctance to enter into informed and robust discussion about the withdrawal or withholding of life-sustaining treatment from critically ill infants.

2.13 Conclusion

This chapter has highlighted the first of several subjective and speculative practices that are currently central features in decision making for premature and

---

242 Seemingly, indeterminate concepts such as best interests, futility and poor quality of life nearly always equate to death. However, there are other possible explanations for the withdrawal or withholding of life-sustaining treatment. One explanation is that such cases only go to court where parents maintain unrealistic and unreasonable hopes of a recovery; thus the courts are utilised as a circuit breaker. In light of the cases that end up in court (where there is very poor prognosis), it may explain why decisions are usually made to withdraw or withhold treatment. For further discussion of the application of the best interests principle through value theory, see David Degrazia, 'Value Theory and the Best Interests Standard' (1995) 9(1) *Bioethics* 50–61.

critically impaired infants. The reason that discussion in this area is often so emotional and controversial is that it relates to paramount human interests, and the consequences of the decisions are both considerable and absolute. The role of moral or legal luck or happenstance in relation to outcomes that define the destiny of human beings and the values that underpin a society must be limited.[243] The unpredictable nature of human experience must accommodate for some degree of flexibility. However, even allowing for this, the best interests principle is an uncharacteristically vague legal standard, so much so that it has been described by one commentator as 'vacuous'.[244]

This situation is unsatisfactory for a number of reasons that extend beyond the well-known rule of legal virtues that require the law to be knowable and clear.[245] This book contends that matters of significant importance, of which life and death is of the highest importance, should be governed with a greater degree of objectivity, transparency and tangibility. If the best interests test is to be preserved, it should be informed by clearer criteria. A wholesale re-evaluation is required. The criteria, if they are to be established, need to be developed and debated by a body with a popular mandate to do so – that is, Parliament.

The next chapter examines the second subjective and arbitrary factor that currently informs end of life decisions for premature and critically impaired infants – clinical guidelines utilised by medical practitioners in the hospital setting.[246]

2.14 References

Ahronheim, Judith C and M Rose Gasner, 'The Sloganism of Starvation' (1990) 335(8684) *The Lancet* 278.

Airedale NHS Trust v Bland [1993] AC 789.

Amarasekara, Kumar and Mirko Bagaric, *Euthanasia, Morality and the Law* (Peter Lang Publishing, 2002).

Annas, George J and Michael A Grodin, *The Nazi Doctors and the Nuremberg Code: Human Rights in Human Experimentation* (Oxford University Press, 1992).

Archard, D W, 'Children's Rights' in E N Zalta et al. (eds), *Stanford Encyclopaedia of Philosophy* (Winter 2002). http://plato.stanford.edu/archives/win2002/entries/rights-children

Aristotle (Translated by Hugh Lawson-Tancred), *De Anima (On the Soul)* (Penguin, 1986).

Aristotle (Translated by T A Sinclair), *The Politics* (Penguin, 1981).

Aristotle (Translated by J A K Thomson), *The Nicomachean Ethics* (Penguin, 1955).

---

243 For further examination of the concept of moral luck, see Thomas Nagel, *Mortal Questions* (Cambridge University Press, 1979).

244 Natasha Cica, 'Sterilising the Intellectually Disabled: The Approach of the High Court of Australia in *Department of Health v J.W.B. and S.M.B.*' (1993) 1(3) *Medical Law Review* 186.

245 Joseph Raz, *The Authority of Law* (Oxford University Press, 1979) 211, 214–216. See, also, Joel Finnis, *Natural Law and Natural Rights* (Oxford University Press, 1980) 270–276.

246 See James Tibballs, 'The Legal Basis for Ethical Withholding and Withdrawing of Life Sustaining Medical Treatment in Children' (2006) 14(2) *Journal of Law and Medicine* 244, 244.

Aristotle (English translation by A L Peck), *On the Generation of Animals* (W Heinemann, 1943).

Aristotle (Translated by Richard Cresswell), *On the History of Animals* (Henry G Bohn, 1862).

Ashby, Michael A and Danuta Mendelson, 'Gardner; re BWV: Victorian Supreme Court Makes Landmark Australian Ruling on Tube Feeding' (2004) 181(8) *Medical Journal of Australia* 442.

Auckland Area Health Board v Attorney General [1993] NZLR 235.

Baby D (No 2) [2011] Fam CA 176.

Baby M (Victorian State Coroner's Office, Record of Investigation into Death, Case No 3149/89, 29 October 1991) VIC.

Barry, Robert L, *The Sanctity of Human Life and its Protection* (University Press of America, 2002).

Bolam v Friern Hospital Management Committee [1957] 1 WLR 582.

Borthwick, C J and R Crossley, 'Permanent Vegetative State: Usefulness and Limits of a Prognostic Definition' (2004) 19(4) *Journal of Neuro Rehabilitation* 381.

Brazier, Margaret, *Medicine, Patients and the Law* (Penguin Books, 3rd edn, 2003).

Children's Act 1989.

Cica, Natasha, 'Sterilising the Intellectually Disabled: The Approach of the High Court of Australia in *Department of Health v. J.W.B. and S.M.B.*' (1993) 1(3) *Medical Law Review* 186.

'Couple's Distress at Baby Ruling', *BBC News*, 21 March 2009. http://news.bbc.co.uk/2/hi/ uk_news/7956450.stm

Curtis, Polly, 'Down's Syndrome Changing Attitudes', *The Guardian* (Online) 1 September 2007. www.theguardian.com/stage/2007/sep/01/theatre3

Day, Elizabeth, 'Baby RB: Heartbreak in Court 50 as Life of a One-year-old Hangs in the Balance', *The Guardian* (Online), 8 November 2009. www.guardian.co.uk/society/2009/nov/08/baby-rb-court-case

Degrazia, David, 'Value Theory and the Best Interests Standard' (1995) 9(1) *Bioethics* 50.

Department of Health and Community Services v JWB and SMB (Marion's case) (1992) 175 CLR 218.

Doyal, Len, 'Dignity in Dying Should Include the Legalization of Non-Voluntary Euthanasia' (2006) 1(2) *Journal of Clinical Ethics* 65.

Dudley v Stephens (1884) 14 QBD 273.

Dwivedi, O P, 'Satyagraha for Conservation: Awakening the Spirit of Hinduism' in J Ronald Engel and Joan Gibb Engel (eds), *Ethics of Environment and Development: Global Challenge, International Response* (University of Arizona Press, 1990).

Dworkin, Ronald, *Taking Rights Seriously* (Harvard University Press, 4th edn, 1977).

Eekelaar, J, *Regulating Divorce* (Clarendon Press, 1991).

Elliston, Sarah, *The Best Interests of the Child in Healthcare* (Routledge Cavendish, 2007).

F v West Berkshire Health Authority [1989] All ER 545.

Faunce, Thomas Alured, *Pilgrims in Medicine: Conscience, Legalism and Human Rights* (Koninklijke Brill NV, 2005).

Faunce, Thomas A and Cameron Stewart, 'The Messiha and Schiavo Cases: Third-party Ethical and Legal Interventions in Futile Care Disputes' (2005) 183(5) *Medical Journal of Australia* 261.

Finnis, Joel, *Natural Law and Natural Rights* (Oxford University Press, 1980).

Fortin, Jane, *Children's Rights and the Developing Law* (Cambridge University Press, 3rd edn, 2009).

Freeman, Michael, 'Whose Life is it Anyway?' (2001) 9 *Medical Law Review* 259.

Gardner, Julian, 'Dilemmas in End-of-life Care: The Maria Korp Case' in Simon Barraclough and Heather Garner (eds), *Analysing Health Policy: A Problem Orientated Approach* (Elsevier, 2008).

Gardner re BMV [2003] VSC 173.

Glass v United Kingdom [2004] ECHR 103 (9 March 2004).

Glover, Jonathan, *Causing Death and Saving Lives* (Pelican Books, 1977).

Gostin, Larry, 'A Moment in Human Development: Legal Protection, Ethical Standards and Social Policy on the Selective Non-Treatment of Handicapped Neonates' (1985) 11 *American Journal of Law and Medicine* 31.

Gunn, M J and J C Smith, 'Arthur's Case and the Right to Life of a Down's Syndrome Child' (1985) (Nov) *Criminal Law Review* 705.

Hagan, Kate, 'Doctors Tread Ethical Minefield, 21 Years On', *The Age* (Victoria), 14 August 2010.

Harmon, Louise, 'Falling Off the Vine: Legal Fictions and the Doctrine of the Substituted Judgment' (October 1990) 100(1) *Yale Law Journal* 1.

Harris, John, 'Human Beings, Persons and Conjoined Twins: An Ethical Analysis of the Judgment in Re A' (2001) 9(3) *Medical Law Review* 221.

Haslam, Robert H A and Ruth Milner, 'The Physician and Down Syndrome: Are Attitudes Changing?' (1992) 7(3) *Journal of Child Neurology*, 304.

Huxtable, Richard and Karen Forbes, '*Glass v United Kingdom*: Maternal Instinct v Medical Opinion' (2004) 16(3) *Child and Family Law Quarterly* 339.

Huxtable, Richard, 'D(en)ying Life: The Sanctity of Life Doctrine in English Law' (2002) 14(3) *Retfoerd* 60.

Iacovelli, G, 'The Evolution of the Hippocratic Oath' (1989) 1(1) *Medicina nei Secoli* 39.

Jackson, Emily, *Medical Law: Texts, Cases and Materials* (Oxford University Press, 2006).

Kennedy, Ian, Patients, Doctors and Human Rights' in Robert Blackburn and John Taylor (eds), *Human Rights for the 1990's: Legal, Political and Ethical Issues* (Mansell, 1991).

Kennedy, Ian, *Treat Me Right* (Oxford University Press, 1988).

Keown, John, *Euthanasia, Ethics and Public Policy: An Argument Against Legislation* (Cambridge University Press, 2002).

Keown, John, 'The Incompetent Patient: Sanctity of Life, Quality Of Life and Vitalism' in Michael Parker and Donna Dickenson (eds), *The Cambridge Medical Ethics Workbook* (Cambridge University Press, 2001).

Keown, John 'The Legal Revolution: From Sanctity of Life to Quality of Life and Autonomy (1997–1998) (14)(2) *Journal of Contemporary Health Law and Policy* 253.

Keown, John, 'Restoring Moral and Intellectual Shape to the Law after Bland' (1997) 113(3) *Law Quarterly Review* 481.

Kerridge, Ian, Michael Lowe and Cameron Stewart, *Ethics and Law for Health Professions* (Federation Press, 4th edn, 2013).

Kuhse, Helga, 'A Report from Australia: Quality of Life and the Death of Baby M' (1992) 6(3) *Bioethics* 233.

Kuhse, Helga, *The Sanctity-of-Life Doctrine in Medicine* (Oxford University Press, 1987).

Kuhse, Helga, 'A Modern Myth. That Letting Die is Not the Intentional Causation of Death: Some Reflections on the Trial and Acquittal of Dr Leonard Arthur' (1984) 1(1) *Journal of Applied Philosophy* 21.

Kuhse, Helga, 'Debate: Extraordinary Means and the Sanctity of Life' (1981) 7(2) *Journal of Medical Ethics* 74.

Kuhse, Helga and Peter Singer, *Should the Baby Live?* (Oxford University Press, 1985).

McGee, Andrew, 'Finding a Way Through the Ethical and Legal Maze: Withdrawal of Medical Treatment and Euthanasia' (2005) 13(3) *Medical Law Review* 357.

McLean, Sheila, *Old Law, New Medicine: Medical Ethics and Human Rights* (Pandora, 1999).

McNeill, Paul M and Bruce S Dowton, 'Declarations Made By Graduating Medical Students in Australia and New Zealand' (2002) 176(3) *Medical Journal of Australia* 123.

McQueen, Moira M and James L Walsh, 'The House of Lords and the Discontinuation of Artificial Nutrition and Hydration: An Ethical Analysis of the Tony Bland Case' (1991–1994) 35 *Catholic Lawyer* 363.

Magnusson, Roger S, 'The Devil's Choice: Re-Thinking Law, Ethics, and Symptom Relief in Palliative Care' (2006) 34(4) *Journal of Law, Medicine and Ethics* 559.

Mann, Jonathan M, Lawrence Gostin, Sofia Gruskin, Troyen Brennan, Zita Lazzarini and Harvey V Fineberg, 'Health and Human Rights' (1994) 1(1) *Health and Human Rights* 6.

Marrus, Michael Robert, 'The Nuremberg Doctors Trial in Historical Context' (1999) 73(1) *Bulletin of the History of Medicine* 106.

Miles, Steven H, *The Hippocratic Oath and the Ethics of Medicine* (Oxford University Press, 2004).

Miola, Jose, *Medical Ethics and Medical Law: A Symbiotic Relationship* (Hart Publishing, 2007).

Montgomery, Jonathan, 'Time for a Paradigm Shift Medical Law in Transition' (2000) 53(1) *Current Legal Problems* 363.

Nagel, Thomas, *Mortal Questions* (Cambridge University Press, 1979).

National Library of Medicine, History of Medicine Division, *Greek Medicine*. www.nlm.nih.gov/hmd/greek/greek_oath.html

NHS Trust v Baby X and others [2012] EWHC 2188 (Fam) (30 July 2012).

NHS Trust v MB [2006] EWHC 507 (Fam) (15 March 2006).

NHS Trust v OT [2009] EWCA Civ 409 (14 May 2009).

Northridge v Central Sydney Area Health Authority (2000) 50 NSWLR 549.

Plato (Translated by Benjamin Jowett) *Crito* (Forgotten Books, 2008).

Plato (Translated by David Gallop) *Phaedo* (Oxford University Press, 1993).

Portsmouth Hospital NHS Trust v Wyatt [2004] EWCA 2247 (Fam) (7 October 2004).

R v Arthur (1981) 12 BMLR 1.

R v Howe [1987] 1 AC 417.

R v Bournewood Community and Mental Health NHS Trust ex parte L [1998] 3 All ER 289.

Re A (children) (conjoined twins: surgical separation) [2000] 4 All ER 961.

Re A (male sterilisation) [2000] 1 FLR 549.

Re B (a minor) (wardship: medical treatment) [1990] 3 All ER (CA) 927.

Re Baby RB (a child) [2009] EWHC 3269 (Fam) (10 November 2009).

Re BWV: Ex parte Gardner (2003) 7 VR 487; *Re MC* [2003] QGAAT 13.

Re C (a minor) (1997) 40 BMLR 31 (Fam Div).

Re C (a minor) (wardship: medical treatment) [1989] 2 All ER 782.

Re F: F v F (Unreported, Supreme Court of Victoria, Vincent J, 2 July 1986).

Re J (a minor) (wardship: medical treatment) [1992] 4 All ER 614.

Re J (a minor) (wardship: medical treatment) [1990] 3 All ER 930.

Re L (Medical Treatment: Benefit) [2004] EWHC 2713 (Fam).

Re Marion (1990) 14 Fam LR 427.

Re Marion (No 2) (1992) 175 CLR 218.

Raz, Joseph, *The Authority of Law* (Oxford University Press, 1979).

Read, Janet and Luke Clements, 'Demonstrably Awful: The Right to Life and the Selective Non-Treatment of Disabled Babies and Young Children' (2004) 31(4) *Journal of Law and Society* 482.

Right Honourable Lord Woolf, 'Are the Courts Excessively Deferential to the Medical Profession?' (2001) 9(1) *Medical Law Review* 1.

Robertson, John A, 'Substantive Criteria and Procedures in Withholding Care from Defective Newborns' in Stuart F Spicker, Joseph M Healy and H Tristram Engelhardt (eds), *The Law–Medicine Relation: A Philosophical Exploration* (Reidel Publishing Company, 1981).

Rousseau, Jean Jacques, *The Social Contract* (Hafner Publishing Company, 1947).

Section 3(1) Children Act 1989.

Section 61B Family Law Act 1975 (Cth).

Section 67ZC of the Family Law Act 1975 (Cth).

Seymour, J, 'Parens Patriae and Wardship Powers: Their Nature and Origins' (1994) 14(2) *Oxford Journal of Legal Studies* 159.

Singer, Peter, *Rethinking Life and Death* (Text Publishing, 1994).

Skene, Loane, *Law and Medical Practice: Rights, Duties, Claims and Defences* (Lexis Nexis Butterworths, 3rd edn, 2008).

Slaveski v Austin Health [2010] VSC 493.

Stewart, Cameron, 'A Defence of the Requirement to Seek Consent to Withhold and Withdraw Futile Treatments' (2012) 196(6) *Medical Journal of Australia*, 406.

Stewart, Cameron, 'Withdrawal of Treatment from Newborns in Australia: Baby D (No 2) [2011] Fam CA 176', *Journal of Bioethical Inquiry* (2011) 8<DOI 10.1007/s11673-011-9321-3> 227.

Stewart, Cameron, 'Withdrawal of Treatment from a Newborn with Congenital Myasthenic Syndrome' (2010) 7(1) *Journal of Bioethical Inquiry* 3.

Stewart, Cameron, 'The Sanctity of Life in Law: Comparisons between Jewish, Catholic, Islamic and Common Law Approaches' in Peter Radan, Denise Meyerson, Rosalind F Croucher (eds), *Law and Religion: God, the State and the Common Law* (Routledge Studies in Religion, Volume 9, 2004).

Stewart, Cameron, 'Legal Constructions of Life and Death in the Common Law' (2002) 2(Summer) *Oxford University Commonwealth Law Journal* 67.

Stone, Julie, 'Withholding Life-Sustaining Treatment' (1995) 145(6686) *New Law Journal* 354.

Tibballs, James 'The Legal Basis for Ethical Withholding and Withdrawing of Life Sustaining Medical Treatment in Children' (2006) 14(2) *Journal of Law and Medicine* 244.

TS & TD v Sydney Children's Hospital ('Mohammed's case') [2012] NSWSC 1609.

Van der Riet, Pamela, Denise Brooks and Michael Ashby, 'Nutrition and Hydration at the End of Life: Pilot Study of a Palliative Care Experience' 2006 14(2) *Journal of Law and Medicine* 182.

Victorian Medical Treatment Act 1988.

White, Ben and Lindy Willmott, 'How Should Australia Regulate Voluntary Euthanasia and Assisted Suicide?' (2012) 20(2) *Journal of Law and Medicine* 410.

Williams, M, J Chesterman and P Grano, 'Challenging Australia's "Closed" Model of Neonatal Care: The Need for Reform following *Re Baby D (No 2)*' (2012) 19(4) *Journal of Law and Medicine* 835.

Willmott, Lindy, Ben White and Donna Cooper, 'Interveners or Interferers: Intervention in Decisions to Withhold and Withdraw Life-Sustaining Medical Treatment' (2005) 27(4) *Sydney Law Review* 597.

'Women Cry "Thank God" as Dr Arthur is Cleared', *The Times* (UK), 6 November 1981.

World Medical Association, *WMA Declaration of Geneva*. www.wma.net/en/30publications/10policies/g1/

3 Non-uniformity in clinical guidelines

The previous chapter examined the best interests principle as applied by the English and Australian courts in deciding whether treatment should lawfully be withheld or withdrawn from premature and critically impaired infants. An analysis of the selected case law and judicial reasoning over the past three decades was presented, highlighting the imprecision of the best interests principle and its inherent subjectivity when applied to end of life decision making.

Chapter 2 also highlighted that the courts seemingly place excessive weight on medical opinion, often against parents' wishes. In addition, the courts were found to apply indeterminate terms such as 'best interests' and a 'balance sheet of burdens and benefits' to allow the lawful withdrawal or withholding of treatment often resulting in death. In light of this, the chapter concluded that the current best interests test is too nebulous and idiosyncratic to constitute a coherent assessment.

This chapter explores another speculative practice that currently informs decisions to withdraw or withhold life-sustaining treatment from premature and critically ill infants. Chapter 3 examines some of the key clinical guidelines and frameworks drafted by a range of bodies that assist medical practitioners in end of life decision making. Further, it highlights the deficiencies and lack of uniformity in clinical guidelines in the UK and Australia. The inaccessibility of clinical guidelines across Australian hospitals warrants particular attention and is discussed later in this chapter. Chapter 3 begins by discussing the earliest possible gestational period at which an extremely premature infant born alive is likely to be resuscitated and provided with life-sustaining treatment.

3.1 The threshold of viability

Generally, end of life treatment decisions are made within the parameters of the hospital setting by doctors in collaboration with parents. As discussed in the previous chapter, cases that require legal intervention in the UK and particularly in Australia are infrequent.[1]

---

1 Particularly in Australia. See, especially, *Baby D (No 2)* [2011] Fam CA 176 and *TS & TD v Sydney Children's Hospital ('Mohammed's case')* [2012] NSWSC 1609.

It has also previously been noted in this book that premature birth is not a new phenomenon. Moreover, although technological advancement in medical science has allowed pre-term infants to survival outside the womb, many of those who do survive do so with severe abnormality or disability.[2] Even with impressive advancements in healthcare and technology, it has not been possible to significantly decrease the number of pre-term births.[3]

Contributing factors to premature births in the UK include high rates of teenage pregnancy[4] and the decision by women to delay pregnancy until later in life. Another significant contributor is in-vitro fertility (IVF) treatment, which can often result in multiple pregnancies and pre-term births as a consequence of the implantation of several embryos simultaneously.

The definition of pre-term birth in its crudest form refers to infants born before a pregnancy has come to full term, between 37 and 42 weeks. However, the variation in development and likelihood of survival outside the womb differs drastically for those born between 22 weeks and 26 weeks onwards. At these earlier stages, the uncertainty of the chance of any life, or a life with severe disability, is considerably ambiguous for medical practitioners and parents alike.

In its 2006 report, the Nuffield Council on Bioethics (NCOB) discussed the survival rates and possible treatment outcomes of infants born at varying gestational ages.[5] In particular, the report considered the likely outcomes of infants born at the 'borderline of viability' – up to and including 25 weeks + 6 days' gestation.[6] Infants born at this stage in England account for '0.3 per cent of all deliveries, both born alive and stillborn', and their survival rate is 'much less than 50 per cent'.[7]

The Nuffield report, which is discussed later in this chapter, found that infants born in the UK at up to 22 weeks + 6 days' gestation are highly unlikely to survive, or even to leave the intensive care unit; thus, resuscitation is usually rejected.[8] The chances of survival marginally increase when a baby remains in

---

2 This is discussed in greater detail in Chapters 4 and 6.

3 There has also been discussion about the increase of premature births in the UK and Australia over the past two decades. See, generally, Anna White, 'Premature Babies: The Pregnant Elephant in the Room is Stress', *The Telegraph* (Online), 17 December 2012. www.telegraph.co.uk/women/womens-life/9748592/Premature-babies-The-pregnant-elephant-in-the-room-is-stress.html

4 Although the UK has tended to have one of the highest teenage pregnancy rates in western Europe, recently, the lowest number of teenage pregnancies (under the age of 18) has been recorded since 1969. See, especially, Office for National Statistics, *Teenage Pregnancies at Lowest Levels Since Records Began* 2 April 2013. www.ons.gov.uk/ons/rel/vsob1/conception-statistics--england-and-wales/2011/sty-conception-estimates-2011.html. See, also, www.theguardian.com/news/datablog/2014/feb/25/new-record-lows-in-teen-pregnancy-rate. More recently, see BBC, News Health, ' Teen pregnancy rate lower still'. www.bbc.com/news/health-26338540

5 Nuffield Council on Bioethics, *Critical Care Decisions in Fetal and Neonatal Medicine: Ethical Issues* (Nuffield Council on Bioethics, 2006). The report and the work of the Nuffield Council is discussed later in this chapter.

6 Ibid 33 [3.8].

7 Ibid 33 [3.8].

8 Ibid 156 [9.16].

the womb until at least 23 weeks + 6 days. Often, only at this period do doctors begin to consider the possibility of providing life-sustaining treatment to extremely premature infants. The Nuffield report asserted that 'where there is greatest uncertainty about the outcome for an individual baby and where the decision on whether treatment is in his or her best interests is most difficult to make'.[9] From 24–26 weeks' gestation the chances of survival, albeit with some disability, improve. Infants born during this period are admitted, treated and given medical support following normal neonatal practice in the UK.

However, those born at 23 weeks' gestation pose the greatest medical and ethical challenge for doctors, and are emotionally confronting for parents. It is infants born at this very precarious stage of gestation who are of particular consideration with regards to allocation of finite healthcare resources in later chapters of this book.

3.2 The very nature of clinical guidelines

It is understood that by their very nature guidelines are broad and are designed to leave room for a degree of clinical discretion. The alternative would be to have very stringent criteria that could potentially lead to poor decision-making outcomes, particularly in a case where an infant may have had a good chance of survival with a reasonable quality of life. Where does that leave clinical guidelines? Stuck between being too general and conversely being too specific?

As will be highlighted throughout this chapter, the guidelines discussed are considerably vague and inconsistent. This view is supported by Doyal and Larcher who state: 'Such documents can be criticised as being too general to be useful, stigmatising to some individuals or groups, and striking the wrong balance between law and morality.'[10] There is a need for uniformity in clinical guidelines in the UK and particularly in Australia where clinical guidelines vary from hospital to hospital, and this is discussed later in this chapter. For now, the next section of this chapter examines the core clinical guidelines and frameworks that have been published to assist and arguably reassure doctors that the legally and ethically charged decisions they make concerning (often extremely) premature and critically ill infants are supported by the medical profession and the law.

3.3 Clinical guidelines: United Kingdom

In recent years, several sets of clinical guidelines on end of life treatment and care have been published in the UK. It is arguable that this high rate of activity in the production and publication of guidelines is encouraging in ensuring that end of life decisions are considered in the most appropriate manner. However, guidelines

---

9 Ibid 75 [5.16].
10 L Doyal and V F Larcher 'Drafting Guidelines for the Withholding or Withdrawing of Life Sustaining Treatment in Critically Ill Children and Neonates' (2000) 83(1) *Archives of Disease in Childhood: Fetal and Neonatal* 60, 60.

are only a discretionary tool to assist medical practitioners with treatment decisions for premature and critically ill infants.

The proliferation of guidelines and frameworks is perhaps a symptom of the variance of thought and treatment approaches in the area of neonatal care. This is reflected in the differing measures applied to pregnancy itself. The Confidential Enquiry into Maternal and Child Health (CEMACH), published in 2009 in the UK, studied perinatal periods internationally. In Australia and New Zealand, the perinatal period begins at 20 weeks' gestation; in Canada, it begins at 22 weeks; and in the UK, data are collected on fetal losses from 20 weeks' gestation.[11]

This book argues that end of life decisions for premature and critically impaired infants, particularly those born extremely premature, should be driven by more objective and transparent criteria. In light of this, the greater the number of clinical guidelines, frameworks and policies published in the UK and Australia, the less clarity, impact and authority any of them will possess. This chapter now turns to examine some of the clinical guidelines from the UK.

3.4 Royal College of Paediatrics and Child Health: *Withholding or Withdrawing Life Sustaining Treatment in Children: A Framework for Practice*

Following a first edition in 1997, in May 2004 the Royal College of Paediatrics and Child Health (RCPCH) published the second edition of its framework in the UK. The preface of the document notes that the title had been changed from 'life-saving treatment to life-sustaining treatment to reflect the fact that treatment this is often given is not curative but supportive'.[12]

The RCPCH framework determines five situations in which it is legal and ethical to consider termination of life-sustaining treatment:[13]

1   Brain dead child – it is agreed within the profession that treatment in such circumstances is futile and the withdrawal of current medical treatment is appropriate.
2   Permanent vegetative state – following trauma or hypoxia, the child is reliant on others for all care and does not react or relate with the outside world. It may be appropriate to withdraw or withhold life-sustaining treatment.
3   No chance – child has such severe disease that life-sustaining treatment simply delays death without significant alleviation of suffering: treatment to sustain life is inappropriate.

---

11 Confidential Enquiry into Maternal and Child Health, *Perinatal Mortality 2007* (CEMACH, 2009) 2.
12 Royal College of Paediatrics and Child Health, *Withholding or Withdrawing Life Sustaining Treatment in Children: A Framework for Practice* (RCPCH, 2nd edn, 2004) 8. This statement perhaps indicates the value placed by the authors on the philosophical tenets that 'all life is sacred' and that 'life must be preserved at all cost', as considered in Chapter 2.
13 Ibid, 10–11.

4 No purpose – child may be able to survive with treatment; the degree of physical or mental impairment will be so great that it is unreasonable to expect them to bear it.

5 Unbearable – the child and/or family feel that in the face of progressive and irreversible illness, further treatment is more than can be borne. They wish to have a particular treatment withdrawn, or to refuse further treatment irrespective of the medical opinion that it may be of some benefit.

The first two categories raise little ambiguity.[14] However, the following three 'situations' documented are fairly open-ended and as such can be interpreted subjectively and with a significant amount of discretion, as they do not conform to a bright line rule.[15] Morris supports this view, noting the overlap between the categories in determining the prognosis of an incapacitated infant: 'the blurring of "no purpose" and "no chance" raises important questions about the notion of "futility" as it is used in a medical – and also in a judicial – context.'[16]

Tibballs further reinforces this point, asserting the categorisation is 'somewhat misguided and confused':

> Although both the 'no purpose' situation and 'the unbearable' situation may be the basis for withholding or withdrawal of treatment, the 'no purpose' situation is also described, confusingly, in terms of the child being unreasonably expected to 'bear the situation'.[17]

Examined in its entirety, the RCPCH framework echoes the voice of the law, and although it is a clinical guideline, the document assumes much of the same language as would a legal judgment. A considerable section of the framework focuses on legal and ethical considerations, including a brief discussion on the unlawfulness of euthanasia.[18]

The balance sheet of burdens and benefits discussed in Chapter 2 is also evident in the framework: 'There is substantial evidence that it is common and accepted practice to withdraw life-sustaining care where parents and medical staff believe that the distress incurred by such care outweighs the benefits.'[19]

---

14 Although the Nuffield Report (2006) does raise the issue of the difficulty of diagnosing brain stem death in infants.
15 For further discussion on the origins and development of the bright line rule, see, especially, Edward L Glaeser and Andrei Shleifer, 'Legal Origins' (2002) 117(4) *Quarterly Journal of Economics* 1193–1229.
16 Anne Morris, 'Selective Treatment of Irreversibly Impaired Infants: Decision Making at the Threshold' (2009) 17(3) *Medical Law Review* 347, 357.
17 James Tibballs, 'The Legal Basis for Ethical Withholding and Withdrawing of Life Sustaining Medical Treatment in Children' (2006) 14(2) *Journal of Law and Medicine* 244, 246.
18 Royal College of Paediatrics, above, n 12, 15–21.
19 Ibid 13.

The framework also sounds a cautionary tone as to the role and involvement of the courts in treatment disputes between parents and doctors:

> If a doctor wishes to continue treatment of a very ill child, but there is room for reasonable doubt about the benefit, the doctor may be in a difficult position if he continues when the parents have withheld or withdrawn consent. A court might say that the doctor did not act in the best child's interests.[20]

The RCPCH framework includes some legislation – for example, the Children Act 1989 and the United Nations Convention on the Rights of the Child 1989 (which cannot be applied by the UK courts) – and then summarises the key findings of relevant judgments:

1   There is no obligation to give treatment that is futile and burdensome.
2   Treatment goals may be changed in the case of children who are dying.
3   Feeding and other medical treatment may be withdrawn from patients who are thought to be in a state of PVS.
4   Treatment may be withdrawn form patients where continued treatment is not in their best interests.[21]

This is illustrated in the RCPCH's discussion on intolerability. Considered at length in the case of *Re J (a minor) (wardship: medical treatment)*,[22] the concept was merely touched on in the framework in the statement that 'a severe/intolerable disability is undefinable'.[23] The framework suggests:

1   Intolerable may mean 'that which cannot be borne' or 'that which people should not be asked to bear'.
2   An individual may believe that he/she is an intolerable burden.
3   An impossibly poor existence may not be recognised by the individual, depending on that person's cognition.[24]

Arguably, the RCPCH framework would have been better served by refraining from defining what had previously been considered undefinable. The first suggestion merely provides a textbook definition of the term 'intolerable'. The second and third suggestions are also unfeasible given that most children, and especially infants, cannot express their treatment wishes or awareness of medical prognosis.

---

20 Ibid 19.
21 Ibid 16–17.
22 *Re J (a minor) (wardship: medical treatment)* [1990] 3 All ER 930. See Chapter 2 for case details.
23 Royal College of Paediatrics, above, n 12, 25.
24 Ibid.

The RCPCH framework and other guidelines are presumably aimed at providing doctors with reassurance that the decisions they make are both lawful and 'Bolam-ised' – that is, 'in accordance with a responsible body of medical opinion'.[25] The framework is likely to prove reassuring to junior doctors confronting ethically and potentially legally charged treatment decisions. This is reflected in the RCPCH framework, which states that juniors should 'administer life-sustaining treatment until senior, more experienced doctors take over'.[26]

McHaffie and Fowlie make the compelling assertion that medical practitioners may find comfort and solace in end of life decision making by receiving 'reassurance and peace of mind from other competent consultants with expert knowledge of neonatology similarly concluding that treatment should be withdrawn'.[27]

The RCPCH framework is only one of several guidelines that have been published in the UK. As illustrated later, there is a considerable amount of overlap between the clinical guidelines. It is questionable whether there is a need for several documents to assist medical practitioners in end of life decision making. Nevertheless, an examination of another set of guidelines follows.

3.5 British Medical Association: *Withholding and Withdrawing Life-prolonging Medical Treatment: Guidance for Decision Making*

The BMA amended and published the third edition of its guidelines in 2007, three years after the RCPCH framework. The BMA handbook provides guidance for the withdrawal or withholding or life-prolonging treatment. It states its main focus as 'decisions to withdraw or withhold life-prolonging treatment from patients who are likely to live for weeks, months or possibly years, if treatment is provided but who, without treatment, will or may die earlier'.[28]

The BMA guidance is not exclusive to infants and focuses on:

> the process through which decisions are made to withdraw or withhold life-prolonging treatment from all types of patients – adults with capacity, adults lacking capacity, young people with capacity and children and young people who lack capacity.[29]

Although the remit of these guidelines is wide, unlike the RCPCH framework, the BMA guidance considers the 'legal and ethical considerations' of decision making in some depth, citing case law and legal judgments.

---

25 *Bolam v Friern Hospital Management Committee* [1957] 1 WLR 582. The Bolam test is discussed in Chapter 2.
26 Royal College of Paediatrics, above, n 12, 1.
27 Hazel E McHaffie and Peter W Fowlie 'Withdrawing and Withholding Treatment: Comments on New Guidelines' (1998) 79(1) *Archives of Disease in Childhood: Fetal and Neonatal* 1, 2.
28 British Medical Association, *Withholding and Withdrawing Life-prolonging Medical Treatment: Guidance for Decision Making* (Blackwell Publishing, 3rd edn, 2007) 1 [1.2].
29 Ibid 2.

The BMA guidance reflects the law with regard to the withholding or withdrawing of medical treatment, making reference to *Bland* in stating: 'Although psychologically it may be easier to withhold treatment than to withdraw that which has been started, there are no necessary legal or morally relevant differences between the two actions.'[30]

Part eight of the guidance considers decision making for children and young people who lack capacity, with an emphasis on the role of parents in the decision-making process. The guidance again reiterates the law, in that although treatment decisions must be discussed with parents, parents' requests for certain treatments do not have to be satisfied.[31] The section then proceeds with a discussion of the situations in which there is a conflict regarding the acceptance or refusal of treatment and care that is deemed to be in the child's best interests.[32]

Compared with the RCPCH framework, the BMA guidance is set on more of a legal footing. The familiar concepts of best interests, futility and the balance sheet of burdens and benefits introduced in Chapter 2 of this book are present in the BMA guidance. The High Court judgment in *Wyatt* is also discussed as a 'reminder of the difficulty of accurately assessing prognosis in seriously ill young children and the importance of keeping treatment decisions constantly under review'.[33] Additionally, it discusses the relationship between intolerability and best interests and the balance sheet approach that the courts are increasingly applying in decisions to withdraw or withhold treatment.

The BMA guidance highlighted: 'In reaching a judgement about best interests, the courts are increasingly using the "balance sheet" approach and this can be a useful exercise for health professionals to consider in the event of disagreement.'[34] This statement suggests that the BMA were considering more than just clinical guidance when authoring their document. Rather, they appear to have been intending to provide doctors with an advance understanding of factors considered by judges when parental–doctor treatment conflicts end up at the doors of the court.

By ensuring that doctors are 'legally' aware, the BMA are reflecting current legal approaches to decision making in life or death matters, where the courts have actively promoted the legal and ethical transfer of responsibility to the medical fraternity. However, the BMA guidance fails to provide any significant contribution to the area of end of life decision making, and seemingly provides a 'reference point' for medical practitioners as to the currency of the law in decisions to withdraw or withhold life-sustaining treatment.

---

30 Ibid 19.
31 Ibid 97 [47.5].
32 Ibid 98 [47.6].
33 Ibid 103 [48.1].
34 Ibid 34 [22.2].

3.6 General Medical Council: *Treatment and Care Towards the End of Life: Good Practice in Decision Making*

The GMC guidelines came into effect on 1 July 2010 in the UK. They are very basic, such that end of care decisions concerning infants and young children are discussed in only two pages.

The guidelines adopt more regimented language and read more like a set of 'rules for doctors' as opposed to the legal stance of the BMA guidelines. In this set of guidelines, the issue of 'quality of life' is not discussed in any great detail, and any discussion of the ethical or moral quandaries in determining quality of life is avoided. They state: 'You must be careful not to make judgements based on poorly informed or unfounded assumptions about the impact of a disability on a child or young person's quality of life.'[35]

The guidelines do attempt to define best interests and use the same terms as the courts, in that: 'Decisions about treatment for children and young people must always be in their best interests. This means weighing the benefits, burdens and risks of treatment for the individual child.'[36] Further, medical practitioners are advised that if:

> you conclude that, although providing treatment would be likely to prolong life, it would cause pain, suffering and other burdens that would outweigh any benefits and you reach a consensus with the child's parents and healthcare team that it would be in the child best interests to withdraw, or not start treatment, you may do so.[37]

The GMC guidelines and the other frameworks discussed thus far fail to provide any robust considerations or observations with regard to premature and critically impaired infants.[38] The EPICure studies from the UK provide some sharp statistics and findings about the relationship between premature birth and quality of life.

---

35 General Medical Council, *Treatment and Care Towards the End of Life: Good Practice in Decision Making* (General Medical Council, 2010) 47 [96].
36 Ibid 45 [92].
37 Ibid 50 [106].
38 Although the guidelines examined thus far do not expressly consider the allocation of limited health resources as an important criterion, there is nothing to suggest or prevent doctors basing their decisions to discontinue treatment on available healthcare funds. The General Medical Council 2012, 'Leadership and Management' (for doctors) guidance does specifically discuss the efficient use and management and allocation of resources. See, especially, General Medical Council, *Leadership and management for all doctors* (General Medical Council, 2012) 31–33. www.gmc-uk.org/static/documents/content/Leadership_and_management_for_ all_doctors-English_ 0414.pdf

3.7 The UK EPICure studies

Two 'population based studies of survival and later health status in extremely premature infants',[39] known as the EPICure studies, have been conducted in the UK. On its website, the team of three neonatal paediatricians describe the aims and scope of their work: 'The whole point of EPICure . . . [is that] it allows us to quantify the outcomes and shows us where we need to target our care.'[40]

EPICure Study 1: 1995

The initial study, known as EPICure 1 was conducted between March and December 1995. Data were collected from all 276 maternity units in the UK and the Republic of Northern Ireland.[41] The study was exclusively concerned with the births of infants born between 20 and 25 weeks + 6 days' gestation, recorded by the respective hospitals. A full record was generated for those that required neonatal admission after birth.

The study recorded 4,004 births up to 25 weeks + 6 days' gestation. Of those, 811 were admitted to intensive care and 314 survived, to be later discharged to go home. The study identified that 'survival ranged from two babies (9% of admissions) at 22 weeks, 26 babies (20%) at 23 weeks, 100 babies (34%) at 24 weeks, to 186 babies (52%) at 25 weeks'.[42]

The results indicate that survival of infants born earlier than 24 weeks is rare. Although important, the EPICure team were unable to provide information about end of life decisions to 'provide active care or whether a decision had been made that the risks were too high and the doctors and midwives would simply make the baby comfortable after birth and not intervene'.[43] Such information was unlikely to be provided given the very real risk of criminal proceedings against doctors.[44] The 1995 study was an ambitious ongoing project, monitoring and recording the health status of those born and those that survived. Local paediatricians reported at one year of age:

> [T]here were continuing medical problems for a proportion of the children at one year of age, 95 (31%) of the children had significant problems in areas such as development, neurology and need for oxygen. 40 children had two or more of these disabilities.[45]

---

39 EPICure, *EPICure: Population Based Studies of Survival and Later Health Status in Extremely Premature Infants*. www.epicure.ac.uk/
40 Ibid.
41 Kamini Yadav and David Field, 'The Limit of Viability: Should We Lower It?' (2011) 100(3) *Neonatology* 295.
42 EPICure, *EpiCure 1995*. www.epicure.ac.uk/epicure-1995/
43 EPICure, *Survival*. www.epicure.ac.uk/overview/survival/
44 *R v Arthur* (1981) 12 BMLR 1, See Chapter 2 for case details.
45 EPICure, *EPICure at One Year*. www.epicure.ac.uk/epicure-1995/epicure-at-one-year/

The follow-up questionnaire was conducted by local paediatricians at two and a half years of age. Of the 314 survivors at birth, six had died after hospital discharge and several others had moved overseas. Further studies were conducted to assess the progress and development of those born in 1995 when they reached the age of 5.5–7 and again at age 11. However, many families and children were untraceable and many more had moved overseas.

The EPICure study was highly publicised as the largest study examining infants born at under 26 weeks' gestation. Its findings were reported in several English newspapers and medical journals, and exclusive access to interviews with the researchers was given to the BBC.[46]

EPICure Study 2: 2006

The findings of the 1995 EPICure study supported the contention that advancements in medical science and technology have improved standards in neonatal care, resulting in infants surviving longer. In 2006, a similar study was conducted to determine whether, ten years on, pre-term infants were surviving for longer, and whether there had been any improvements in the risk of those born premature, consequently suffering severe disability. The second EPICure study aimed to:

> tell us how effective advances in Neonatal care have been. It will also tell us more about the lung development of very tiny babies. The professional approach of different baby units will also be considered. This will build on the knowledge gained through the hard work of the EPICure families and study group in the original study.[47]

Data were collected on births throughout England of infants born between 22 and 26 weeks + 6 days. The second study also considered mothers and their pregnancies, rather than exclusively monitoring the development of infants born alive and being discharged. In addition, microscopic evidence of cord attached to the placenta in the womb was examined, to look for inflammation and infection prior to birth.[48]

The aims and continued focus of the research team is commendable. The task of a coordinated national effort in data collection and clinical observation in collaboration with maternity and intensive care units represented a significant

---

46 See, especially, K L Costeloe et al., 'The EPICure Study: Outcomes to Discharge from Hospital for Infants Born at the Threshold of Viability' (2000) 106(4) *Pediatrics* 659–671. See, also, BBC One, *Miracle Baby Grows Up* 17 September 2004. http://news.bbc.co.uk/2/hi/programmes/panorama/3655050.stm

47 EPICure, *EPICure 2*. www.epicure.ac.uk/epicure-2

48 Ibid. The extension of the study to include pre-natal health of the infant and mother is beneficial. As will be considered in greater detail in Chapter 7, preventative measures against premature birth, by focusing on the health and wellbeing of mothers, is critical in reducing extremely premature birth.

challenge. This comprehensive view was represented in the results, which reflected the reality of pre-term births: while the survival rate of those born between 22 and 26 + 6 days had improved by 13% (up from 40% in 1995), of the 152 infants born at 22 weeks, only three survived.

The findings, published recently in the *British Medical Journal*, are invaluable and provide a stark reminder of the limits of medical science, which, while advancing rapidly, cannot totally defy nature.[49] As the vice president of the RCPCH, Dr Simon Newell, poignantly said, 'We can only protect so much from the effects of immaturity.'[50] Although the results of the EPICure studies highlight a pessimistic outlook for those born at the edge of viability, the publication of and intense media attention surrounding the findings is a positive step towards public awareness of the realities that extremely premature and critically impaired infants and their families face.[51]

The impact on those surviving with severe disability can be profound, affecting the individual, their families and society through the continued financial demands involved in satisfying the day-to-day requirements of such individuals.[52] Professor Marlow asserts: 'As the number of children that survive pre-term birth continues to rise, so will the number who experience disability throughout their lives.'[53] Professor Marlow also highlights: 'Intensive care for small babies is expensive, and providing care for children with disabilities as they grow up is also expensive, impacting the demand for health, education and social care services.'[54]

While the allocation of finite health resources is an uncomfortable topic in regard to making life and death decisions, serious discussion in this area is critical. It is necessary to break the taboo about placing a price or value on life in order to have a pragmatic and honest discussion about end of life decision making and the allocation of limited healthcare resources.[55] This is discussed in Chapter 6; however, for now the discussion returns to an examination of the final set of clinical guidelines from the UK.

49 See, generally, Moore et al., 'The Epicure Studies: Better Survival, Better Outcomes?' (2011) 96(Suppl 1) *Archives of Disease in Childhood: Fetal and Neonatal* 16.
50 James Gallagher, 'Severely Premature Babies: More Survive Being Born Early' BBC 5 December 2012. www.bbc.co.uk/news/health-20583678
51 This is discussed in greater detail in Chapter 4.
52 This is discussed in Chapter 6.
53 Dennis Campbell, 'Premature Babies Study Shows Survival Rates on Rise' *The Guardian* (Online), 5 December 2012. http://m.guardian.co.uk/society/2012/dec/05/survival-rates-premature-babies-rise. The costs associated with the upbringing of severely disabled infants is discussed in detail in Chapter 6.
54 Thomas Moore, 'Premature Babies: Dilemmas Over Care Grows' Sky News 5 December 2012. http://news.sky.com/story/1020756/premature-babies-dilemma-over-care-grows
55 The main premise of this book is that resource allocations should be a cardinal consideration in end of life decision making for extremely premature and critically impaired infants. By encouraging public discussion and awareness about the increasing demand for and limited supply of healthcare funds, discussions about end of life decisions can be driven with greater objectivity and efficiency.

3.8 British Association of Perinatal Medicine: *Management of Babies Born Extremely Preterm at Less Than 26 Weeks of Gestation: A Framework for Clinical Practice at the Time of Birth*

Published in 2008 with the stipulation that it was not 'a set of instructions, but a framework to highlight the range of evidence and opinion that needs to be considered by staff and parents',[56] the British Association of Perinatal Medicine (BAPM) began on an encouraging note.

Relying heavily on the statistics following the EPICure studies, the BAPM framework provided the following recommendations to assist doctors on end of life decision making for critically ill infants:

1   Babies born with certain gestational age of under 23 weeks – in the best interests of the baby and standard practice, resuscitation not to be carried out: based on the 1995 EPICure study only two survived, one suffering severe disability. The 2006 study revealed a high occurrence of major morbidity.
2   Babies born with certain gestational age of 23–23 + 6 days – where a fetal heart is heard, a professional experienced in resuscitation should be available. However, express parental express wishes not to resuscitate should be honoured: based on the 1995 EPICure study 80% of those born at this gestational age died in hospital. The 2006 study revealed the survival rate had not significantly improved.
3   Babies born with certain gestational age of 24–24 + 6 days – resuscitation should be commenced unless both parents and practitioners consider that the baby will be severely compromised. The critical issue is the baby's lung and heart response using a mask: based on the 1995 EPICure study of those born at this age, given intensive care, 66% died. The 2006 study found survival increased by 12%.
4   Babies born with certain gestational age of 25 weeks or more – survival is greater than of those born in 1995, and therefore resuscitation is appropriate: based on the 1995 study 48% died, but 27% survived with no identifiable impairment at the age of six years. The 2006 study revealed an increase of 13% in survival from 54% to 67%.

The BAPM framework failed to address concerns that doctors may have in managing the expectations and discussions about end of life care with parents and families of pre-term infants. The framework does not advance the existing discussion about end of life decision making for critically impaired infants in any meaningful way; arguably, it republishes the findings from the EPICure studies. Before turning to explore clinical guidelines in Australia, this chapter considers

---

56 Wilkinson et al., 'Management of Babies Born Extremely Preterm at Less Than 26 Weeks of Gestation: A Framework for Clinical Practice at the Time of Birth' (2009) 94(1) *Archives of Disease in Childhood: Fetal and Neonatal* 2.

the much publicised Nuffield Council of Bioethics (NCOB) 2006 report, which also failed to meet the expectations with which it was conceived.

3.9 Nuffield Council on Bioethics: *Critical Care Decisions in Fetal and Neonatal Medicine: Ethical Issues*, 2006: a missed opportunity for the UK?

The NCOB is a multidisciplinary, independent body in the UK. The council was established by joint funding and cooperation of the Nuffield Foundation,[57] the Wellcome Trust and the Medical Research Council. The council aims to 'advise policy makers and stimulate debate in bioethics' and its work has been recognised internationally.[58]

The council consists of several eminent professors from disciplines such as medicine, science, philosophy and law. It has successfully completed several projects on topics of significance to societal development and medico-ethical debate, including an examination of ethical dilemmas in dementia, public health, research involving animals and, most currently, the disclosure of information in relation to donor conception. The 2006 report, entitled *Critical Care Decisions in Fetal and Neonatal Medicine: Ethical Issues*, is of particular relevance and importance to this book.

The report examined 'ethical, social and legal issues that arise when making critical care decisions'.[59] Although the report is to be commended for re-introducing the issues surrounding end of life decision making into the public domain, it has produced little reform since its publication several years ago. The 2006 report arose out of an impressive multidisciplinary working party chaired by Professor Brazier. Other members of the party included eminent professors in medicine, nursing and philosophy, as well as a disability commissioner, an economist and a lawyer.

Although the nine-chapter report was primarily 'targeted at policy makers', it was written with a broad audience in mind.[60] The report examined ethical, social and legal issues concerning end of life decision making for infants. The fact that the report and the further exploration of the issues were considered necessary in 2006 indicates that existing practices and published guidelines are insufficient, ambiguous and need reform. This book argues that, almost a decade on, there has been little development or reform in this area. Thus, the need for clarity, transparency and uniformity in end of life decision making for premature and critically ill infants remains a pressing matter.

---

57 Hereafter referred to as the NCOB. The Nuffield Foundation is a charity founded by Lord Nuffield in 1943 and William Morris to contribute to and improve issues of societal importance such as education and social wellbeing. Nuffield Foundation, *About the Nuffield Foundation*. www.nuffieldfoundation.org/About-the-foundation

58 Nuffield Council on Bioethics, *About*. www.nuffieldbioethics.org/about

59 Nuffield Council on Bioethics, above, n 5, 3 [1.4].

60 Ibid 5 [1.10].

As the NCOB is an independent body, its 2006 report provided an ideal platform for candid and clear discussion on neonatal end of life decision making. The report presented the opportunity to introduce coherent recommendations for legislative reform, and the public interest and media attention attracted by the findings of the report could have been beneficial in discussing the issue of resource allocation. However, the report avoided the robust reforms necessary to inject the clarity and objectivity that is required. Instead, it endorsed the current abundance of clinical guidelines published by national bodies and supported existing opaque concepts such as best interests, futility and intolerability.

The report emphasised the need for a continued 'partnership of care' between key stakeholders, parents and the healthcare team, as recommended by the RCPCH and the BAPM.[61] It also strongly endorsed the guidelines and recommendations of the RCPCH and BAPM and the EPICure study findings. The NCOB working party rejected the need for legislation on decision making for extremely premature infants born at the edge of viability (23 weeks), despite commenting that 'clearer guidance would be helpful to both parents and professionals'.[62]

Having endorsed several sets of the current guidelines and frameworks in the UK, interestingly the NCOB devised yet another set of guidelines and best practice as to thresholds for resuscitation and withholding or withdrawing of treatment from critically ill infants based on gestation age. The report suggested:[63]

> At 25 + weeks – intensive care should be initiated as babies born at this time have a high survival rate, unless it is known that the infant will be affected by a severe abnormality.
>
> At 24–24 + 6 days – normal practice should be that the baby will be offered full intensive care and support from birth unless the parents and clinicians agree that such treatment is not in the baby's best interests.
>
> At 23–23 + 6 days – future outcome predictions are difficult and precedence should be given to the wishes of the parents regarding resuscitation and intensive care.
>
> At 22–22 + 6 days – standard practice should be not to resuscitate, unless it is considered to be in the baby's best interests.
>
> At below 22 weeks – no baby should be resuscitated unless for experimental reasons and for approved research studies.[64]

The Nuffield report suggested that intensive care should not be offered at certain gestational periods, but did not present any new recommendations. Morris noted that the gestational periods at which the report recommends that

61 Ibid 23 [2.48].
62 Ibid 154 [9.14].
63 Ibid 155 [9.16].
64 Ibid 156 [9.19].

infants not be resuscitated almost mirror those of the RCPCH framework. The Nuffield report categorises infants born before 25 weeks' gestation and affected by abnormality as having 'no chance'. This is similar to the 'no purpose' or 'unbearable' categories in the RCPCH framework. In these instances, the infant is judged to have a quality of life that makes treatment the least favourable option.[65]

The report generated a range of responses from national medical bodies high-lighting the variance of opinion on guidelines, their effectiveness and require-ments. Some members of the BMA considered the proposed guidelines to be 'too restrictive, undermining of professional judgement'[66] and argued that they set out 'blanket rules – smothering clinical discretion'.[67]

In contrast, the Royal College of Obstetricians and Gynaecologists (RCOG) stated that the working party should seriously consider 'the role of active euthan-asia in neonatal critical care'. Where the BMA considered greater subjectivity in approach appropriate, the RCOG may have welcomed a more objective test, similar to that of the Groningen Protocol used in the Netherlands, which allows infants to be euthanised.[68]

However, the working party 'unreservedly rejected active ending of neonatal life, even when such a life would be considered to be intolerable'.[69] Any discussion on active euthanasia was avoided by applying the 'slippery slope' argument that such would open the floodgates to adult euthanasia.[70] In taking this stance, the Nuffield report resonated the law, stating that there is 'no reason to distinguish between withdrawing treatment and decision not to start it, provided the decision is made in the best interests of the baby'.[71]

The report continued to endorse the law relating to the concept of 'double effect', concluding: 'Provided treatment is guided by the best interests of a baby, and had been agreed in the joint decision making process, potentially life-shortening but pain relieving treatments are morally acceptable.'[72]

Although the report acknowledged the 'frequently cited resource constraints of the National Health Service'[73] associated with the treatment of infants born at 23 weeks, it avoided any further discussion by claiming that such decisions should be made not on the basis of economic considerations, but on clinical judgments based on the best interests of the baby.[74] This book argues that, given the standing of the multidisciplinary working party and the media platform on

65 Morris, above, n 16, 347, 356.
66 Carolyn April and Michael Parker, 'End of Life Decision-making in Neonatal Care' (2007) 33(3) *Journal of Medical Ethics* 126, 126.
67 Margaret Brazier and David Archard, 'Letting Babies Die' (2007) 33(3) *Journal of Medical Ethics* 125, 125.
68 This will be considered in Chapter 7.
69 Nuffield Council on Bioethics, above, n 5, 157 [2.37].
70 Brazier and Archard, above, n 67, 125, 125.
71 Nuffield Council on Bioethics, above, n 5, 154 [9.14].
72 Ibid 20 [2.38].
73 Ibid 84 [5.45].
74 Ibid 22 [2.43].

which the report was presented, an open and thorough discussion about the efficient application of medical resources would have been invaluable.

Overall, the report adopted an inoffensive approach to issues that required, and continue to require, robust and open discussion. This may have been a strategic decision to avoid any condemnation from the public or from statutory bodies. Brazier and Archard, both members of the working party, 'felt it right to respect the feelings of those most intimately involved in decisions about premature babies and who may want the opportunity to spend time caring for a dying baby'.[75]

In its foreword, the party stated that it 'embarked on its task with some trepidation'. This was evident throughout the report, which, as a result, failed to discuss the issues surrounding end of life decision making concerning infants or to offer any vigorous reform or recommendations, thus confirming the status quo.

While Brazier and Archard believed the report attempted to 'start an honest debate about these issues',[76] this book contends that the report was ineffective in its aim: an honest and open debate, by its very nature, challenges established ideas. In this case, this would have involved discussing matters that were ethically and morally thought-provoking, which the report failed to do.

Overall, the guidelines and frameworks considered thus far from the UK are repetitive, and likely to cause further confusion to parents already facing an emotionally testing time. Thus, there is a need for uniform guidelines that are utilised by all hospitals in the UK, at least as a starting point. This chapter now turns to consider clinical guidelines in Australia.

3.10 Clinical guidelines Australia: the Royal Australasian College of Physicians: Paediatrics and Child Health Division: *Decision Making at the End of Life in Infants, Children and Adolescents* (2008)

To date, there are no freely available extensive clinical guidelines that have been published by any national Australian or New Zealand body that exclusively consider withdrawal or withholding of treatment of infants. The closest document is the Royal Australasian College of Physicians (RACP) guidelines, which are modelled on the Royal College of Paediatrics and Child Health (RCPCH) from the UK, discussed earlier. In its documents the RACP focuses and places emphasis on the role of the family and the shared role of both parents and doctors in the decision-making process:

> Collaborative decision making is the safest and most robust model, incorporating and balancing the observation, knowledge and insights of both the family/whanau and the members of the treating team. This model allows a variety of responses and can adapt to most circumstances. It also provides

---

75 Brazier and Archard, above, n 67, 125, 126.
76 Ibid.

an inherent system of 'checks and balances' against extremes in decision making, while providing support and validation for the conclusions of the decision making.[77]

The RACP document further states that the role of the health team is:

to care for the family/whanau, while facilitating the process of decision making around the child's care and maintaining a relationship of trust and respect . . . Health professionals have a duty to argue their views concerning management choices but there is also an obligation to respect group decisions and the decisions of the family, regardless of personal beliefs.[78]

The emphasis on 'collaborative decision making' with families is evidenced in the RACP's acknowledgment of the best interests principle:

Clinicians and guardians, usually parents, have a duty to make all key decisions in the best interests of the child. The treating team must always see itself as the advocate for the interests of the child and be prepared to manage differences with the parents from this perspective.[79]

Given that the central notion of decisions to withdraw or withhold life-sustaining treatment are based on what is 'best' for the infant, it is surprising that the principle of 'best interests' is not defined or discussed in the guidelines. Further, the guidelines highlight the possibility of conflict between medical practitioners and parents when making treatment decisions, and the potential for such disagreements to require legal intervention. In light of this, the guidelines fail to consider instances in which continuation or discontinuation of life-sustaining treatment would be in the best interests of an infant but they describe three situations whereby the appropriateness of continuing treatment is questionable as:

1　Where death is imminent.
2　Treatment would be ineffective making life intolerable because of pain and suffering.
3　Life would be shortened regardless of treatment and non-treatment would allow for increased comfort.[80]

The RACP guidelines do correctly state that there are 'no legal or morally relevant differences between withholding or withdrawal of treatment'.[81] Although the three situations just described are seemingly 'standardised' terms of intolerability

---

77　Royal Australasian College of Physicians, *Decision Making at the End of Life in Infants, Children and Adolescents* (Royal Australasian College of Physicians, 2008) 11.
78　Ibid 8.
79　Ibid 6.
80　Ibid 9.
81　Ibid 9.

and relief of pain and suffering as often applied by the court, the fact of legal sanction is not referred to in the RACP guidelines.

While the sentences 'where (when) death is imminent' and 'treatment would be ineffective' suggest futile treatment, and 'making life intolerable' suggests imposition of burdens rather than benefits, the terminology lacks clarity and is inadequate.

The document briefly considers neonatal treatment decision making under a section entitled 'Specific issues: neonatal period'. Although not entirely specific to those born at the edge of viability, the document mentions:

> In the circumstances of infants with an extremely small chance of survival it may be appropriate not to offer treatment such as with infants at 22–23 weeks' gestation particularly in poor condition.[82]

It further states:

> There is no legal obligation to offer treatment which is not medically indicated or which is futile, although taking this step in the absence of agreement should be considered only after all avenues have been exhausted.[83]

The guidelines fail to explain the meaning of futility and define the nature of 'other avenues' that must be exhausted. Although worthy, the emphasis on parental involvement suggests that there is an urgent need for uniform, homogeneous guidelines to assist doctors with end of life treatment decisions. This book posits that uniform national guidelines would encourage further parental involvement with greater trust, consistency and transparency in end of life decisions by the medical institution charged with the infant's care.

Overall, the RACP guidelines are too basic, provide little clinical guidance and lack any 'clout' – they are merely a document with unclear definitions and no prescribed course of action. When such decision are being made, with consequences that are so absolute, such a considerable amount of latitude is concerning.

3.11 Australian guidelines: each hospital to its own

In marked contrast to the UK, with its abundance of information and the repetitive and intersecting guidelines freely accessible to all, in Australia approaches to end of life decision making in premature and impaired infants appear to be specific to individual hospitals and look to be a 'closed model' of care.[84] Guidelines within hospitals on withdrawing or withholding life-sustaining treatment are often confidential and internal, and are unavailable to the public. Moreover, such careful

---

82 Ibid 21.
83 Ibid 21.
84 Michael Williams, John Chesterman and Philip Grano, 'Challenging Australia's "Closed" Model of Neonatal Care: The Need for Reform following *Re Baby D (No 2)*' 2012 19(4) *Journal of Law and Medicine* 835–85.

guarding of these policies provides little transparency for parents, who may be seeking information and understanding about decisions that are being made about their infant, often with significant and absolute consequences – death.

Overall, the one aspect of uniformity that exists between Australian guidelines is their variability. Individual hospital guidelines or frameworks vary in each hospital (even within one state) and are not mandated or audited by a national body within the medical community. Further, the guidelines do not describe treatment options based on any objective criteria and could possibly be considered to be 'motherhood' statements.

The variation between hospital clinical guidelines implies that there is a lack of consistency in end of life decision making in Australian hospitals. This variation creates further potential subjectivity in decision making to withdraw or withhold life-sustaining treatment from critically impaired infants. This runs the risk of parental confusion, ambiguity and a lack of trust and confidence in medical management, whereby parents may consider that in a different hospital their infant might receive treatment more in line with their own views.[85]

Although there is no clear solution to avoid parental loss of trust in the medical team, this book argues that the development of uniform national clinical guidelines can mitigate the risk of loss of parental or community trust in the decisions of healthcare institutions and/or medical practitioners to withdraw or withhold life-sustaining treatment. A uniform set of national guidelines would alleviate at least some of the subjectivity and allow a greater level of trust and confidence in medical teams by the assurance that all hospitals nationally are utilising the same clinical guidelines as a starting point in the often complex task of deciding whether life-sustaining treatment should be withdrawn or withheld.

The documents that guide doctors on end of life decisions are arguably symptomatic of the high level of autonomy of hospitals to set their own guidelines. However, the lack of any uniformity in clinical guidelines allows for an inappropriate level of medical discretion and autonomy in end of life decision making for premature and impaired infants. As individuals in our society, we all expect to travel to any state or hospital within the country and receive a similar standard of care. Why, then, should we not expect similar processes or procedures to be followed when making end of life decisions?

3.12 Perinatal care at the borderlines of viability: a consensus statement based on New South Wales and Australian Capital Territory consensus workshop (2005): another missed opportunity?

Arguably, the nearest that Australia came to developing uniform guidelines for critically ill infants was almost a decade ago with a 'consensus statement'. The

---

85 The role of parents in decision making is discussed in Chapter 4.

objectives of the 'statement' provided a good starting point for discussions for uniform guidelines; however, national engagement and collaboration was required for the statement to have realised its potential, conceivably resulting in national uniform guidelines.

The workshop was attended by nominated representatives from each of the ten neonatal intensive care units across New South Wales (NSW) and the Australian Capital Territory (ACT) across the disciplines of obstetrics, midwifery, neonatology, neonatal nursing and allied health professionals. In addition, individuals from parental groups, medical and nursing colleges and rural and regional practices were invited to participate in the generation of a consensus statement.

Lui et al. acknowledged the number of international guidelines on end of life treatment decisions for premature infants, and the associated 'grey zones' of uncertainty whereby end of life decisions are the most fragile.[86] Further, and most importantly, the group noted the lack of satisfactory guidelines for Australia and considered the need for such guidelines, consequently leading to a consensus workshop with participants from NSW and the ACT. Its findings were published in the *Medical Journal of Australia* in 2006. The aims of the workshop were twofold:

1   To produce consensus statements to supply clinicians and parents dealing with challenging scenarios encountered at the borderlines of viability.
2   To agree on accurate, meaningful and consistent information across NSW and the ACT for clinicians, parents and prospective parents of extremely premature infants.[87]

After studying the outcomes at 2–3 years of age of 897 premature infants born between 22 weeks' gestation and 25 weeks and 6 days' gestation in NSW and ACT, the group concluded that the viability of an infant born at 23 or fewer weeks of gestation was minimal and the risk of morbidity so high that resuscitation was not appropriate, while for an infant born at 26 weeks or more gestation resuscitation should be routine. However, for an infant born between 23 and 26 weeks' gestation, there was a 'grey zone' of discretion for which clinical treatment could be variable according to the clinicians and parents.

Overall, the findings of the workshop did not differ to those of the EPICure studies, or other work conducted in the UK. The group concluded that 'at gestational ages between 23–25 weeks + 6 days treatment is discretionary'.[88]

86 Lui et al., 'Perinatal Care at the Borderlines of Viability: A Consensus Statement Based on a NSW and ACT Consensus Workshop' (2006) 185(9) *Medical Journal of Australia* 495, 498.
87 Ibid 495.
88 Brian Darlow, 'The Limits of Perinatal Viability: Grappling with the Grey Zone' (2006) 185(9) *Medical Journal of Australia* 477, 478.

Provision of treatment or withholding of treatment would be appropriate at the following gestational periods:

1   at 23 weeks + 0–6 days – active treatment discussed but discouraged with parents
2   at 24 weeks + 0–6 days – option of non-treatment offered to parents
3   at 25 weeks + 0–6 days – active treatment offered but option of non-treatment offered – particularly in presence of adverse fetal factors
4   at 26 weeks and above – obligation to treat very high unless exceptional circumstances.

The consensus statement also asserted that where the family of a pre-term infant opts for non-intervention at 23–25 weeks' gestation, the following should be available:[89]

1   All hospitals should have guidelines for communication with parents in situations in which the family had opted for no intervention.
2   Counselling should be carried out by, or at least in consultation with, senior clinical staff.
3   If the birth occurs in a non-tertiary centre, access to senior staff in a tertiary centre for consultation should be available.
4   Clinical staff should be well versed in preparing parents for palliative care.
5   Appropriate support for grieving and post-death arrangements.

The group members were unanimous on the need for a good partnership of care between parents and doctors, and determined that good communication was of key importance.[90] The group discussed the importance of non-directive counselling offered to parents of those born in the 'grey zone' (at the borderline of viability). Commendably, the group did candidly discuss the varying attitudes and views of caregivers and decision makers: parents, doctors and nurses. The group agreed that 'consistent, transparent information should be shared between parents and members of the perinatal team'.[91]

As promising as the intention of the workshop and consensus statement initially appears, it has been subject to clinical and ethical critique. While Darlow generally supported the statement, it was criticised for claiming that consensus agreement of at least 90% of the participants had been reached. The number of agreeing participants was only 72% on the matter of withholding treatment on parental request for an infant 25 weeks + 0 –6 days' gestation. In addition, the composition of the multidisciplinary group was mainly health professionals, with no ethical, legal or religious representation.[92]

89 Lui et al., above, n 86, 495, 498.
90 Darlow, above, n 88, 477, 478.
91 Lui et al., above, n 86, 495, 499.
92 Darlow, above, n 88, 477–479.

Another commentator, French, questioned how much and whose opinions should be afforded the greatest weight in treatment decision making – medical professionals or parents – stating:

> [I]f parents dealing with an otherwise uncomplicated labour at 23 weeks gestation request initiation of intensive care, having had discussions and being duly informed of the possible outcomes, would these families be offered full support for their infant even if it were not the recommendation of the attending neonatologist or obstetrician?[93]

The critical evaluations of the consensus statement have some merit. Despite the workshop highlighting the need for 'accurate, meaningful and consistent information', the final statement is perfunctory in nature. While the statement provides that families of pre-term infants should be given counselling or support, it is illuminating that the workshop omitted to include ethical, legal or religious representatives. This arguably unduly narrowed the breadth of opinions that were considered.

The lack of such representation in the workshop was flawed. Given that medical practitioners and parents are often guided or comforted by the counsel of the very groups that were not represented in the workshop, a more holistic approach that included legal, ethical and religious representatives would have given the consensus statement greater legitimacy and authority.

The creation and publication of this consensus is important, particularly given the absence of any national guidelines in Australia. Arguably, the workshop provided an ideal opportunity for the development of national uniform guidelines in Australia. However, while the workshop was attended by primarily clinical representatives from NSW and the ACT, national engagement, including representatives from all other states and territories, was imperative for a true and informed 'consensus statement'.

It is not suggested that creating a working group and developing a uniform framework is by any means an easy task; however, the NSW/ACT consensus statement can be utilised as a springboard for a more refined and definitive framework. A good starting point would be to decipher and consider both the valuable data and information and the failings of the NSW/ACT consensus statement.

3.13 Academic discussion in this area

As discussed earlier in this chapter, by its very nature a set of guidelines or a framework is discretionary. However, several commentators support the contention of this chapter that greater consistency in guidelines is needed. In his paper

---

93 Noel French, 'Consensus statement on Perinatal Care' (2007) 43(6) *Journal of Paediatrics and Child Health* 492, 493.

in the *Singapore Medical Journal*, Foo highlights that the paediatrician Whitelaw recommends 'near certainty of death or no meaningful life' as the benchmark for decision making. He also states: 'No meaningful life is a virtual certainty of complete incapacity not just a handicap.'[94]

Other academics have suggested proposals and frameworks to address the ambiguity and low impact of clinical guidelines that have been published. Lamb suggests a more robust approach, employing the term 'slippery slope' to describe situations in which a specific course of action that may be seen as ethical actually leads to other courses of action that are unethical.[95] Pinter also agrees with this 'slippery slope' concept in relation to guidelines, and noted that, without 'sharp and precise boundaries', there will be a deterioration of ethical decision making.[96]

Further, Zutlevics proposed a 'cooperative discursive' framework with essential features such as ample time (where possible), a diverse and inclusive group of moral decision makers who have an equal opportunity to contribute to the discussion informing decision making, and rational and principled decision making.[97]

In contrast, McHaffie et al. assert that there is no need for stringent guidelines to clarify roles and responsibilities, and instead recommend a 'flexible package of care, tailored to specific need'.[98]

More recently, in his book *Death or Disability?* neonatologist Dominic Wilkinson has 'critized guidelines for treatment decisions that focus on the best interests of the child, since it seems to me that such guidelines are unable to provide practical guidance to clinicians'.[99] Wilkinson considers current guidelines for impaired infants, 'vague, and difficult to apply in practice, even where the prognosis for a child was known with certainty'.[100]

Wilkinson has provided some valuable points of discussion and has articulately proposed a threshold framework, which the author (and, it should be added, this book) hopes 'is a first step towards developing more detailed and specific guidelines'.[101] In the threshold framework for decision making, Wilkinson suggests a minimum of two thresholds, which the author refers to as an 'upper and lower threshold setting',[102] the upper threshold relating to 'mandatory treatment' and

94 K B Foo 'Medico-legal and Ethical Problems Associated with Treatment of Children Born with Congenital Malformations' (1994) 35(2) *Singapore Medical Journal* 184, 188.
95 David Lamb, *Down the Slippery Slope: Arguing in Applied Ethics* (Routledge, 1988).
96 A B Pinter, 'End-of-life Decision Before and After Birth: Changing Ethical Considerations' (2008) 43(6) *Journal of Pediatric Surgery* 430–436.
97 Tamara Zutlevics, 'Pursuing the Golden Mean – Moral Decision Making for Precarious Newborns' (2009) 27(1) *Australian Journal of Advanced Nursing* 75–81.
98 McHaffie et al., 'Deciding for Imperilled Newborns: Medical Authority or Parental Autonomy?' (2001) 27(2) *Journal of Medical Ethics* 104–109.
99 Dominic Wilkinson, *Death or Disability? The 'Carmentis Machine' and Decision-making for Critically Ill Children* (Oxford University Press, 2013) 303.
100 Ibid 261.
101 Ibid 261.
102 Ibid.

the lower threshold to 'inappropriate treatment'. The threshold framework includes a holistic discussion of parental discretion, quality of life and other influencing factors in decision making such as the allocation of resources.[103] The author acknowledges the need for 'guidelines that reflect the fundamental ethical underpinnings of decisions' but also to 'respect the range of different views within a community about how we should evaluate the risks and benefits of future life, and of death'.[104]

3.14 The need for uniform guidelines

In addition to the insufficiently defined best interests principle applied by the courts discussed in the previous chapter, clinical guideline variation illustrates the potential subjectivity and ambiguity in current decision making to withdraw or withhold life-sustaining treatment from premature and critically impaired infants.

As noted in Chapter 2, the courts have demonstrated a deference to medical opinion. When considered in isolation, this regard for the opinion of treating physicians is understandable to a certain degree. Judges are not medically trained and cannot make medical prognoses. However, this deference potentially undermines the cardinal rule of law's virtues in the form of transparency, consistency and predictability in the operation and application of important human endeavours.

Further, end of life decisions may be unduly dependent on the subjective attitudes, beliefs and values of the treating practitioner or parents, especially where the treatment wishes of the patient are unclear.[105]

Although it cannot be denied that every individual case has its own unique characteristics, this should not be confused with a lack of need for a unified national framework. On the contrary, a unified framework would allow the intricacies of each case to be given a thorough examination against a common denominator. This is of key importance in moving forward to a better system of decision making with greater transparency and consistency, particularly given that the majority of withdrawal or withholding of treatment decisions are made in the hospital setting.

While it is acknowledged that the development of uniform clinical guidelines will not remove much of the medical uncertainty for critically imperilled infants, uniform guidelines would inject some degree of objectivity to end of life decisions.

Given that end of life decision making is so emotionally and ethically charged and open to a great deal of subjectivity, a better model would be to create and utilise a unified body of guidelines that are applied nationally. As such, it is invaluable to consider more structured, consistent and transparent guidelines that

103 Ibid 303.
104 Ibid.
105 Dominic Wilkinson and Robert D Truog, 'The Luck of the Draw: Physician-related Variability in End-of-life Decision Making in Intensive Care' 2013 39(6) *Intensive Care Medicine* 1128–1132.

are mandated as hospital policies or procedures, which could potentially prevent parent–doctor 'disagreements' escaping the hospital corridors and becoming disputes that end up at the doors of the court.

3.15 Conclusion

This book posits that present guidelines for withholding and withdrawing life-sustaining treatment for infants in the UK and Australia are inadequate. They are not supported by current common law and lack clarity and precision. There is an urgent need to reformulate national guidelines.

An overarching uniform framework would inject clarity, consistency and transparency into decisions to withdraw or withhold life-sustaining treatment. This is of considerable importance in creating a more open and honest dialogue between parents and doctors. Additionally, removing some of the subjectivity that informs end of life decisions will allow for greater parental trust and confidence in healthcare institutions and treating practitioners.

Moreover, when withdrawing or withholding life-sustaining treatment is the best option, uniform and clear standards will allow the finite period of time to be better spent on providing the appropriate care and perhaps saving parents from some emotional turmoil where treatment simply prolongs an infant's inevitable death.

It will be recalled from the previous chapter that the law places great emphasis on medical opinion and has relied on the clinical guidance of medical bodies when making end of life decisions. In *Bland*, Lord Goff relied on the *Bolam* test – holding that a doctor will act with the benefit of guidance from a responsible and competent body of relevant professional opinion – and the advice and guidance of the BMA ethics committee to reach his conclusion to withdraw and withhold treatment.[106]

In addition, in *Re C*,[107] the courts' decision to withdraw treatment from an infant born with spinal muscular atrophy was made after careful analysis of the RCPCH guidelines. Sir Stephen Brown highlighted the need to make a decision with the child's best interests as the paramount consideration.[108]

Somewhat aberrantly, it appears that judges rely on medical opinion and doctors rely on case law decisions when developing guidelines to assist doctors in decision making. Like the case law and judicial deference to medical opinion considered earlier, guidelines provide yet another non-prescriptive or directional formality to medico-legal dilemmas concerning end of life decision making for premature and impaired infants.

---

106 *Airedale NHS Trust v Bland* [1993] AC 789.
107 *Re C (a minor)* [1997] 40 BMLR 31 (Fam Div).
108 See, further, Michael Fertleman and Adam Fox, 'The Law of Consent in England as Applied to the Sick Neonate' (2003) 3(1) *Internet Journal of Pediatrics and Neonatology*. http://archive.ispub.com/journal/the-internet-journal-of-pediatrics-and-neonatology/volume-3-number-1/the-law-of-consent-in-england-as-applied-to-the-sick-neonate.html#sthash.pX6ODMbI.uRnuOQGt.dpbs

This is an ethical and moral quandary, fraught with controversy. The reliance demonstrated by both the medical and legal professions on each other in guiding and deciding life and death decisions is arguably an illustration of both professions' unwillingness to take the lead in any real or meaningful dialogue towards decisions in this area. Medical practitioners and judges both apply ill-defined terms such as 'best interests', 'futility' and 'benefits and burdens', and both have demonstrated inconsistent and loose application of such.

The abundance of information and frameworks in the UK and the variation (within hospitals even within the same state) in clinical guidelines in Australia is confusing, and one unified set of guidelines in each country that is applied nationally is required. Both the UK and Australia have either missed or avoided taking the opportunities to have frank discussions about more robust decision-making reforms.

Premature and critically impaired infants cannot express their inherent right to autonomy or advocate their treatment wishes. Thus, the role and limits on decision making between key caregivers and decision makers (that is, chiefly, doctors, parents and the judiciary) in decision making for critically impaired infants is imperative. This issue is examined in the next chapter of this book.

3.16 References

Airedale NHS Trust v Bland [1993] AC 789.

April, Carolyn and Michael Parker, 'End of Life Decision-making in Neonatal Care' (2007) 33(3) *Journal of Medical Ethics* 126.

Arnett, George, 'New Record Lows in Teen Pregnancy Rate', *The Guardian* (Online) 26 February 2014. www.theguardian.com/news/datablog/2014/feb/25/new-record-lows-in-teen-pregnancy-rate

Baby D (No 2) [2011] Fam CA 176.

BBC One, *Miracle Baby Grows Up* 17 September 2004. http://news.bbc.co.uk/2/hi/programmes/panorama/3655050.stm

BBC, News Health, '*Teen pregnancy rate lower still*' 25 February 2014. www.bbc.com/news/health-26338540

Bolam v Friern Hospital Management Committee [1957] 1 WLR 582.

Brazier, Margaret and David Archard, 'Letting Babies Die' (2007) 33(3) *Journal of Medical Ethics* 125.

British Medical Association, *Withholding and Withdrawing Life-prolonging Medical Treatment: Guidance for Decision Making* (Blackwell Publishing, 3rd edn, 2007).

Campbell, Dennis, 'Premature Babies Study Shows Survival Rates on Rise' *The Guardian* (Online), 5 December 2012. http://m.guardian.co.uk/society/2012/dec/05/survival-rates-premature-babies-rise

Confidential Enquiry into Maternal and Child Health, *Perinatal Mortality 2007* (CEMACH, 2009).

Costeloe, K L, Enid Hennessy, Alan T Gibson, Neil Marlow and Andrew R Wilkinson, 'The EPICure Study: Outcomes to Discharge from Hospital for Infants Born at the Threshold of Viability' (2000) 106(4) *Pediatrics* 659.

Darlow, Brian, 'The Limits of Perinatal Viability: Grappling with the Grey Zone' (2006) 185(9) *Medical Journal of Australia* 477.

Doyal, L and V F Larcher 'Drafting Guidelines for the Withholding or Withdrawing of Life Sustaining Treatment in Critically Ill Children and Neonates' (2000) 83(1) *Archives of Disease in Childhood: Fetal and Neonatal* 60.

EPICure, *EpiCure 1995*. www.epicure.ac.uk/epicure-1995

EPICure, *EPICure 2*. www.epicure.ac.uk/epicure-2

EPICure, *EPICure at One Year*. www.epicure.ac.uk/epicure-1995/epicure-at-one-year

EPICure, *EPICure: Population-Based Studies of Survival and Later Health Status in Extremely Premature Infants*. www.epicure.ac.uk

EPICure, *Survival*. www.epicure.ac.uk/overview/survival

Fertleman, Michael and Adam Fox, 'The Law of Consent in England as Applied to the Sick Neonate' (2003) 3(1) *Internet Journal of Pediatrics and Neonatology*. http://archive.ispub.com/journal/the-internet-journal-of-pediatrics-and-neonatology/volume-3-number-1/the-law-of-consent-in-england-as-applied-to-the-sick-neonate.html§hash.pX6ODMbI. uRnuOQGt.dpbs

Foo, K B, 'Medico-legal and Ethical Problems Associated with Treatment of Children Born with Congenital Malformations' (1994) 35(2) *Singapore Medical Journal* 184.

French, Noel, 'Consensus Statement on Perinatal Care' (2007) 43 (6) *Journal of Paediatrics and Child Health* 492 .

Gallagher, James, 'Severely Premature Babies: More Survive Being Born Early' 5 December 2012, BBC. www.bbc.co.uk/news/health-20583678

General Medical Council, *Leadership and Management for all Doctors* (General Medical Council, 2012) 31. www.gmcuk.org/static/documents/content/Leadership_and_management_for_all_doctors_-_English_0414.pdf

General Medical Council, *Treatment and Care Towards the End of Life: Good Practice in Decision Making* (General Medical Council, 2010).

Glaeser, Edward L and Andrei Shleifer, 'Legal Origins' (2002) 117(4) *Quarterly Journal of Economics* 1193.

Lamb, David, *Down the Slippery Slope: Arguing in Applied Ethics* (Routledge, 1988).

Lui, Kei, Barbara Bajuk, Kirsty Foster, Arnolda Gaston, Alison Kent, John Sinn et al., 'Perinatal Care at the Borderlines of Viability: A Consensus Statement Based on a NSW and ACT Consensus Workshop' (2006) 185(9) *Medical Journal of Australia* 495.

McHaffie, Hazel E and Peter W Fowlie 'Withdrawing and Withholding Treatment: Comments on New Guidelines' (1998) 79(1) *Archives of Disease in Childhood: Fetal and Neonatal* 1.

McHaffie Hazel E, Ian A Laing, Michael Parker and John McMillan, 'Deciding for Imperilled Newborns: Medical Authority or Parental Autonomy?' (2001) 27(2) *Journal of Medical Ethics* 104.

Moore, Thomas, 'Premature Babies: Dilemmas Over Care Grows' 5 December 2012, Sky News. http://news.sky.com/story/1020756/premature-babies-dilemma-over-care-grow

Moore, Thomas, S Johnson, E Hennessy, P Chisholm and N Marlow, 'The Epicure Studies: Better Survival, Better Outcomes?' (2011) 96(Suppl 1) *Archives of Disease in Childhood: Fetal and Neonatal* 16.

Morris, Anne, 'Selective Treatment of Irreversibly Impaired Infants: Decision Making at the Threshold' 2009 17(3) *Medical Law Review* 347.

Nuffield Council on Bioethics, *About*. www.nuffieldbioethics.org/about

Nuffield Council on Bioethics, *Critical Care Decisions in Fetal and Neonatal Medicine: Ethical Issues* (Nuffield Council on Bioethics, 2006).

Nuffield Foundation, *About the Nuffield Foundation*. www.nuffieldfoundation.org/About-the-foundation

Office for National Statistics, *Teenage Pregnancies at Lowest Levels Since Records Began* 2 April 2013. www.ons.gov.uk/ons/rel/vsob1/conception-statistics—england-and-wales/2011/sty-conception-estimates-2011.html

Pinter, A B, 'End-of-life Decision Before and After Birth: Changing Ethical Considerations' (2008) 43(6) *Journal of Pediatric Surgery* 430.

R v Arthur (1981) 12 BMLR 1.

Re C (a minor) [1997] 40 BMLR 31 (Fam Div).

Re J (a minor) (wardship: medical treatment) [1990] 3 All ER 930.

Royal Australasian College of Physicians, *Decision Making at the End of Life in Infants, Children and Adolescents* (Royal Australasian College of Physicians, 2008).

Royal College of Paediatrics and Child Health, *Withholding or Withdrawing Life Sustaining Treatment in Children: A Framework for Practice* (RCPCH, 2nd edn, 2004).

Tibballs, James, 'The Legal Basis for Ethical Withholding and Withdrawing of Life Sustaining Medical Treatment in Children' (2006) 14(2) *Journal of Law and Medicine* 244.

Tracy, S K, M B Tracy, J Dean, P Laws and E Sullivan, 'Spontaneous Preterm Birth of Liveborn Infants in Women at Low Risk in Australia over 10 Years: A Population-Based Study' (2007) 114(6) *BJOG: An International Journal of Obstetrics & Gynaecology* 731–735.

TS & TD v Sydney Children's Hospital ('Mohammed's case') [2012] NSWSC 1609.

White, Anna, 'Premature Babies: The Pregnant Elephant in the Room is Stress', *The Telegraph* (Online), 17 December 2012. www.telegraph.co.uk/women/womens-life/9748592/Premature-babies-The-pregnant-elephant-in-the-room-is-stress.html

Wilkinson, Andrew R, Jag Ahluwalia, Andy Cole, Doreen Crawford, Janet Fyle, Ann Gordon et al., 'Management of Babies Born Extremely Preterm at Less Than 26 Weeks of Gestation: A Framework for Clinical Practice at the Time of Birth' (2009) 94(1) *Archives of Disease in Childhood: Fetal and Neonatal* 2.

Wilkinson, Dominic, *Death or Disability? The 'Carmentis Machine' and Decision-making for Critically Ill Children* (Oxford University Press, 2013).

Wilkinson, Dominic and Robert D Truog, 'The Luck of the Draw: Physician-related Variability in End-of-life Decision Making in Intensive Care' 2013 39 (6) *Intensive Care Medicine* 1128.

Williams, Michael, John Chesterman and Philip Grano, 'Challenging Australia's "Closed" Model of Neonatal Care: The Need for Reform following *Re Baby D (No 2)*' 2012 19(4) *Journal of Law and Medicine* 835.

Yadav, Kamini and David Field, 'The Limit of Viability: Should We Lower It?' (2011) 100(3) *Neonatology* 295.

Zutlevics, Tamara, 'Pursuing the Golden Mean – Moral Decision Making for Precarious Newborns' (2009) 27(1) *Australian Journal of Advanced Nursing* 75.

4 The role, impact and importance of key caregivers and decision makers

Chapter 3 critiqued the role of clinical guidelines and end of life decision making for premature and critically ill infants. It examined the guidelines and frameworks created and implemented in hospitals in the UK, and their variation in Australia. The chapter noted that there are exclusive clinical guidelines in the UK for premature and critically ill infants. Chapter 3 also critically evaluated the 2006 Nuffield Council of Bioethics Report and its missed opportunity to make any robust recommendations to improve the existing, and repetitive, wealth of guidelines and frameworks in the UK. It was noted that in Australia each hospital exercises an unhealthy degree of autonomy, with life and death decisions made based on internal policies, inaccessible to the wider public. Chapter 3 argued that there is a need for greater uniformity in clinical guidelines in the UK and Australia, thus allowing for end of life decisions for impaired infants to at least begin from the same baseline.

Chapter 4 examines the roles, views and influencing factors in end of life decision making of key caregivers and decision makers – chiefly parents, doctors and judges. It is these primary groups that are affected or involved in the decision-making process for premature and critically ill infants.[1] This chapter begins by examining the intertwined dynamic that exists between parents and doctors in end of life decision making. It then considers how the dynamic changes when the decision making is taken out of the hospital setting and moves into the court.

Discussion in the area of end of life decision making for premature and critically impaired infants is invariably emotive and controversial due to the final consequences of such decisions. Infants cannot express their own will and are entirely dependent on others to make decisions for them. Thus, caregivers and decision makers (that is, doctors, judges and parents) must assume this authority, and they occasionally take actions that detract from the rights and interests of the infant. In some cases, these actions lean towards the perceived duties and interests of the caregiver or decision maker rather than the patient. Dunn acknowledged this, stating:

---

1 The wider community is also affected by end of life decisions – namely, where treatment is continued and the infant is suffering with severe disability. This is discussed in Chapter 6.

[W]hether it be to have a prenatal diagnosis or to have a caesarean section or to submit to life-saving interventions, we must never lose sight of that most fundamental right of all, the right to choice, and the right not to have what doctors sometimes naively assume our patients will or should want.[2]

Many medical journals provide global empirical research in the form of surveys, questionnaires and polls that have been conducted to ascertain medical professionals' attitudes and perceptions towards end of life decision making for premature and impaired infants.[3] There are also some invaluable empirical studies, largely conducted by McHaffie in the UK, documenting parental experiences in end of life decision making for impaired infants, many of which are discussed in this chapter.[4]

This book argues that the views of caregivers and decision makers in treatment decisions concerning premature and impaired infants should not be explicitly or implicitly determinative in life and death decision making. In seeking to better understand this area, it is first important to identify, in concrete terms, the interests that are affected. Then the respective weight that should be accorded to each of them can be discussed. This requires an examination of the ideals and values involved, and also a determination of the relevant caregivers and decision makers.

There are often competing and equally valid rights, duties and interests at play, which will produce different answers depending on the questioner. Heimer supports this observation with regards to parents:

Parents stake their claim on their right to family autonomy, privacy and freedom of religion and on their ultimate responsibility for the child. It is they who must bear the burden of raising a disabled child, balancing its needs against those of other family members.[5]

---

2 Peter Dunn, 'Appropriate Care of the Newborn: Ethical Dilemmas' (1993) 19(2) *Journal of Medical Ethics* 82, 82.

3 See, e.g., Rebagliato et al., 'Neonatal End-of-life Decision Making: Physicians' Attitudes and Relationship with Self-reported Practices in 10 European Countries' (2000) 284(19) *Journal of American Medical Association* 2451–2459; D Duffy and P Reynolds, 'Babies Born at the Threshold of Viability: Attitudes of Paediatric Consultants and Trainees in South East England' (2011) 100(1) *Acta Paediatrica* 42–46; Cuttini et al., 'End-of-life Decisions in Neonatal Intensive Care: Physicians' Self-Reported Practices in Seven European Countries' (2000) 355(9221) *The Lancet* 2112–2118.

4 A number of McHaffie-led studies are discussed in this chapter; for comprehensive research undertaken by McHaffie in this area, see, especially, Hazel E McHaffie, *Crucial Decisions at the Beginning of Life* (Radcliffe Medical Press, 2011). For a comprehensive discussion of the views of medical practitioners and nurses in end of life decision making for extremely premature infants, see, especially, Hazel E McHaffie and Peter W Fowlie, *Life, Death and Decisions* (Hochland & Hochland Ltd, 1996).

5 Carol A Heimer, 'Competing Institutions: Law, Medicine, and Family in Neonatal Intensive Care' (1999) 33(1) *Law and Society Review* 17, 31.

6 Ibid.

On the other hand, physicians' 'claims are based on their traditional rights to make treatment decisions on possession of arcane medical knowledge and on experience treating other infants with similar problems'.[6] Further:

> And the state, through legislatures, regulatory bodies and courts, argue that its interest in the lives and health of its citizens takes precedence over parents' right to control their own children. As Parens Patriae it claims to be a disinterested protector of infant citizens.[7]

Kerridge, Lowe and Stewart also highlight that *parens patriae* powers in Australia 'is the notion of the sovereign as the "father of the nation"'.[8] As such, 'the Supreme Courts of the States and Territories have the power to consent to treatments on behalf of incompetent adults and children under their inherent jurisdiction'.[9]

Should certain caregivers and/or decision makers be regarded as functionaries in the process? Is the *ad hoc* system currently applied in hospitals to make life and death decisions the most effective and efficient? These are some of the key questions addressed in this chapter. The next section explores some of the factors that affect and influence parents, who are primarily 'one-time players' in decisions to withdraw or withhold life-sustaining treatment from premature or critically impaired infants.

4.1 Parents: conflicting interests and views

The parents of infants born severely premature or with severe abnormality are affected significantly in decisions about the withdrawal or withholding of life-sustaining treatment. The period during which such decisions are made is marked by measures of joy and sorrow, as parents are asked to consider the loss of a child, and as they grapple with the consequences of their decision in the process. For many adults, the concept of death or dying may be unfamiliar as this may be their first experience of losing a loved one.[10]

A study published in the UK by McHaffie in 2001 found that 'contemplating tragic outcomes, watching a baby die, burying their own child, these are extraordinary experiences for young people to live through'.[11] In addition, many

---

7 Ibid.
8 Ian Kerridge, Michael Lowe and Cameron Stewart, *Ethics and Law for Health Professions* (Federation Press, 4th edn, 2013) 395.
9 Ibid. See, also, Lainie Freidman Ross, *Children, Families, and Health Care Decision Making* (Oxford University Press, 1998), in particular Chapter 7, 'The child as patient' 131–152; and David Archard, *Children: Rights and Childhood* (Routledge, 2nd edn, 2004), in particular Chapter 11, 'Family and state' 153–167.
10 For a more in-depth examination of parental experiences after the death of a baby, see Nancy Khoner and Alix Henley, *When a Baby Dies: The Experience of Late Miscarriage, Stillbirth and Neonatal Death* (Pandora Press, 1991).
11 McHaffie et al., 'Deciding for Imperilled Newborns: Medical Authority or Parental Autonomy?' (2001) 27(2) *Journal of Medical Ethics* 104, 106.

young parents 'lamented their lost youth and innocence . . . they were now permanently separated from their peers, and could not regain their carefree approach to life'.[12]

Ostensibly, parents of premature or critically impaired infants in the end of life decision-making process are deserving of the utmost compassion. However, to rely entirely on such a view would be misguided. Such a one-dimensional assessment does not explain the varying reactions of parents in these situations, and fails to capture the most complete picture of parents, the emotions they experience and the decisions they come to make.

The influence of media, development of medical science and technology

There has been a shift in societal attitudes towards the family structure. This has corresponded to the increased accessibility of contraception, women's rights and personal autonomy on matters such as abortion and planned pregnancies.[13] Twentieth-century innovation and developments have allowed infants to defy nature, and have given parents and doctors capacity to play a significant role in an infant's ultimate future. Shelp explains the situation prior to these developments:

> Medicine, for all practical purposes, was impotent to effectively intervene to rescue life or transform a sick baby into a healthy one. Parents necessarily received what the natural lottery of human reproduction delivered. Cure and/or habilitation [sic] to a normal life were beyond the control of both parents and medicine.[14]

Often parents have their hopes and aspirations tied up in their child. Relationships, career choices and life experiences all contribute to parents having a vested interest in the birth of a child. There are many reasons that people want, need and have children. Nearly all of these are admirable, although others may be regarded as selfish. By way of example of the last, financial reasons, reasons that uphold notions of social status, familial pressures and the internal dynamics of individual relationships may contribute to the drive to reproduce.[15]

---

12 Ibid.
13 But see Rebecca Smith, 'Women Finding Access to Contraception Difficult', *Telegraph* (Online) 11 May 2012. www.telegraph.co.uk/health/healthnews/9257070/Women-finding-access-to-contraception-difficult.html. See, also, Mazza et al., 'Current Contraceptive Management in Australian General Practice: An Analysis of BEACH Data' (2012) 197(2) *Medical Journal of Australia* 110–114.
14 Earl E Shelp, *Born to Die? Deciding the Fate of Critically Ill Newborns* (Free Press, 1986) 77.
15 There may be societal pressures on couples to reproduce; see, e.g., Christine Crowe, '"Women Want It": In-vitro Fertilization and Women's Motivations for Participation' (1985) 8(6) *Women's Studies International Forum* 547–552. Further, cultural or religious reasons may mean that women are under pressure to reproduce. Susan Martha Kahn asserts that Jewish citizens derive from

Prospective parents may regularly speculate on the future goals they wish to see their child achieve. During the pregnancy, soon-to-be parents often begin to consider names, the suburbs in which they would like to raise their children, the schools their children might attend and the activities in which they hope their children will participate. The thought of a difficult or premature pregnancy or of bearing a child with a severe abnormality does not sit comfortably alongside the ideals or hopes of prospective parents. As Shelp explains: 'It is frightening for parents to think that this pregnancy might result in the birth of an infant with serious impairment that could effectively shatter all the hopes and dreams they have for this child.'[16]

Scientific and technological progress has enabled significant advances. However, with these achievements have come greater expectations as to what can be delivered to the patient. Moreover, as technology has advanced, women have been able to embark on pregnancy later in life, and those who may once have been considered infertile now have the opportunity to become mothers.

This raises an important question: just because we *can* save impaired infants from death, does this mean we *should* save impaired infants (especially those born at extreme prematurity) from death or severe disability? Guyer suggests that, 'some parents push too hard for treatments that are medically inappropriate'.[17] Others may rely on 'reproductive technologies in order to conceive a baby and then expect that other technologies will rescue and maintain their baby'.[18]

In the quest for a 'good story', the media often publish stories and bold headlines about 'miracle babies'. Parents often passionately cling to such stories of babies surviving against all odds, believing that their baby can do the same. This sentiment is candidly echoed by Guyer:

> Sometimes media hyperbole focuses on a single micropremmie – 'The Size of a Coke Can!' – or on a baby whose radical surgery – 'Infant Heart, the Size of a Walnut, Rebuilt and Running' – stands as testimony to a surgeon's technical prowess but not to what constitutes an appropriate reaction to nature's inevitable anatomical mistakes.[19]

Arguably, medical professionals have become victims of their own success. By now being able to save infants who may have died as little as two decades ago, there is often an unrealistic expectation that doctors will keep these critically ill infants alive. Dr Andrew Watkins, Director of the NICU at the Mercy Hospital in

immigration, conversion to the Jewish faith or by birth. Thus, 'Israeli Jewish women are left as the primary agents through which the nation can be reproduced as Jewish . . . Jewish women are under extraordinarily pressure to reproduce, whether they are married or unmarried.' See, especially, Susan Martha Kahn, *Reproducing Jews: A Cultural Account of Assisted Conception in Israel* (Duke University Press, 2000) 4.

16 Shelp, above, n 14, 54.
17 Ruth Levy Guyer, *Baby at Risk* (Capital Books, 2006) 50.
18 Ibid.
19 Ibid.

Melbourne, carries a similar view: 'There is no pleasure in the irony that the NICU is a victim of its own success; 20 years ago, 28 weeks was the limit of viability for premature babies.' He went on to say:

> Today, sophisticated advances in biomedical engineering, with cots that light up like cockpits . . . the result is that younger than ever babies are now surviving . . . needing beds for longer.[20]

A study conducted in New Zealand highlighting the survival rate of infants born weighing 501–1500 grams over a 50-year period found marked improvements. Infants born with a birth weight of 501–1000 grams saw a survival rate increase from less than 10% in 1959 to 80% in 2009.[21] This vast improvement in survival rate has not been confined to New Zealand. Both the UK and the University of Washington reported increased survival rates for infants of this weight for between 1965 and 1975.[22]

Given the improvements in survival rates, it is understandable that parents today may push for aggressive treatment. This may also be true of situations in which the continuation of treatment is futile, but where parents are hoping that their child will also be a 'miracle baby', as read about in tabloid newspapers.

Although very rarely seen, two such 'Sunday features' recently in Australia should be commended for attempting to present a more nuanced view of infants born at the edge of viability.[23] Additionally, 2011 saw the BBC air a documentary, *The Price of Life*, by science writer Adam Wishart in the UK. Wishart spent six months in the NICU of the Birmingham Women's Hospital, where he was given unrestricted access to interview parents and doctors and, in doing so, document the very different experiences of families and medical staff in making end of life decisions for infants born extremely premature – at 23 weeks.[24]

These newspaper articles and documentary are an exception to the rule in representing a realistic view of life in, and beyond, the NICU. However, generally, the bulk of media reporting fails to discuss the realities that face infants and their

---

20 Kathy Evans, 'The Edge of Life', *The Melbourne Magazine, The Age* (Australia), Issue 90, April 2012, 38, 40.
21 Battin et al., 'Improvement in Mortality of Very Low Birth Weight Infants and the Changing Pattern of Neonatal Mortality: The 50-Year Experience of One Perinatal Centre' (2012) 48(7) *Journal of Paediatrics and Child Health* 596, 597.
22 Ibid 598.
23 Segments of both articles and the documentary will be discussed throughout this chapter. Tracey McVeigh, 'I Would Have Wanted Him to Die in My Arms', *Sunday Herald Sun Magazine, The Herald Sun* (Australia) 17 April 2011; Kathy Evans, 'The Edge of Life', *The Melbourne Magazine, The Age* (Australia), Issue 90, April 2012; *The Price of Life* (Directed by Adam Wishart, BBC Productions, 2011).
24 Considerations of the allocation of limited healthcare resources for infants born extremely premature and critically impaired are discussed in Chapter 6.
25 See, further, Jag Ahluwalia, Christoph Lees and John J Paris, 'Decisions for Life Made in the Perinatal Period: Who Decides and on Which Standards?' (2008) 93(5) *Archives of Disease in Childhood: Fetal and Neonatal* 332, 332.

families. Critically, there is often a failure to highlight the real survival rates and discuss the denominator against which survival can be measured.[25]

As highlighted in Chapters 1 and 3, infants who survive without any disability and against medical odds are unusual rather than the norm. In representing the exception, the media reinforces the contention of this book: that there is a need for greater transparency and objectivity in relation to end of life decision making for premature and impaired infants. Greater public awareness is required to realistically highlight life particularly for extremely premature infants born at 23 weeks' gestation, thus removing some of the emotion that is often attached to birth and newborn babies. The significant impact of the internet and the media in decision making is supported by recent empirical research from Moro et al., in which the authors noted that one mother found 'the information she gathered on the internet impacted her ability to hold out hope that her daughter would survive'.[26]

Today, due to the media reporting stories of survival and presenting an unbalanced view, parents are often surprised to discover that they have a premature infant and that, as a result of its prematurity, it is likely to have severe disabilities. Hammerman et al. support this point, asserting: 'they [parents] must struggle with many conflicting emotions. On the one hand there is the love, concern and hope for their baby's wellbeing counterbalanced by the grief, disappointment and guilt over the reality of their imperfect infant.'[27]

Religious and cultural beliefs

Varying religious beliefs affect parental attitudes and views of withdrawal or withholding of treatment and death. Hammerman et al. conducted a study on attitudes of pregnant women towards medical decision making for critically ill infants. The subjects of the study were Israeli-born Muslim and Jewish women in their mid-twenties to thirties. Based on the level of religious observance of the women, the research found that 'mothers who described themselves as ultraortho-dox/fundamentalist constituted a higher proportion of those selecting maximally aggressive medical intervention (25% v 17% of the total population)'.[28] In comparison, mothers who considered themselves more secular and would select minimal intervention accounted for 31% as opposed to 20% of the general population.[29]

The study highlighted that women with more religious and fundamental beliefs considered that the principle of sanctity of life was of utmost importance, regardless of the child's disability. One respondent in the Hammerman-led study

26 Moro et al., 'Parent Decision Making for Life Support Decisions for Extremely Premature Infants: From the Prenatal through to End-of-Life Period' (2011) 25(1) *Journal of Perinatal and Neonatal Nursing* 52, 57.

27 Hammerman et al., 'Decision-making in the Critically Ill Neonate: Cultural Background v Individual Life Experiences' (1997) 23(3) *Journal of Medical Ethics* 164, 167.

28 Ibid 165.

29 Ibid.

asserted that 'even the most severely handicapped child has a soul and all care must be taken to ensure his survival. In fact I have heard that "special" children have the loftiest souls.'[30] Women who considered themselves more secular indicated that the key influencing factor in their decision making was the quality of life the infant would have and his or her inability to enjoy life and all it had to offer.

Thus, religious affiliation and decision making for premature and critically ill infants appear to be commonly linked. Often parents believe that life and death decisions should be left in God's hands. They are of the belief that God is the ultimate decision maker, not them. Many parents consider doctors to be 'representatives of God in the healing process'.[31]

However, this line of thought is fraught with contradiction: if God is the decision maker, how can doctors, medical science and medical equipment, which are ultimately 'keeping the infant alive', all be held in the hands of a higher power, greater than man?

Paris et al. agree with this line of thought, stating: 'the child is trapped in technology from which death is the only exit. When the inevitable NICU death does occur, those involved assure themselves "We did everything possible. It was God's decision, not ours".'[32] A recent American study published in 2011 indicates a more literal application of God as the ultimate referee. One family in the study led by Moro believed that the decision as to whether the infant survived should be left entirely in God's hands, and that the only way to allow 'God to handle it' was to remove the infant from the ventilator and allow God to decide the child's fate.[33] One religious parent, interviewed for a Melbourne newspaper, described having thoughts about the conversations he would have with God in the future: 'I can't wait to meet him (God).'[34]

The common denominator: hope

Human beings often make the most important decisions in their lives based on emotion. Marriage is a key example of this; those who are about to wed probably do not consider divorce statistics or allow information regarding unhappy marriages to deter them. Such life-changing decisions are generally made following one's desires, rather than based on rational thought processes. Decisions regarding the withdrawal or withholding of life-sustaining treatment from premature and critically impaired infants are generally founded on parental emotion and an instinctive desire to protect and unconditionally love their newborn. This is illustrated in a case study documented in Wishart's BBC programme.

---

30 Ibid 168.
31 Ibid.
32 Paris et al., 'Approaches to End-of-life Decision-making in the NUCI: Insights from Dostoevsky's The Grand Inquisitor' (2006) 26(7) *Journal of Perinatology* 389, 389.
33 Moro et al., above, n 26, 52, 56.
34 Evans, above, n 20, 38, 43.

In this case study, the parents of baby Simone, the only survivor of triplets, born at 23 weeks, spoke of their hope of taking their child home. The baby's mother, 23-year-old Kelly, stated, 'It gives you hope seeing her move, she's a little fighter.'[35] She added: 'she looks normal, kicking, moving, wriggling about, crying, it's weird . . . she's come too far to give up now.'[36]

In the same documentary, another parent, police officer Craig, discussed his fears of setbacks: 'if you get your hopes up too much you might get knocked down – so it's best to keep it level and don't get too excited . . . and then good news is good news.'[37] The importance of 'framing' conversations with parents about outcomes in a manner that will be understood rationally has been discussed by Janvier, and will be considered later in this chapter.[38]

For parents, emotions play a significant role in decision making. Humans instinctively desire to love and nurture their loved ones, particularly infants. These instinctive desires are enshrined in cultural mores: the creation of a successful family unit and good parenting are considered to be worthy goals. This is further demonstrated by the abhorrence with which society regards those who harm or kill children. Many parents of premature and critically ill infants hold on to hope, even when the prognosis is bleak. Arguably, hope is an intangible entity that no doctor or court of law can take away from parents, and as such it is something parents may not let go of until the very last moment.

This assertion is supported in one of McHaffie's 2001 studies, in which it was noted that one couple were staunch believers that their child would survive, and 'not wanting to jeopardise her chances, they refused to have her out of the incubator to cuddle her until the last few minutes of life'.[39] Further, Moro's empirical study found one mother's hope that 'the infant would survive fuelled the mother's determination to make physicians try to save the infant in the delivery room. While this mother thought there was less than 1% chance that her daughter would live, she indicated that she had hope until the last moment.'[40] Another mother of triplets in the same study 'reported feeling hopeful even after the first infant died because there were two who survived'.[41]

Parental ethnicity

Parental ethnicity and cultural beliefs also play a significant role in decision making. A study conducted in 2004 by Roy et al. in the UK found that Jewish and

35 *The Price of Life* (Directed by Adam Wishart, BBC Productions, 2011), 00.18.25.
36 Ibid 00.23.54 and 00.24.10.
37 Ibid 00.49.29.
38 Annie Janvier, 'Can We Improve Parental Decision Making for Perinatal and Neonatal Decisions?' (Speech delivered at the Ethical, Legal and Social Implications of Neonatal Intensive Care Units Conference, Geneva, 4–5 June 2012). www.brocher.ch/en/events/ethical-legal-and-social-implications-of-neonatal-intensive-care-units
39 H E McHaffie, A J Lyon and P W Fowlie, 'Lingering Death after Treatment Withdrawal in the Neonatal Intensive Care Unit' (2001) 85(1) *Archives of Disease in Childhood: Fetal and Neonatal* 8, 9.
40 Moro et al., above, n 26, 52, 55.
41 Ibid.

African families were more likely to request aggressive treatment. The study further found that over a period of 45 months, of the 1807 infants who were admitted to the NICU, 85% died. Withdrawal of life-sustaining treatment was the cause of death for 58% of those imperilled infants who died.

Discussions were undertaken with parents before treatment was withdrawn, with 72% of cases agreeing with withdrawal. Of those parents: 'White parents, those from the Indian subcontinent and Afro-Caribbean parents (20 of 23) were more likely to agree to withdrawal of LST (life-sustaining treatment) than Black African or Jewish (8 of 16) parents.'[42] Additionally, 'of the 11 sets of parents who refused the option of withdrawal of LST, three (including two orthodox Jewish families) gave religion as the primary reason'.[43]

The study also found that only 54% of black African parents, compared with almost all of the white parents, agreed to withdrawal of life-sustaining treatment, giving their religious and personal beliefs as the key deciding factor.[44] Boneh et al., acknowledging that parental attitudes are often determinative of the decisions they make, recommend doctors to:

> be aware of the parents' cultural attitude to decisions regarding end of life. They need to explore the willingness of the family of the newborn to make decisions regarding withholding or withdrawing therapy and to counsel families using appropriate terminology.[45]

Life experience is also a factor in end of life decision making for parents. For many mothers, life experiences and societal attitudes in their maternal country of origin are influential factors in decision making. Hammerman noted that women from former Soviet Russia, where approximately 10% of women have experienced an abortion at least once during childbearing age, had a less restrictive approach to withdrawal of treatment decisions:

> [I]mmigrant mothers in the USSR were much less aggressive in their approach to treating critically ill, damaged neonates, probably reflecting prevalent attitudes in a country where families are generally limited to one to two children and where abortion is considered an acceptable method of contraception.[46]

Thus, the considerations so far suggest that, while parents believe they are the chief advocates for their child's life and its protection, and have the highest

---

42 Roy et al., 'Decision Making and Modes of Death in a Tertiary Neonatal Unit' (2004) 89(6) *Archives of Disease in Childhood: Fetal and Neonatal* 527, 528.
43 Ibid.
44 Ibid 529.
45 Boneh et al., 'Clinical, Ethical and Legal Considerations in the Treatment of Newborns with Non-Ketotic Hyperglycaemia' (2008) 94(2) *Molecular Genetics and Metabolism* 143, 147.
46 Hammerman et al., above, n 27, 164, 168.

authority to decide 'what is best for their child', parents' decisions regarding treatment are often made based wholly on their own subjective interests and beliefs. This is supported by the study from McHaffie et al., which described one scenario in which parents felt compelled to leave their dying baby alone due to a cultural belief that witnessing their child's ears turning blue would signify the end of meaningful life.[47]

Kopelman and Kopelman discussed a case with similar cultural obstacles in America.[48] The case concerned Baby S, an infant born at 26 weeks' gestation to graduate student parents from India. The infant suffered several conditions due to premature birth and had a 70% chance of survival, with the strong possibility of problems (ranging from mild to profound). A week after birth, the parents requested that treatment be withdrawn, an opinion that was not shared by the attending doctors.

While the doctors were optimistic about the prognosis, the parents believed that once they returned to India, they would not have financial access to the level of care their son would possibly require. Further, they feared hostility due to a cultural stigma relating to abnormalities.[49] Ordinarily, such a conflict of opinion would have been referred to the courts; however, in this case, doctors, social workers and nurses, independent of the courts, concluded that pursuing treatment would not be in the best interests of the infant.

Baby S's condition deteriorated and he passed away before treatment was revoked. However, the case provides an example of the impact of cultural beliefs in life and death decisions. In most developed countries, laws are not tailored to specific cultures.[50] While they are, and should be, respectful of myriad cultural beliefs, they are not dictated by them. However, there may be exceptional instances, such as the one discussed earlier, in which too much emphasis could be placed on cultural preferences or personal bias.

Looking at Baby S's case, it is questionable whether the same decision would have been reached had the infant not been born to parents returning to a developing nation, particularly given the parents' reliance on arguments for withdrawal of treatment that centred on cultural stigma and limited access to financial resources for further care.

Parental bias and judgments may not be physically visible to the outside world, but it can still affect parental decision making. An example of such personal bias

---

47 McHaffie et al., above, n 11, 104, 108.
48 L M Kopelman and A E Kopelman, 'Using a New Analysis of the Best Interests Standard to Address Cultural Disputes: Whose Data, Which Values?' (2007) 28(5) *Theoretical Medicine and Bioethics* 373, 373.
49 Disability or congenital abnormalities are often viewed as punishment for past 'sins' committed in Indian culture. See, generally, Anita Ghai, 'Disability in the Indian Context: Post-colonial Perspectives' in Mairian Corker and Tom Shakespeare (eds), *Disability/Postmodernity: Embodying Disability Theory* (Continuum, 2002) 88–100.
50 For a discussion about the organisation of society and cultural beliefs, see Avner Greif, 'Cultural Beliefs and the Organization of Society: A Historical and Theoretical Reflection on Collectivist and Individualist Societies' (1994) 102(51) *Journal of Political Economy* 912–950.

has been examined by Shelp, who discussed a case involving a premature infant born with severe respiratory issues, and who also suffered with a non-functioning micro penis, which could have been removed, allowing the infant to be raised as female. However, Shelp found, 'rather than cope with a perceived failure of his masculinity, the father, with the consent of the mother, refused treatment of the infant's respiratory disease'. Although treatment was provided, the infant died.

A profound observation from this case is that 'the defect need not be visible to others or affect the brain in order to provoke a judgment that death of the newborn is a desirable end'.[51] Another factor that plays a role in the decision-making process for parents is the pain and suffering of the child, to which the discussion now turns.

Infants' pain and suffering

During their initial consultations with medical teams about prognosis, parents may instinctively have a firm vision and make an immediate determination that their neonate's life must be preserved at all costs. Moro highlighted that all mothers initially indicated 'they wanted everything done for their infant in the delivery room'.[52]

Interestingly, Moro also found that neither parents nor doctors explicitly defined what 'everything done' meant.[53] This is an important point and further discussion or research in this area would be valuable. As will be considered later in this chapter, parent and doctor perceptions vary extensively as to what treatments can and should be offered to premature and critically ill infants. The term 'everything done' is subjective, and for a medical team that has assessed the prognosis for the infant, 'everything done' could be interpreted as alleviating pain or suffering and providing the infant with palliative care and comfort.

Conversely, for parents 'everything done' may mean aggressive treatment, even when there is no positive response by the infant. Moro found: 'despite the mother's insistence that the physician do everything, she felt that they did not provide appropriate care . . . "it seemed like when they, took her to the table to try, they put a mask on her and handed her back".'[54]

Similarly, McHaffie found that parents discussed a constant need to 'beg the staff to do all they could in the face of frequent comments implying treatment was futile'.[55] A critical turning point for many parents from wanting the medical team to 'do everything' to save their infant to agreeing to the withdrawal of treatment is conversations with the medical team regarding the pain and suffering endured by their infant. In the Wishart documentary, parents Lucy and Craig expressed their reservations for aggressive treatment for their daughter Matilda,

---

51 Shelp, above, n 14, 63.
52 Moro et al., above, n 26, 52, 55.
53 Ibid 57.
54 Ibid 55.
55 Hazel E McHaffie, Andrew J Lyon and Robert Hume, 'Deciding on Treatment Limitation for Neonates: The Parents Perspective' (2001) 160 *European Journal of Pediatrics* 339, 341.

stating: 'she has to have a quality of life, if it comes to it we have to let nature takes its course.'[56]

Both Moro's study and those conducted by McHaffie highlight the significance of pain as a key factor in end of life decision making for parents and doctors. In the McHaffie study, some parents expressed a desire to 'ameliorate their child's suffering', and one mother stated: 'I just wanted the best for my daughter. I didn't want her to suffer anymore.'[57]

Visible deterioration such as skin colour changes, noises of exasperation and 'clear information' about prognosis also influenced withdrawal decisions.[58] In another study, McHaffie found that, when infants were taken off ventilation and began to struggle to breathe independently, parents found this distressing.[59] One mother described her son's condition while treatment was being withdrawn from him: 'He was coughing, spluttering, gasping . . . the minute he (the doctor) was coming over (to check that his heart has stopped) he started again. I was just not looking . . . My arm was numb.'[60] She went on to say that the medical team told her to 'go and have a lie down, this could go on for hours, but I couldn't even move. I was just so damned scared. I think it was more his noises that haunt me than the colour of his blue hand.'[61]

Doctors may attempt to protect parents from the beginning of the dying process when their infant is removed from ventilation, either due to a sense of paternalism or empathy or out of an awareness of the fragile emotional state of parents at this time. Studies have shown that, as difficult as it may be, parents prefer to be given the facts and told in very certain terms exactly what the dying process entails. In failing to do so, many parents lose trust in the treating physician. This is explored below.

The 'dying process'

McHaffie, Lyon and Fowlie explored parental perceptions of the dying process between three and 13 months after neonatal or infant death from treatment withdrawal. The study was conducted across three regional units in east Scotland, and its findings were published in 2001. The findings are noteworthy: 68% of those interviewed were satisfied with the manner in which the 'dying process' was handled, while only 8% found the process unsatisfactory. These statistics should provide the medical fraternity with reassurance that, generally, the process is perceived to be handled with emotional sensitivity. However, 22% of parents expressed discomfort about the length of the dying process.[62]

56 *The Price of Life*, above, n 35, 00.28.48.
57 McHaffie, Lyon and Hume, above, n 55, 339, 341.
58 Ibid 342.
59 McHaffie, Lyon and Fowlie, above, n 39, 8, 10.
60 Ibid.
61 Ibid.
62 Ibid 8.

After grappling with emotionally challenging decisions and accepting that their infant is too imperilled to survive, some parents wanted the 'dying process' to be as quick as possible. In McHaffie's study, one couple could not 'face watching their son die' and simply wanted to be informed if he deteriorated any further.[63]

Other parents felt the need and duty to be with their infant right up to the dying moment. However, these parents then risked being traumatised by the duration of the dying process and the distress and physical changes that occurred. As McHaffie explains, one infant's parents 'believed that death would be instantaneous when the ventilator was withdrawn and they were completely unprepared for the 21 hours they had with the living child'.[64] For other parents, the process varied from three to 36 hours.

Although unpleasant for any parent, once their infant had died, 16% of those interviewed wished they had made the decision to withdraw treatment sooner and that the entire process had been shorter. For some couples, the quick or 'rapid death, reinforced the accuracy of the medical prognosis'.[65] Another couple went even further, stating 'they wished their child had been "euthanized" early on and they all had been spared the agonising experience they had endured'.[66] Three other couples 'found it unhelpful when the doctors did not give the child something to end life sooner, to lessen the baby's suffering and their own distress'.[67]

The infants' suffering is not always the foremost consideration. The recent Moro-led study highlighted the case of one mother of triplets, who, having endured the death of two of them, 'did not want her last infant to only live for a few weeks or months'. She said: 'since I already had to bury the other two . . . maybe I should let them all go together.'[68] While this may seem a selfish comment for a mother to make, it reflects a necessary form of emotional self-preservation.

Some parents began to doubt their decision to withdraw treatment when the dying process took longer than anticipated. As discussed earlier in this chapter, parents continued to hold on to hope and the possibility that their infant was going to 'fight on' until the very end. Parents' thoughts revolved around questions such as 'if the baby was fighting so hard to live should they give him/her every chance? Was he or she trying to tell them that they [sic] wanted to live?'[69]

63 Ibid 9.
64 Ibid 10.
65 Ibid.
66 Ibid.
67 Ibid 11.
68 Moro et al., above, n 26, 52, 55.
69 McHaffie, Lyon and Fowlie, above, n 39, 8, 10.

Disability: perceptions and realities

The area of disability activism is wide-reaching[70] and beyond the scope of this book. However, it is necessary to discuss briefly how disability affects individuals and families when decisions to continue treatment are made. It has been noted thus far in this book that there is a strong likelihood of disability when an infant is extremely premature and survives. The uncertainty of initial survival and then the severity of the disability the infant is likely to suffer are just two of the issues that make end of life decision making for this group of infants so controversial and challenging. Moral values and interpretations of quality of life vary, and perceptions of disability and its severity are also subjective.[71] Varying levels of cognition, intellect and disability may be given more or less weight, depending on who is assessing such quality of life.[72]

For example, physical impairment may be less important to an individual than mental impairment. Millions of individuals wear corrective lenses in glasses due to a visual impairment, but would be unlikely to question their 'quality of life' or consider themselves limited in choices or lifestyle. In contrast, a lower intelligence quotient (IQ) or learning disability is more likely to affect an individual's life choices, career and socioeconomic outcomes. Saigal and Tyson's studies indicate that parents and doctors may report a higher level of disability and lower quality of life than the affected person. Further, 'Parents views on QoL [quality of life] may be negatively influenced by the burden of caregiving, stress, and their own mental, social, and economic status.'[73]

Zutlevics also points that 'the impact on families and particular affected individuals from disability is also highly variable'. Disability activists are concerned about a 'general misapprehension that people with moderate or greater physical and intellectual disabilities cannot lead lives of quality'.[74] Further, Zutlevics makes another compelling point that aligns with the main argument of this book; she asserts that 'more than disability, more crippling is societal attitudes and inadequate resources to assist such individuals'.[75] This is of particular relevance to this book,

---

70 For a discussion on disability activism in Australia, see, generally, Margaret Cooper, 'The Australian Disability Rights Movement Lives' (1999) 14(2) *Disability & Society* 217–226. For further discussion on disability activism in the UK, see, generally, Colin Barnes, 'Disability Activism and the Struggle for Change Disability, Policy and Politics in the UK' (2007) 2(3) *Education, Citizenship and Social Justice* 203–221.

71 For further discussion, see, also, Saigal et al., 'Self-perceived Health-related Quality of Life of Former Extremely Low Birth Weight Infants at Young Adulthood' (2006) 118(3) *Pediatrics* 1140–1148.

72 Nicolas Porta and Joel Frader, 'Withholding Hydration and Nutrition in Newborns' (2007) 28(5) *Theoretical Medicine and Bioethics* 443, 433.

73 Saroj Saigal and Jon Tyson, 'Measurement of Quality of Life of Survivors of Neonatal Intensive Care: Critique and Implications' (2008) 32(1) *Seminars in Perinatology* 59, 62. See, also, Saroj Saigal, 'Quality of Life of Former Premature Infants during Adolescence and Beyond' (2013) 89(4) *Early Human Development* 209–213.

74 Tamara Zutlevics, 'Pursuing the Golden Mean – Moral Decision Making for Precarious Newborns' (2009) 27(1) *Australian Journal of Advanced Nursing* 75, 77.

75 Ibid.

which argues that the allocation of limited public resources should be an objective consideration in end of life decision making for extremely premature and critically impaired infants. This is discussed in detail in subsequent chapters.

Research from the UK in 2010 found that premature infants were 'more at risk of lower IQ, poorer cognitive function, learning disabilities and behavioural problems than full term babies'.[76] In the BBC documentary mentioned earlier, Wishart also highlighted that 'life-saving' treatments can often cause more harm than good: 'tubes can lead to lung diseases, drugs to assist with development can cause cerebral palsy and medication for the heart can cause fragile guts to collapse.'[77]

In the documentary, Wishart also provided an illustrative example of the first-hand experience of an individual born at the edge of viability, at 23 weeks. Twenty-one-year old Heather candidly discussed her disabilities and her perception of quality of life. Heather could only use her left arm, and unless the 'carers come to the house she is stuck in bed all day'.[78] Heather suffered severe depression, had considered suicide and did not see anything positive in her life.[79] Due to her heavy reliance on her parents, she feared losing them and worried about what life would be like when they died: 'I am massively scared about when my parents die, so, so, so scared, I rely on them so much . . . each year I get more scared.'[80]

The documentary, which also aired in Australia, is commendable, and provided much needed transparency and a real portrayal of life for those born as, or caring for, extremely premature and impaired infants. Heather continues to be directly affected by her parents' decision to push for aggressive treatment to keep her alive at 23 weeks, and her parents are just as affected by their decision.

The birth of her daughter at 23 weeks served as the impetus for Catherine Rutherford to become a nurse practitioner in the Birmingham NICU. She discussed the difficulty parents face when making such life-changing decisions at the time of birth: 'at that point in time you have no understanding of what people are telling you, because you have a baby, your child in front of you and you want that child to survive.'[81]

While Catherine did not openly discuss any doubts or regrets she may have had about her decision not to withdraw treatment, another mother interviewed in an Australian Sunday magazine did. Alexia Pearce spoke honestly about her decision to keep her premature Nathan alive: 'If I'd known then what I know now about what extremely premature babies have to go through, I wouldn't have chosen that for my little boy.'[82] Alexia expressed guilt over her decision: 'even though it was

76 McVeigh, above, n 23, 17.
77 *The Price of Life*, above, n 35, 00.30.02.
78 Ibid 00.31.17.
79 Ibid 00.32.08.
80 Ibid 00.33.22.
81 Ibid 00.33.01.
82 McVeigh, above, n 23, 16.

made with the best intentions . . . no mother or father wants to see their child suffer. But because of the choices I made, I feel he's suffered, and still does.'[83]

Gunderman and Engle highlight the varying perceptions individuals have about disability and quality of life:

> Judgements about what constitutes an acceptable quality of life may vary from physician to physician and family to family. One family may judge even relatively mild sensory, cognitive and motor impairments unacceptable, while another may eagerly welcome a child that others would regard as neurologically devastated.[84]

Eichenwald et al. described an opposing view held by some parents, in which doctors may decide contrary to initial discussions to continue treatment when an infant is considered to 'appear healthy'. The authors found that some parents showed anger and frustration that their initial 'agreement' to withdraw treatment had now been breached. Parents stated that they could not 'manage an impaired child' and that their doctors had a 'duty to respect their wishes'.[85]

However, the competing view is that such selective withdrawal decisions may be inequitable. Wilkinson also agrees with this position: that decisions to withdraw treatment based on potential disability could be argued to be discriminatory or 'based on a false assessment of the quality of life of those with such disabilities'.[86] Both views reflect the significant levels of subjectivity in both the withdrawal and continuation of treatment decisions by parents.

Relationships of trust and confidence with the medical team

The one certainty in end of life decision making for premature and critically ill infants is the uncertainty of the prognosis and survival. Lantos et al. note that 'prognosis will always depend on a combination of factors, and will always be somewhat uncertain for any particular baby'.[87]

Critically, at this stage, the lack of certainty of outcomes means that doctors often cannot give parents certainty even about the dying process. As discussed earlier, the dying process for infants varies considerably. Doctors attempt to communicate clinical information in the most sensitive manner to parents. There is a fine line between parents trusting the treating doctor and having confidence in his or her medical opinion, and parents losing faith

83 Ibid 17.
84 Richard B Gunderman and William A Engle, 'Ethics and the Limits of Neonatal Viability' (2006) 236(2) *Radiology* 427, 429.
85 Eichenwald et al., 'Physician and Parental Decision Making in Newborn Resuscitation' (2008) 10(6) *Virtual Mentor* 616, 616.
86 Dominic Wilkinson, 'Is it in the Best Interests of an Intellectually Disabled Infant to Die?' (2006) 32(8) *Journal of Medical Ethics* 454, 455.
87 Lantos et al., 'Withholding and Withdrawing Life Sustaining Treatment in Neonatal Intensive Care: Issues for the 1990s' (1994) 71(3) *Archives of Disease in Childhood: Fetal and Neonatal* 218, 220.

and belief in medical judgment when medical predictions and probabilities become possibilities.

Due to the uncertain nature of predicting outcomes for premature and critically impaired infants, parents often doubt their own decisions and those of the medical team, right up to and after death. McHaffie highlighted a case in which one family 'recalled being told three times that when successive treatments were withdrawn their child would die. When forecasts proved wrong the parents lost trust in medical expertise and as a result the child's eventual death took them by surprise.'[88]

There is no clear solution to avoid parental loss of trust in the medical team. Often both stakeholders, parents and doctors, tread very carefully, knowing that the decision-making process will be more harmonious when they work together. However, several studies have highlighted that parents prefer open and honest discussion with doctors, even when it entails the communication of uncomfortable or confronting information.

Moro noted one mother who 'reported that communication and relationship with providers impacted . . . experiences of decision making'.[89] Other mothers have expressed similar views.[90] Further, 'parents need more than just information' and 'relationships between both parties can be forged on trust'.[91] Moro argued that 'trust can be built by admitting uncertainty'.[92] McHaffie echoed a similar sentiment, giving the example of one parent who stated: 'If they had just told us that (there was no hope before they resuscitated him on day six), we wouldn't have had to go through all this agony for the next three weeks until he died.'[93]

However, doctors are often not in a position to make such predictions, and 'parents seem able to tolerate a degree of uncertainty and they demonstrate trust in expertise of senior clinicians . . . [O]ne of the main contributing factors to their [parents'] insecurity is a lack of concrete evidence of a bleak outcome.'[94]

Therein lays the problem. Often there is no concrete evidence, and decisions about prognosis and predictions are based on retrospective data and statistics. This also explains why, when one infant 'survives' and continues to flourish in his or her life, he or she is referred to as a 'miracle baby'.

Parents continue to hold on to hope throughout the entire process. Moro et al. found that 'hope can be very powerful and provide a source of strength for parents even in the most dismal circumstances . . . [In the end,] parents want their health care providers to be honest yet hopeful.'[95]

In the Wishart documentary, Lucy, mother of Matilda, born at 23 weeks, felt 'we have to trust in what the professionals tell us about how much trauma and

---

88 McHaffie et al., above, n 11, 104, 106.
89 Moro et al., above, n 26, 52, 58.
90 Ibid.
91 Ibid.
92 Ibid.
93 McHaffie, Lyon and Fowlie, above, n 39, 8, 11.
94 McHaffie, Lyon and Hume, above, n 55, 339, 343.
95 Moro et al., above, n 26, 52, 58.

pain she will suffer'.[96] However, a counterpoint to be made is that, when parents and doctors disagree on treatment decisions, there is a likelihood of volatility and distrust of the medical team.[97]

Overwhelmingly, the studies suggest that for parents to trust treating doctors, those doctors have to communicate to parents, in a firm and honest manner, the harsh realities of the infants' prognosis, the confronting truth of the dying process and what to expect.

Do parents carry guilt and the burden of responsibility in decision making?

After being so closely involved in the decision to withdraw or withhold life-sustaining treatment to their infants, parents may feel guilt or carry a heavy sense of burden and responsibility during the process itself. For many parents, the thought of 'giving up' may cause emotional discomfort and does not align with external community ideals. There may also be familial influences at play.[98]

Bracegirdle agrees with this view, stating that 'parents feel pressurised by family, friends and the media to allow technology to keep trying, and thus may feel compelled to carry on with treatment when they do not feel that the benefit exceeds the harm'.[99] In more extreme situations, there may be no parental emotional attachment to an infant, yet there remains a continued push for medically futile treatment.[100]

Wishart documented the perception of baby Simone's father that his role as a father was to 'protect' his child: 'I'm supposed to be a dad, supposed to protect her, daddies are supposed to look after their little girls.'[101] He went on to explain that he would feel as if he was killing her: 'If she's suffering, it's bad not to (withdraw treatment) but I couldn't do it, I've killed my own child, couldn't live with that.'[102]

Another couple, Claire and Paul, stated that they had wanted their daughter, Holly, resuscitated after Claire's waters broke at 23 weeks. Holly died soon after birth and was cradled by her parents, who were given the choice to hold her while she remained attached to tubes and had her heart rate sustained by artificial ventilation, or without tubes. Her father Paul asserted: 'at least we tried, if things don't pan out at least we can say we had the choice and we went for it.'[103]

---

96 *The Price of Life*, above, n 35, 00.26.29.
97 Dominic Wilkinson, 'The Self-Fulfilling Prophecy in Intensive Care' (2009) 30(6) *Theoretical Medicine and Bioethics* 401, 405.
98 Carl A Kuschel and Alison Kent, 'Improved Neonatal Survival and Outcomes at Borderline Viability Brings Increasing Ethical Dilemmas' (2011) 47(9) *Journal of Paediatric and Child Health* 585, 588.
99 Karen E Bracegirdle, 'A Time to Die: Withdrawal of Paediatric Intensive Care' (1994) 3(10) *British Journal of Nursing* 513, 514.
100 Lantos et al., above, n 87, 218, 221.
101 *The Price of Life*, above, n 35, 00.18.33.
102 Ibid 00.22.24.
103 Ibid 00.05.06.

Returning to empirical research, McHaffie's study reported that medical teams of doctors and nurses assumed that decisions to withdraw or withhold life-sustaining treatment from infants were 'too weighty a burden for parents to bear . . . only three per cent of doctors and six per cent of nurses thought parents should take the ultimate decision.'[104] There is much literature that supports the statistics from McHaffie's study. For example, Pinter suggests that 'to prevent unnecessary guilt, we (doctors) should always be careful to avoid giving parents the sense that the decision is completely theirs'.[105] Tripp and McGregor convey a similar sentiment:

> Although both parents and professionals have rights, it is usually going to fall to the professional team, to elicit how much of their 'rights' parents want to exercise – bearing in mind the responsibility and potential for guilt that comes with a right determination.[106]

Further, a doctor's 'willingness' to take on the responsibility of being the decision maker is an 'important mechanism to allay parental guilt'; 'parents may actually welcome the opportunity to be completely relieved of the decision and turn to the courts.'[107] Arguably, this is an exception to the norm, and most parents do not turn to the courts, or only do so as a last resort. This is particularly true in Australia, where only two cases have required judicial intervention in recent times.[108]

Contrary to this opinion, many parents feel that the decision falls within their responsibility as parents. As discussed further later, 56% of parents in the McHaffie study believed that they had made the decision.[109] More recently, the 2011 study from Moro et al. found that only one out of the five mothers interviewed expressed feelings of burden in the decision-making process.[110]

Although the decision carries much emotional strain, many parents felt that the experience, although unpleasant, challenged or changed their previous views or beliefs. One parent in the study had previously been a devout pro-life supporter, but, after experiencing her newborn's suffering, acknowledged that such decisions were fraught with uncertainty.

It is noteworthy to consider the summary of parental responsibility in end of life decisions for infants to be found in Paris et al., conceptualised against the backdrop of Dostoevsky's classic novel *The Brothers Karamazov*. In the novel, personal responsibility was not considered an option, as 'collective' family decisions

---

104 McHaffie et al., above, n 11, 104, 105.
105 A B Pinter, 'End-of-life Decision Before and After Birth: Changing Ethical Considerations' (2008) 43(6) *Journal of Pediatric Surgery* 430, 433.
106 Tripp J and D McGregor, 'Withholding and Withdrawing of Life Sustaining Treatment in the Newborn' (2006) 91(1) *Archives of Disease in Childhood: Fetal and Neonatal* 67, 69.
107 Ibid.
108 *Baby D (No 2)* [2011] Fam CA 176; *TS & TD v Sydney Children's Hospital ('Mohammed's case')* [2012] NSWSC 1609.
109 McHaffie et al., above, n 11, 104, 105.
110 Moro et al., above, n 26, 52, 58.

were made. Paris et al. suggest that a similar approach could be taken by families in decision-making scenarios. This is often the case in practice – the mother makes treatment decisions, taking into account the views of the infant's father and members of the wider family.

Making life and death decisions is far from easy. The difficulties that parents face in wanting treatment withdrawn, or in accepting responsibility for the decision, are of particular magnitude. The guilt associated with actively requesting that a newborn die is a heavy burden, particularly when that newborn is your own child.[111] Paris et al. illustrate this point, stating:

> For parents that choice is not so easy. They look at the physician and ask, Doctor, do you mean you want our permission to kill our baby? How could parents agree to that? How could they endure the guilt of having given up on their child?[112]

The authors suggest that life and death decisions for premature and critically impaired infants are best made without putting parents in the position such that they feel considerable guilt or responsibility. They suggest that a more assertive approach on the part of doctors, without much 'choice' or 'active involvement' for parents, in the decision-making process is better for parents:

> Do not ask the parents, 'If your baby suffers a cardiac arrest, do you want us to try to save him?' Such a question gives parents false hopes and unrealistic expectations, expectations that inevitably lead to demands for more and more interventions and the risk of further complications.[113]

Interestingly, Shapiro described a darker side to the guilt that parents may carry from deciding to withdraw treatment. The author described parents feeling that wanting or allowing a loved one to die was a 'dirty secret' that they carried.[114] It is uncommon that such feelings would be discussed frankly and openly, and indeed, in the wider community, it is considered taboo for parents to express such sentiments. Instead, Shapiro asserts that in these cases, family members may do the opposite to what they really want, driving out taboo feelings by passionately advocating for treatment to be continued.

Montello and Lantos further suggest that there may be 'strange communication', wherein individuals may feel discomfort in expressing their true desires or wishes.[115] This may be considered an unspoken message: the more vehemently parents advocate for treatment to continue, the more they may want treatment not to continue. However, this is perhaps a dangerous assumption to make, as

111 Paris et al., above, n 32, 389.
112 Ibid 390.
113 Ibid.
114 Martha Montello and John Lantos, 'The Karamazov Complex: Dostoevsky and DNR Orders' (2002) 45(2) *Perspectives in Biology and Medicine* 190, 194.
115 Ibid.

there is potential for severe miscommunication, through a lack of honest communication. A better view may be to push for doctors to engage in a more open and honest dialogue and provide clinical information, while also maintaining a degree of empathy for parents in making treatment decisions.

Perceptions of 'making the decision' or being 'involved' in the decision-making process vary between parents. Gillam and Sullivan point out that 'involvement in decision making could lead to guilt and repentance and yet did not regard not being involved as a way to resolve the potential difficulty'.[116]

Parents are thus in a difficult situation. The 'doctor knows best' paternalism evident in some of the cases examined in Chapter 2 suggests that in the early 1970s and 1980s decision making was predominantly left to the medical professionals.[117] Today, while some parents may find a lack of involvement in the decision-making process easier, the majority would probably disagree. Studies conducted by Orfali and Gordon involving American and French mothers found: 'on the one hand they want to be involved and became angry if they are not given control over many medical aspects of the baby's care . . . but no mother in our sample ever requested more active involvement in life and death decisions.'[118] Seemingly, mothers of impaired infants 'want some control over a dreadful situation, but none of them expressed an eagerness to take over the terrible act of deciding'.[119]

As considered earlier in this chapter, parents take several indicators and factors into account when making end of life decisions. Some rely on religious or cultural beliefs, leaving decisions in God's hands and negating any 'responsibility' for making the decision. Others make treatment withdrawal decisions based on their infants' visual deterioration and a desire to end their pain and suffering.

McHaffie et al. found that a majority of parents did not feel guilt or doubt about the decision to withdraw treatment. Only one mother in their study referred to any feeling of guilt, with this being related to her individual feeling, possibly selfishness, in not wanting her infant to die, 'when she knew it was in his best interests'.[120] Further, Pignotti asserts that the overwhelming consensus in Europe is that parents play a crucial role in decision making for their children, based on the 'assumption that, in exercising their authority, they are acting in their child's best interests'.[121]

Pignotti's study also indicated that, rather than wanting to be 'spared' the trauma of decision making, parents were 'appalled' at the idea that decisions

---

116 Lynne Gillam and Jane Sullivan, 'Ethics at the End of Life: Who Should Make Decisions about Treatment Limitation for Young Children with Life-Threatening or Life-Limiting Conditions?' (2011) 47(9) *Journal of Paediatrics and Child Health* 594, 596.

117 Pinter, above, n 105, 430, 433. See also *R v Arthur* (1981) 12 BMLR 1.

118 Kristina Orfali and Elisa J Gordon, 'Autonomy Gone Awry: A Cross Cultural Study of Parents' Experiences in Neonatal Intensive Care Units' (2004) 25(4) *Theoretical Medicines and Bioethics* 329, 348.

119 Ibid.

120 McHaffie, Lyon and Hume, above, n 55, 339, 343.

121 Maria S Pignotti, 'Extremely Preterm Births: Recommendations for Treatment in European Countries' (2008) 93(6) *Archives of Disease in Childhood: Fetal and Neonatal* 403, 405.

about their infants could be made without their involvement.[122] This leads to a final consideration of the role and impact and influence of parents in end of life decision making for premature and critically impaired infants

Parents as decision makers: fact or fiction?

Parental autonomy in decision making for their children is important and the law provides parents with a significant amount of discretion on such matters. However, as Stewart noted, 'in the case of minors, the rights of parents to consent or to refuse medical treatment are not absolute'.[123] This prevailing legal opinion seems to have longstanding global consensus. This was evinced in an American president's commission 30 years ago, when it was stated that 'parental authority must occasionally be superseded by clinicians when it is determined that the parent's decisions are at odds with societal consensus about what best serves a child's interests'.[124]

From the case law and discussion presented in this chapter thus far, it is clear that parents find it difficult to accept that the best possible therapy is often non-treatment. Many journeys across different terrain are taken by parents and wider family units in arriving at the reality that their infant will not survive, or that survival will not provide a fruitful life. Nevertheless, a majority of parents perceive that ultimately the final decision to withdraw or withhold life-sustaining treatment is theirs.

McHaffie et al. reported that 56% of parents felt that the ultimate decision was theirs. The 7% who did not make the ultimate decision wished they had done so.[125] Further, parents felt that this decision had to be made by them as part of their responsibility as a parent. However, most parents cannot make an informed and independent decision to withdraw or withhold life-sustaining treatment due to their lack of medical skills, training and information. Gilliam and Sullivan assert that 'many parents wanted to participate [in decision making], but not decide, citing lack of medical knowledge and the possibility for emotional factors to overwhelm a rational decision'.[126]

Thus, any decisions regarding infants must be made in collaboration between the parents and the medical team. For this reason, transparent, honest and informative relationships between parents and doctors are crucial.[127] However, parents are often aware of the inequality that exists between medical staff and parents. McHaffie found that discussions or disagreements between staff about treatment decisions happened 'behind the scenes', yet when discussing options

---

122 Ibid.
123 Cameron Stewart, 'Who Decides When I Can Die? Problems Concerning Proxy Decisions to Forego Medical Treatment' (1997) 4 *Journal of Law and Medicine*, 386, 387.
124 Jeffrey P Burns and Christine Mitchell, 'Is There Any Consensus About End-of-life Care in Pediatrics' (2005) 159(9) *Archives of Pediatrics and Adolescent Medicine* 889, 890.
125 McHaffie et al., above, n 11, 104, 105.
126 Gillam and Sullivan, above, n 116, 594, 596.
127 This point is supported by Bracegirdle, above, n 99, 513, 514.

with parents, the medical team stage a united front. Often doctors excluded certain information from parents that they deemed 'irrelevant' to decision making, to strengthen a particular professional opinion or recommendation about treatment.[128] This will be discussed in greater detail later in this chapter.

This leads to an important question: Who is really making the decision? It would seem that doctors 'stage' the communication process with parents, making parents believe they are casting the deciding vote. Given that parents are those most affected by decisions to withdraw treatment, both at the time and for years later, perhaps this staging allows parents to draw some closure, solace and comfort in believing themselves to have made the choice, enabling them to bid farewell to their child with a sense of benevolence and duty.

The discussion so far has focused on parental involvement in decision making to withdraw or withhold life-sustaining treatment from premature and critically impaired infants. It has been noted that the medical team takes into account parental wishes and that parents play an active role in the decision-making process. However, situations arise in which parents oppose the treatment options that doctors deem best. In such instances, doctors must work together with parents to help them understand their options.[129]

It is established in law and medicine that parents cannot seek to demand or refuse life-sustaining treatment for a critically ill infant. As considered in Chapter 2, parental wishes are noted and carefully considered. However, the prevailing interests of the child are given paramount importance. Ahluwalia et al. make the point that 'decisions are to be jointly made on the basis of the infant's best interests, with clinicians and parents entering into what has been described as a "partnership of care"'.[130] While parental wishes are of importance, they are not overriding; thus the 'treating physician continues to have an independent responsibility towards the newborn's well-being'.[131] Nevertheless, while they should not dictate the fate of the infant, parental wishes must be given considerable weight, particularly given the impact of such decisions on parents and the wider family circle.[132]

As one of the key caregivers, parents' decisions and perceptions are influenced by many factors. All these variables are subjective, and no two families reach their conclusions identically or experience their infant's death in the same way. When examined as a group from a macro level, given their subjectivity, parents could be considered unpredictable and confused. This is understandable, taking into consideration their position as the most immediate and emotionally connected to the premature or critically impaired infant. In seeking to navigate the decision-making process, and in looking for objective advice, parents will turn to the next

---

128 McHaffie et al., above, n 11, 104, 107.
129 This has also been noted as an important factor with regard to clinical guidelines discussed in Chapter 3.
130 Ahluwalia, Lees and Paris, above, n 25, 33, 333.
131 Ibid.
132 This is discussed in Chapter 6.

most immediate caregiver and decision maker – their doctors and medical advisors, who are considered in the next section of this chapter.

4.2 Doctors: conflicting interests and views

The previous section considered the conflicting interests, views and emotional challenges that parents face in the end of life decision-making process. By contrast, medical practitioners might be seen as the more able group in taking a clear and dispassionate approach in decision making. However, as will be discussed later, this is not necessarily the case.

As the examination of the case law in Chapter 2 highlighted, between the early cases in the 1980s, in particular Dr Arthur's case, and the more recent case law there has been a shift in both parent and doctor attitudes and perceptions of the role and duties of the medical profession.[133] A move towards a 'rights'-driven culture and greater awareness of personal autonomy may have contributed to this change in the doctor–patient dynamic.[134] There is potential for conflict between parents and doctors, evidenced in the case law wherein treatment withdrawal disputes have turned to the courts for resolution. Moreover, there is clear inequality between the two groups, with one group possessing expert medical knowledge, while the other does not. This inequality is reinforced by a doctor's sense of empowerment, driven in part by the development of new technologies and the expansion of neonatology as a field of medicine. Arguably, saving from death those infants still young enough to die and be considered a miscarriage or even aborted has perhaps allowed doctors to feel a sense of authority and benevolence.

Guyer supports this view, asserting that the parent–doctor collaborative decision-making process is often quite to the contrary: 'What happened in the NICU was not collaboration but collision. Some doctors were loath to give up their positions as the primary decision makers, and even today some continue to cling to old paternalism.'[135]

Conversely, Truog believes that doctors are losing their 'professional autonomy' by being forced to provide treatment they consider futile. He further states that patients' relatives place heavy and inappropriate demands on doctors, and that the traditional hierarchy of doctor and patient is being eroded.[136] Gampel extends

---

133 This has entailed a shift from withdrawing treatment at a parent's request such as in the case of Baby John Pearson, to doctors resisting treatment that they consider to be futile, even when parents request treatment continuation.

134 Professor Julian Savulescu has researched and examined the area of medical decision making, rationalism and autonomy in detail, taking into account medical, legal and philosophical theory. See, further, Julian Savulescu, 'Autonomy, the Good Life, and Controversial Choices' in Rosamond Rhodes, Leslie P Francis and Anita Silvers (eds), *Blackwell Guide to Medical Ethics* (Blackwell Publishing, 2007) 17–37; Julian Savulescu, 'Liberal Rationalism and Medical Decision-making' (1997) 11(2) *Bioethics* 115–129.

135 Guyer, above, n 17, 40.

136 Robert D Truog, 'Futility in Pediatrics: From Case to Policy' (2000) 11(2) *Journal of Clinical Ethics* 136–141.

this point further, asserting that placing such demands of continuation or discontinuation of treatment on doctors could be seen as making doctors 'slaves to whatever patients want'.[137]

The traditional view of the medical profession is that it is driven by ideals of paternalism, beneficence and non-maleficence. Further, the belief is that a doctor will always do good for his or her patients and will never harm them.[138] However, this is a simplistic notion. Doctors, like parents or any other human being, are exactly that – human. Like parents, they are the sum of their life's experiences and at least partially driven by the same emotions and prejudices. The decisions that medical practitioners make in their professional setting are thus also affected by these factors, and are not intangible or exclusively independent.

Further to this, each doctor's personal beliefs and attitudes will differ, and consequently their ultimate treatment decisions for premature and critically impaired infants may vary considerably.[139] Craig iterates: 'there are times when two doctors, each with the best interests of the patient at heart, would treat in diametrically opposite ways.'[140] End of life decision making for critically impaired infants is thus influenced by medical practitioner subjectivity, highlighting the contention of this book – that there is a need for greater transparency in decisions to withdraw or withhold treatment based on more objective grounds. A driving force and a significant consideration in this regard should be the allocation of limited resources.[141] An examination of some of the factors affecting medical practitioners in end of life decision making follows.

Religious beliefs and cross-country attitudes

Having considered the role played by religious beliefs in influencing parents, this section considers whether doctors are also subject to such influences. Cross-country empirical research suggests that end of life decision making for infants varies within Europe, with the secularity of certain countries also a determining factor.

The EPICure studies from the UK, considered in Chapter 3, and a EURONICS study across Europe overwhelmingly indicate that doctors acknowledge that there must be 'limits' to the amount of intervention they provide to premature infants.[142] However, this is the only issue on which there is consensus. The studies reveal a surprising range of views as to the gestational age such decisions should be made.

---

137 Eric Gampel, 'Does Professional Autonomy Protect Medical Futility Judgments?' (2006) 20(2) *Bioethics* 92, 97.

138 See, further, Anne Morris, 'Selective Treatment of Irreversibly Impaired Infants: Decision Making at the Threshold' (2009) 17(3) *Medical Law Review* 347, 363.

139 Victor Yu, 'Ethical and Moral Dilemmas in Neonates' (2005) 1(2) *World Journal of Pediatrics* 88, 88.

140 Gillian M Craig, 'On Withholding Nutrition and Hydration in the Terminally Ill: Has Palliative Medicine Gone Too Far?' (1994) 20(3) *Journal of Medical Ethics* 139, 139.

141 This is considered in Chapter 6.

142 Warrick et al., 'Guidance for Withdrawal and Withholding of Intensive Care as Part of Neonatal End-of-life Care' (2011) 98(1) *British Medical Bulletin* 99, 110.

It is noted that some variability is understandable, given the differing jurisdictions and educational backgrounds. Warrick asserts that the 'highest rate of physicians in agreement was in the Netherlands, the UK and Sweden'.[143] This is perhaps predictable, particularly given the progressive societal attitudes and secular democracies of these countries. The lowest rate of withdrawal of treatment decisions were in Spain and Italy, probably reflecting the strong Catholic influences operating in these countries. If correct, this supports the view of a religious influence in medical decision making.

Further, Rebagliato et al. provide some important data that support this correlation.[144] They found that 33% of doctors in Italy believed that all human life is sacred and therefore that all premature infants should be treated aggressively regardless of severe disability as a consequence. The study also found that greater consideration to 'quality of life' was made by female doctors who were either Protestant or did not consider religion as an important factor in their lives.[145]

The resuscitation of premature infants is mandatory in Italy, and the law strongly advocates a pro-life stance, even in instances of an induced late abortion.[146] This creates a potential for internal conflict for an Italian doctor, where he or she may believe that withdrawal of treatment is in the best interests of the newborn. In such cases, the doctor's decision is bound by the dominant faith, prevailing tenet of sanctity of life and the illegality of withdrawal of intensive care treatment in that country.[147]

Doctors of the Jewish or Muslim faith have also been found to make end of life decisions based on their faith, sometimes justifying withdrawal of treatment based on Jewish law rather than considering the lawful authority of the country in which they reside. Warrick et al. highlight that 'in the Jewish faith active withdrawal of care, e.g. discontinuation of ventilation is forbidden. In clinically stable infants with a poor prognosis, withholding treatment is unacceptable as one should not judge the quality of another's life.'[148] Although, in a situation in which an infant is likely to die, Jewish law does state that 'one must not impede the natural departure of the dying soul'.[149]

Decision-making processes of this nature are tricky. Doctors are seemingly not only being guided subjectively by their religious beliefs, but also by religious laws that may not have any bearing on the laws of the relevant jurisdiction. Morris reinforces that subjective factors play a significant role in decision making and that treatment decisions are often swayed by the social and religious values of the consulting medical practitioner. Morris claims that in situations in which the

---

143 Ibid.
144 Rebagliato et al., 'Neonatal End-of-life Decision Making: Physicians' Attitudes and Relationship with Self-reported Practices in 10 European Countries' (2000) 284(19) *Journal of the American Medical Association* 2451, 2451.
145 Ibid 2455.
146 Ibid 2458.
147 Pignotti, above, n 121, 405.
148 Warrick et al., above, n 142, 110.
149 Ibid.

doctor held religion in high regard, the decision to withhold or withdraw treatment was less likely.[150]

Interestingly, Morris posits that although doctors in the UK strongly believed that parents should be involved in decision making, they felt that the ultimate treatment decision rests with them (doctors). Significantly, she states that 'ownership' of the final decision provides doctors with the opportunity to give greater weight to their own personal non-clinical views.[151]

A study published in the *Journal of Perinatology* in 2007 found that American doctors made treatment withdrawal decisions based on their own interpretation of the 'grey zone' of gestational period. Eighty-five per cent of neonatologists in the study stated that resuscitation should be enforced anywhere between 22 and 26 weeks' gestation.[152] In this study, the disparity of gestational 'grey zones' and doctors' personal fear of litigation were the subjective factors that most determined treatment decisions, while religious beliefs or practices were less significant for this group of doctors. The study found that 'the litigiousness of parents may result in resuscitation of infants against the physician's better judgement'.[153]

By contrast, French neonatologists do not share a similar fear of litigation; on the contrary, they feel empowered to make decisions, often without seeking any parental involvement. French doctors perhaps perceive giving parents rights and choices in decision making as 'opening the flood gates' to issues of liability and arbitration. Orfali supports this view: 'French neonatologists seem actually reluctant about any legal change that could restrict their action; and their attempts to provide rules for self-regulation are a way of obviating the need for changes in the law.'[154] The French medical system widely perceives the American legal system as an 'anti-model'. Orfali finds:

> opposition to what they consider to be a perversion in the American legal system. Liability issues in the US are highly publicised in France, and are viewed as an anti-model contributing to on-going disputes between patients, parents, families and doctors.[155]

Doctors' perceptions of death, disability and decision making

Of the caregivers and decision makers discussed in this chapter – parents, doctors and judges – medical professionals have the most exposure to death. It is not

---

150 Morris, above, n 138, 364.
151 Ibid 365.
152 A R Weiss et al., 'Decision Making in the Delivery Room: A Survey of Neonatologists' (2007) 27(12) *Journal of Perinatology* 754.
153 Ibid 758.
154 Kristina Orfali, 'Parental Role in Medical Decision Making: Fact or Fiction? A Comparative Study of Ethical Dilemmas in French and American Neonatal Intensive Care Units' (2004) 58(10) *Social Science and Medicine* 2009, 2012.
155 Ibid.

uncommon for neonatologists and other medical professionals to experience the death of one or several patients in any given 'working week'. While doctors may be thought to be accustomed to this, particularly considering that decisions to withdraw life-sustaining treatment are common in the NICU, this is often not the case.

A study conducted by neonatologist Dr Peter Barr from NSW, Australia, supports the view that there is a correlation between withdrawal or withholding life-sustaining treatment and doctors' personal fears of death and dying. In the study, doctors were asked to consider forgoing life-sustaining treatment where its goal was to relieve pain and suffering or where further treatment was considered futile and burdensome on the infant. Given the sensitivity and possible illegality of the issue, the surveys were anonymously completed by both Australian and New Zealand neonatologists registered in units across both countries in 2004.[156] Barr avoided any issues of contention:

> What I indicated to them was that I was asking them something that was medico-legally illegal. And so I asked them to put that concern to one side for the purposes of answering the questions. So it's a self-report questionnaire, rather than ask them what they do in practice.[157]

However, Barr's assertion is not entirely correct, given the findings and purpose of the questionnaire. The findings were not 'hypothetical', but were more likely to relate to 'clinical practice'. Of the 138 surveys distributed, 78 were returned. Ninety-five per cent of neonatologists stated that they would provide adequate medication to control pain and suffering, even if the dosage was too high and caused hastened death.[158] Barr found that of the eight facets of 'fear of death' listed in the survey, 'doctors with a greater fear of the dying process and greater fear of premature death are more likely to accept hastening a newborn infant's death when further treatment is non-beneficial or overly burdensome'.[159] Conversely, 'those with a greater fear of being destroyed are less likely to condone such an action'.[160]

Further, the survey found that an overwhelming number of doctors were prepared to forgo treatment or provide pain relief with the intention of hastening death. Barr stated: 'ANZ neonatologists seem to support the moral notion that it is sometimes "better to kill than let die" even though the former is unlawful and seems not to respect the "sanctity of life".'[161]

---

156 Peter Barr, 'Relationships of Neonatologists' End-of-life Decisions to their Personal Fear of Death' (2007) 92(2) *Archives of Disease in Childhood: Fetal, Neonatal Edition* 104–107.
157 Barbara Miller, '1 in 3 Doctors Would Break the Law to Euthanase Disabled Babies: Survey', *AM*, 7 February 2007 (Peter Barr). www.abc.net.au/am/content/2007/s1842041.htm
158 Gudrun Shultz, *One-Third of Australian Doctors Would Euthanize Sick Babies, Survey Finds* (8 February 2007) LifeSitenews.com. www.lifesitenews.com/news/archive/ldn/2007/feb/07020806
159 Barr, above, n 156, 104, 106.
160 Ibid
161 Ibid.

Barr demonstrates that it is possible to have an open, honest dialogue outside the closed doors of hospital meeting rooms, allowing non-medical professionals to understand what 'really happens'.[162] However, the information arising out of this dialogue does not sit comfortably with everyone. In his article, Schultz reported that Barr's study found that 'one third of Australian doctors would euthanise sick babies', causing pro-life activists to condemn the findings and question the rights of doctors to 'kill another person'.[163]

Subjectivity is also evident when doctors make decisions to treat premature infants in the face of severe lifelong disability. While some doctors make decisions to treat aggressively in light of their religious beliefs, others may take quality of life considerations into account. Orfali's study, for example, found that French neonatologists considered the survival of an infant with severe disability or impairment to be the 'worst risk' of continuing treatment.[164]

As discussed earlier in this chapter, perceptions of disability and the future prospects for premature and critically impaired infants are also factors that affect the decisions of treating doctors. Considering that the doctor will not have to bear the stress and financial burden of raising the disabled child, the doctor's subjectivity in providing aggressive treatment to (often extremely) premature and critically impaired infants who will survive with severe disability is perhaps egotistical. This treatment choice may be a protection for the doctor's own moral conscience, with little regard for the financial and emotional costs to the family and society once the child has left the NICU.[165]

In this regard, the French stance should be contrasted. The Orfali-led study found that 'the acceptability of disability led to very pessimistic evaluations of the infant's current and future condition'.[166] One doctor interviewed for the study stated: 'when one imposes such severe handicap on parents, one has a responsibility towards society.'[167] French doctors thus appear to have a radically different approach to disability and premature infants; that is, they recognise the burden to society once a child has left the NICU, and consider that the preservation of life at all costs is not absolute. This point is supported by Orfali's findings: 'statistically there are more divorces and things like that . . . the same clinicians operate in the NICU and the follow up clinics gives them a kind of legitimate expertise: they know by experience the consequences of their medical intervention.'[168]

Another example of this wide-angle approach is that French neonatologists believe that their involvement and medical intervention is directly responsible for any arising repercussions and that it is their 'professional duty to correct them in the appropriate way'.[169] One doctor stated: 'the professional duty of neonatologists

---

162 Loane Skene, *Law and Medical Practice: Rights, Duties, Claims and Defences* (Butterworths, 1998) 247.
163 Shultz, above, n 158.
164 Orfali, above, n 154, 2018.
165 This is discussed in Chapter 6.
166 Orfali, above, n 154, 2018
167 Ibid.
168 Ibid 2019.
169 Ibid.

is to give parents a child in good condition. I have always thought we should limit treatment instead of giving (the parents) a handicapped child.'[170] The French approach is undoubtedly paternalistic, although markedly different from the other examples of judicial and medical paternalism discussed earlier in this book. French neonatologists distinguish themselves in their confidence and clarity in linking their professional obligations to the infant and its family to those they owe to society.

As considered in Chapter 1, France is considered to be the birthplace of neonatology, the purpose of which was to help to rebuild France's decimated population. While it may be expected that its long history in the field would make French medical professionals leaders in advocating for saving imperilled infants, such a view would ignore that neonatology did not derive from a sense of principle to save individual infants. Rather, the development of neonatology was driven by considerations of the state – a tradition that modern-day French neonatologists appear to be carrying forward.

Different parents, different treatment decisions: are parents treated differently by doctors?

At a conference held in Geneva in 2012, Chicago-based neonatologist William Meadow discussed the socioeconomic factors and attendant cultural attitudes of African American mothers such as often presented at his hospital. Many mothers that have infants born at 23 weeks passionately express their desire for resuscitation at birth. Meadow recalled one woman stating 'save my baby and treat me seriously as a woman in a bad situation'.[171]

However, when doctors are of the medical opinion that any treatment would be futile, they often allow parents to believe that they have 'done everything they can' to save their baby. Such 'sham attempts' allow parents to believe that everything that could possibly have been done to save their infant has been done, and they are grateful that the doctors 'tried'. This again highlights the imbalance of power between doctors and parents. However, in this instance, the play on power and the dispersal of information may actually save parents from heartache and guilt and assist them through the grieving process. Doctors also make decisions to treat more aggressively based on the likelihood of a mother experiencing pregnancy again. This has become a more relevant issue in recent times with the development of reproductive technologies such as IVF.[172]

---

170 Ibid.
171 William Meadow, 'Practice Variations in the Care of Critically Ill Neonates: Good, Bad or Simply Inevitable? (Speech delivered at the Ethical, Legal and Social Implications of Neonatal Intensive Care Units, Geneva, 4–5 June 2012). www.brocher.ch/en/events/ethical-legal-and-social-implications-of-neonatal-intensive-care-units
172 This is particularly true of Australia; see, e.g., Melissa Davey and Philip Ly, 'Over-50 Mums on the Rise', *The Age* (Online) 15 June 2013. www.theage.com.au/national/over50-mums-on-the-rise-20130614-2o9uc.html

Older parents who have used reproductive technologies may be more willing to accept a child with severe disability, as the pregnancy may be their last chance of having a child. Meadow commented that 'older mothers may consider wanting the child to survive even at odds of 5% survival with 100% disability'.[173] He further noted that this group of parents are more likely to be accepting of technology, given its utilisation to conceive in the first place.

According to Meadow, doctors were more willing to apply aggressive treatment for longer periods if the mother of the infant was older, or had conceived by IVF treatment after several years of infertility.[174] This attitude towards withdrawal of treatment could be perceived as discriminatory in nature. Moreover, such discrimination is not exclusive to the age or fertility history of the parent; it is also apparent in doctors' perceptions of pre-term infants as patients.

Are pre-term infants treated differently from other patients?

While one might predict that there would be a strong desire on the part of doctors to protect infants given their vulnerable status, a study conducted by Canadian neonatologist Annie Janvier found that doctors and medical students did not prioritise treatment for premature infants above other patients. The study, which comprised an anonymous questionnaire, posed a scenario with eight critically ill patients ranging from a 24-weeks'-premature infant to an 80-year-old patient suffering dementia and a recent stroke. The patients in between this range included a two-month-old with meningitis, a 14-year-old with leukaemia and a 20% chance of disability, a 35-year-old with brain cancer and a 100% chance of disability if operated on, and a seven-year-old with cerebral palsy and learning difficulties.[175]

Janvier noted 842 respondents, including neonatologists, obstetricians and emergency doctors, and students across the disciplines of anthropology, law, medicine and bioethics. She found that of the hypothetical patients, pre-term infants ranked seventh out of eight, only ahead of the 80-year-old stroke victim.[176] The median order ranked the two-month-old with meningitis as the patient who both medical practitioners and students would resuscitate if they could only treat one of the eight patients. Sixty-one per cent of respondents ranked the 35-year-old with only a 5% chance of survival and a 100% chance of disability if operated on higher than the 24-week infant.

---

173 Meadow, above, n 171.
174 Ibid.
175 Annie Janvier, 'Neonates are Treated Differently from Older Children and Adults' (Speech delivered at the Ethical, Legal and Social Implications of Neonatal Intensive Care Units, Geneva, 4–5 June 2012). www.brocher.ch/en/events/ethical-legal-and-social-implications-of-neonatal-intensive-care-units
176 The order from first to eighth was: two-month-old with meningitis, seven-year-old with multiple disabilities, 14-year-old with leukaemia, full-term baby with brain malformation, 50-year-old trauma victim, 35-year-old with brain cancer, 24-week pre-term infant and 80-year-old stroke victim.

This study indicates that premature infants may be treated differently by medical practitioners. Janvier suggests that one reason for this may be that women are able to abort a pregnancy at a similar gestational age; hence, a premature infant may not be considered as having the same legal rights or status as other patients, even though born alive. This aligns with Singer's view that 'infants lack personhood, autonomy and self-consciousness, and that as such medical professionals and students 'devalue' them as members of society'.[177] This further reinforces the power that doctors possess in making selective treatment decisions, and reiterates the potential consequences of their subjectivity.

The framing effect

Subjectivity and variability extend further, to the type of information that medical practitioners consider important for parents to know and understand. This can vary between doctors in one unit and across different departments, depending on whether their focus is on withdrawal of treatment and palliative care or intensive care.[178] This is indicative of a possible internal power struggle between clinicians and departments in having the 'final influencing role' in life and death decisions.

McHaffie et al. found that doctors gained confidence and authority in decision making through their personal experience. The experience gained then played a pivotal role in influencing recommendations in similar cases. Further, the development of strong communication skills to present a coherent and well-reasoned case directly influenced parents' perceptions and views on treatment decisions. McHaffie et al. acknowledged that this is a dangerous path for doctors to take, and referred to 'recommendations becoming self-fulfilling prophecies', leading to complacency in making decisions in which results can vary significantly.[179] This view has been supported more recently by Wilkinson, who highlighted that such self-fulfilling prophecies 'may compromise honest communication with families by causing doctors to mislead families about the patient's chance of survival'.[180]

Janvier has discussed the 'framing effect',[181] which is a technique of carefully managing the flow of critical information to parents. Janvier suggested that many parents only remember 25% of the information they receive from the doctor. Accordingly, information and its absorption by parents is dependent on how a doctor 'frames' the conversation, thus having a framing effect.[182] Using this technique, doctors might explain to parents that half of infants born at 23 weeks die and half survive. From this communication, parents tend to only hear the

177 Peter Singer, *Rethinking Life and Death* (Text Publishing, 1994) 201.
178 Jox et al., 'Medical Futility at the End of Life: The Perspectives of Intensive Care and Palliative Care Clinicians' (2012) 38(9) *Journal of Medical Ethics* 540, 542.
179 McHaffie et al., above, n 11, 104, 106.
180 Wilkinson, above, n 97, 401, 407.
181 Janvier, above, n 38.
182 Ibid.

latter, positive, part of what is said – the half that survive. Presumably, the selective retention of information on the part of parents is based on hope, as discussed earlier in this chapter.

Further, Janvier found that 'there were differences in what doctors considered to be "important" information and what the parent perceived as important'. Individuals generally prefer decreasing numbers, and consider what Janvier refers to as the 'yuck factor' last. However, the 'yuck factors' are what many doctors consider the most important; these include future prognosis, type of disability, pain and suffering. As such this is often the information that is most confronting to parents.[183] Perhaps a better view would be to present parents with pictures, crosses and ticks rather than charts, graphs and percentages. Instinctively, parents will seek even the slightest improvement or positivity in figures. Catherine Rutherford, interviewed by Wishart, confirms this view: 'as a parent you hear what you want to hear, you cling onto that 5%.'[184]

Parents are in an unfamiliar, unpleasant environment, often feeling inundated with information, framed by medical professionals to convey selected information.[185] This information leads to decisions that may have irrevocable consequences and therefore it should be balanced between rationality and humanity. It may be the case that such subjectivity in decision making overshadows the patient – the infant. It must not be forgotten that such decisions and conversations are ultimately to determine whether the premature or impaired infant lives or dies.

With this is mind, Janvier makes a valuable point. She points out that it is important to assist parents to understand numbers and data for them to make rational decisions, using both their head and their heart.[186] Indeed, Janvier can be regarded an appropriate authority on this matter, considering her own experiences of making treatment decisions following the birth of her daughter Violet at 24 weeks' gestation.[187]

As she reports, although both she and her husband were neonatologists, their experiences and focuses differed. While she concentrated and relied on clinical statistics, data and her medical knowledge, her husband placed greater emphasis on emotions and any signs of movement or life. Their daughter survived, and the author acknowledges the importance that emotions play in decision making. As previously mentioned in this chapter, some of life's most precious and influential moments centre on emotion, and although emotions cannot be relied on solely in cases of making such significant decisions, they should not be disregarded. As Higginson and Janvier state, 'medical research narrowly focuses on issues that can

---

183 See, also, Wendy Yee and Sue Ross, 'Communicating with Parents of High-Risk Infants in Neonatal Intensive Care' (2006) 11(5) *Paediatric Child Health* 291–294.
184 *The Price of Life*, above, n 35, 00.34.17.
185 A better view is held by Dr Ross Haslam, Associate Professor of Neonatal Medicine at the Women's and Children's Hospital in Adelaide, Australia, who described rephrasing withdrawal of care more sensitively to parents as 'redirecting' care to palliative care.
186 Janvier, above, n 38.
187 Kimberley Pfeiffer, 'The Ethics of Caring: Expressing Humanity towards Babies Born at the Borderline of Viability' (2008) 20(2) *Bioethics Research Notes* 21, 23.

be measured . . . [However,] most decisions in life are not based on measurable quantities.'[188]

It is evident from the discussion thus far that doctors hold the 'trump card' and, as in any transaction in which there is room for negotiation, doctors will cajole, coerce or attempt to influence parents to their way of thinking. This is supported by Moro's empirical research, in which a nurse stated that 'she felt that the physician's presentation of . . . information [chances of survival] was leading and may have affected decision making [for the parents]'.[189] Further, many parents focused on the information with which they were provided by doctors, and were sensitive to whether information was expressed negatively or positively.[190] This suggests that, although doctors have the medical knowledge and power to dictate and sway parental decision making, often in the midst of emotional turmoil, a better approach may be to empower parents with information that is clear, understandable and honest, injecting some balance into the parent–doctor power dynamic. Kuschel and Kent support this view, in that 'the relative emphasis of the information provided needs to be gauged against the needs of the family and an assessment of what is appropriate for the infant's situation'.[191] The authors acknowledge that 'it is critical that clinical staff are as objective as possible when information is provided yet empathetic to the circumstances of the family, as the tone or delivery of the message can have as great an impact as the content'.[192]

The roster lottery

In Chapter 3, the examination of clinical guidelines and frameworks concluded that there are no uniform guidelines in the UK or Australia. There is an abundance of non-exclusive guidelines to which to refer; however, the non-binding nature of these reflects that decisions regarding treatment are unaudited and rarely challenged. Within the same states governed and funded by the same health systems, different hospitals exercise their prerogatives based on religious or cultural factors.[193] The scope of subjectivity extends to the doctor treating patients within one unit. Some doctors may treat more aggressively than others, allowing their own beliefs and views to override the wishes of parents, and possibly the best interests of the infant.

Given the number of variables and the amount of practitioner subjectivity in end of life decisions, the term 'roster lottery' seems appropriately fitting here. In its crudest form, this term highlights the depth of medical practitioner subjectivity,

188 Jason D Higginson, 'Emotion, Suffering and Hope: Commentary on "How Much Emotion is Enough?"' (2007) 18(4) *Journal of Clinical Ethics* 377, 378.
189 Moro et al., above, n 26, 52, 58.
190 Ibid.
191 Kuschel and Kent, above, n 98, 585, 587.
192 Ibid.
193 Examples of religious affiliated hospitals in Melbourne, Australia, are the Mercy and St Vincent's Hospital.

where decisions may be based primarily on their own values and belief systems. Which doctor is on call when a 23-week infant is delivered can potentially be the deciding factor in whether treatment is withdrawn, withheld or continued.

One result of this might be that parents decide to 'shop around' for a hospital and particular doctor who they believe is more inclined to treat or not treat in accordance with their own values and beliefs. Such decision making is random, unethical and indefensible, given that decisions are being made about life and death, with the consequences being absolute. Wilkinson and Troug assert that arbitrary decision making may be particularly prevalent when the patient's values are unclear.[194] This certainly seems to be the case in making decisions for premature infants. The authors further acknowledge that varying attitudes can 'impact on actual decisions'.[195] Having considered the extent of doctors' subjectivity in end of life decision making, it is appropriate to pose the question: Should the role of doctors and the autonomy that they are given be reduced?

Should doctors be considered as functionaries?

The beginning of this chapter discussed the shift in societal attitudes from an acceptance of the traditional 'doctor knows best' approach towards a more autonomous and rights-driven culture in which patients feel confident in challenging medical opinion. Indeed, as detailed earlier, the former approach suffers from inconsistency and subjectivity on the part of medical practitioners making life and death decisions. Supported by a wealth of academic literature, incumbent in the acceptance of the shift towards the latter rights-driven approach is a consequent requirement to question the medical profession and its essential function.

Certain standard ethical practices are understood by doctors and patients alike as unacceptable. Examples include not having sexual relations with patients and not disclosing confidential patient information. Why, then, are doctors who base their decisions on their own personal and religious beliefs allowed to slip through the ethical net? Foster believes that for medicine to be practised to its full potential, doctors need to be more holistic and autonomous. He asks, 'how can they [doctors] be equipped to deal effectively with the complex bundles of contradictions they call their patients?'[196] Conversely, ethicist and medical practitioner Julian Savulescu points out that to be a doctor requires a willingness to be 'able to offer appropriate medical interventions that are legal, beneficial, desired by the patient and a part of a just healthcare system'.[197] He goes on to say: 'if we do not allow moral values or self-interest to corrupt the delivery of the just and legal delivery

---

194 Dominic Wilkinson and Robert D Truog, 'The Luck of the Draw: Physician-related Variability in End-of-life Decision Making in Intensive Care' (2013) 39(6) *Intensive Care Medicine* 1128, 1128.
195 Ibid 1131.
196 Charles Foster, 'Why Doctors Should Get a Life' (2009) 102(12) *Journal of Royal Society of Medicine* 518, 519.
197 Julian Savulescu, 'Conscientious Objection in Medicine' (2006) 332 *British Medical Journal* 294, 295.

of such health services, we should not let other values, such as religious values, corrupt them either.'[198]

Savulescu's view is persuasive. An objective, fair system of medical treatment is crucial. Taxpayers, who fund public health systems, should be confident that treatment will be dispensed in a fair, just and objective manner, precluding doctors' subjective values or judgments. As Savulescu points out, 'public servants must act in the public interest, not their own'.[199]

The role of doctors should be functional. Savulescu states 'a primary goal of a health service is to protect the health of its recipients'.[200] He takes this expression further, arguing that 'doctors who compromise the delivery of medical services to patients on conscience grounds must be punished through removal of licence to practise and other legal mechanisms'.[201]

It is important to note that to 'protect the health of recipients' is not necessarily the absolute extension of treatment, particularly in the case of premature birth, where survival is unlikely or carries a risk of severe and debilitating disability. It may be that the best way to protect fragile patients is not to prolong their inevitable death or pain and suffering. Given the significant role that subjective beliefs and values play in decision making, it would be appropriate to reduce doctors' decision-making powers, placing greater emphasis on clinical and technical factors dictated by an overseeing body or governed by stricter sanctions and protocols to which doctors must adhere. Doyal and Wilsher support this view, highlighting the need for public policy on treatment decisions, to overcome the 'rules of thumb' that doctors apply to cases, based on their own 'personal convictions'.[202]

Bagaric and Amarasekara assert that, although doctors' views should be considered, they should by no means be the vehicle that drives decision making in a particular direction: 'there is no reason to think that doctors have a higher level of moral insight that the rest of the community. Certainly, their views should not be discounted . . . however, they should not be given any extra weight.'[203]

As discussed in Chapter 2, the medical profession plays a crucial role in determining and defining the principles of best interests and futility[204] – concepts

198 Ibid.
199 Ibid 297.
200 Ibid 296.
201 Ibid.
202 L Doyal and D Wilsher, 'Towards Guidelines for the Withholding and Withdrawal of Life Prolonging Treatment in Neonatal Medicine' (1994) 70(1) *Archives of Disease in Childhood: Fetal and Neonatal* 66, 69.
203 Mirko Bagaric and Kumar Amarasekara, 'Euthanasia: Why it Doesn't Matter (Much) What the Doctor Thinks and Why There is No Suggestion that Doctors Should Have a Duty to Kill' (2002) 10(2) *Journal of Law and Medicine* 221, 227.
204 See, further, Lindy Willmott, Ben White and Jocelyn Downie, 'Withholding and Withdrawal of "Futile" Life-Sustaining Treatment: Unilateral Medical Decision-making in Australia and New Zealand', (2013) 20(4) *Journal of Law and Medicine* 907–924. The authors highlight that, in multidisciplinary literature, there is a range of definitions used for the concept of futility, including 'will not work' to 'not worth doing'.

on which the courts rely when hearing treatment disputes. Doctors define and characterise the very concept of futility, as Stewart eloquently stated: 'part of the problem with the concept of futility is that it is a subjective notion masquerading as a form of professional, objective and scientific assessment.'[205] Yet, because this concept arises out of the medical profession, often no other caregiver or decision maker, not even a judge, will contest or overrule a doctor's definition of futility or decision to withdraw or withhold treatment. This display of professional sovereignty is clear, Stewart asserts:

> The medical concept of futility is based on a similar concept of sovereignty: in situations of end of life care, it is the medical profession who control the definition of futility and therefore control what treatments are provided to the exclusion of other claims for control.[206]

Doctors thus have the overwhelming power in making life and death decisions. The gravity of this power has been commented on by Willmott, White and Downie,[207] who provide four compelling observations about the current practice and power that medical practitioners in Australia and New Zealand have in relation to treatment decisions:

1   There is no general duty on doctors to provide treatment that they consider to be futile.
2   Doctors do not need consent from the patient or a substitute decision maker, or authorisation from the courts or elsewhere to withdraw or withhold treatment they consider to be futile.
3   They are the decision makers as to when their duty to treat ends, and for determining when treatment is futile.
4   There is no obligation on the part of the treating doctor to facilitate the resolution of a dispute in this way [by means of a court/tribunal]. The onus rests on the family or other party objecting to the treatment being withheld or withdrawn.

These observations reinforce the need for clarity in the roles that doctors play. The medical practitioner's role should be reduced from decision maker to medical enabler in the decision-making process, and their activities, whether undertaken or not, should adhere to certain protocols and be accountable, auditable and subject to rigorous review and penalty.[208] The discussion in this chapter now turns to the role and impact of the judiciary in end of life decision making for premature and critically impaired infants.

205 Cameron L Stewart, 'A Defence of the Requirement to Seek Consent to Withhold and Withdraw Futile Treatments' (2012) 196(6) *Medical Journal of Australia* 406, 406.
206 Cameron Stewart, 'Futility Determination as a Process: Problems with Medical Sovereignty, Legal Issues and the Strengths and Weakness of the Procedural Approach' (2011) 8(2) *Journal of Bioethical Inquiry* 155, 156.
207 Willmott, White and Downie, above, n 204, 914–915.
208 Stewart, above, n 206, 155, 157, 162.

4.3 The judiciary: over-reliance on medical opinion

The rule of law commands that courts are the ultimate decision-making body in relation to legal disputes, including those relating to premature and critically impaired infants. Thus, there is no question that judges have the final say. However, the rule of law also requires that laws are clear, certain, knowable and predictable. As noted in Chapter 2, the current application of the best interests principle in decisions to withdraw or withhold life-sustaining treatment is ill-defined, insufficient and too vague to provide guidance in this area. Moreover, the judicial function in relation to end of life decision making is seemingly undermined by the deference that judges have to medical opinion.

It is widely accepted in society that the ultimate arbiter, which should be the most independent and objective, is the judiciary. Decisions and justice should be blind to the preferences or subjectivity of others. However, as has been illustrated thus far in this book, and most acutely in this chapter, end of life decision making for impaired infants is often determined by a range of subjective factors. Chapter 2 highlighted that when parents and doctors disagree on whether treatment should be withdrawn or withheld, the courts are required to make a determination. Less common in Australia than in the UK, some of these decisions merely require the sanction of the court, whereas others require active determination.

In the Australian landmark case of *Re Marion*, concerning the lawful sterilisation of an intellectually disabled girl (discussed in Chapter 2), the High Court noted that 'the medical profession very often plays a central role in the decision to sterilize as well as in the procedure itself'. The court considered that although the matter was not merely a 'medical issue, nevertheless the question has been "medicalized" to a great degree'.[209] In fact, the High Court acknowledged that 'as with all professions, there are those who act with impropriety as well as those who act bona fide but within a limited frame of reference'.[210] The High Court further stated the need for input and counsel from a variety of experts in varying professions, noting that 'the consequences of sterilization are not merely biological but also social and psychological'.[211]

However, despite the encouraging and rational points raised by the High Court in *Marion's case*, decisions in sterilisation cases and more importantly here in infant withdrawal cases overwhelmingly continue to yield to medical opinion only.[212]

Where a determination has been required by the courts, overwhelmingly judges have agreed with medical opinion to withdraw treatment, often with absolute

209 *Department of Health and Community Services v JWB and SMB (Marion's case)* (1992) 175 CLR 218, 251.
210 Ibid.
211 Ibid.
212 See, further, G Carlson, M Taylor, J Wilson, J and J Griffen, *Menstrual Management and Fertility Management for Women Who Have Intellectual Disability and High Support Needs: Analysis of Australian Policy* (Department of Social Work and Social Policy, University of Queensland, 2nd edn, 1994).

consequences – leading to the death of the infant. This raises questions as to the weight placed on medical opinion by the courts, and in turn raises some compelling questions of bias and impartiality. The judiciary seemingly defer to medical opinion, despite the gravity of these life and death decisions. This is evinced in the case of *A National Health Service v D*,[213] in which Justice Cazalet stated that 'it is well established that there can be no question of the court directing a doctor to provide treatment which he or she is unwilling to give and which is contrary to that doctor's clinical judgement'.[214]

So far in this book, a number of factors have been considered that support the contention that there is a need for greater transparency and objectivity in decision making for premature and impaired infants. The following observations have been highlighted:

1   The imprecise and ill-defined best interests principle – Chapter 2.
2   The lack of uniformity or coherence of clinical guidelines – Chapter 3.
3   The subjectivity of medical practitioners and parents in end of life decision making – Chapter 4.

In addition to the points listed here, the judiciary's deference to the medical profession and reliance on medical opinion is also of concern. Indeed, Coggon asserts that such deference might 'permit the doctor to do what he wants, unhindered because of the application of the notoriously troublesome *Bolam* test and an excessively deferential judiciary'.[215]

Arguably, parents seeking the continuation of medical treatment against medical opinion are fighting a losing battle on two fronts: first, in the hospital where medical professionals have expertise far beyond that of parents, allowing non-medical and subjective criteria into the decision-making process to withhold or withdraw treatment; second, in the court room, where judges' decisions to withdraw or withhold treatment reflect their heavy reliance on medical opinion. This suggests that the medical profession has a significant amount of power and authority in the decision-making process, both in the hospital setting and in court.[216]

The effect of this excessive weight given to medical opinion has been acknowledged and noted by the medical profession, and as such has possibly further empowered them due to their awareness that the highest authority, the law, is unlikely to question their clinical judgment or opinion. Fortin highlights

213   *A National Health Service Trust v D* [2000] 2 FLR 677.
214   Cited in Skene, above, n 162, 357.
215   Cited in Muireann Quigley, 'Best Interests: The Power of the Medical Profession, and the Power of the Judiciary' (2008) 16(3) *Health Care Analysis* 233, 234. The Bolam test is discussed in Chapter 2.
216   See, further, Sabine Michalowski, 'Reversal of Fortune – Re A (Conjoined Twins) and Beyond: Who Should Make Treatment Decisions on Behalf of Young Children?' (2001) 9 *Health Law Journal*, 149, 168.

that 'there seemed little point in parents seeking the courts judicial assessment of situation involving children – since the answer would always be that the doctors were to be guided by their own clinical judgement', leading 'doctors and their lawyers to conclude that since a court would never direct them to act against their clinical judgment, they themselves did not need court authority to override parents objections'.[217]

Lord Woolf also acknowledged the judiciary's preference for, or excessive weighting on, medical opinion, and identified the risks this can pose in presiding over treatment disputes in the courts. He rightly cautioned:

> It is unwise to place any profession or other body providing services to the public on a pedestal where their actions cannot be subject to close scrutiny. The greater the power the body has, the more important is this need.[218]

Such an acknowledgment is remarkable for its frankness, and is a cautionary note for the potential to abuse such power. Stewart points out: 'the power wielded by the courts is open to public scrutiny. The power wielded by doctors in nursing homes and hospitals is not.'[219] In light of this, and with reference to decision making as it affects the withdrawing or withholding of treatment from critically ill infants, this book recommends that doctors be considered functionaries, and that the judiciary should take ultimate responsibility for decisions that have such absolute consequences.

Nevertheless, as highlighted throughout this book thus far, given the symbiotic relationship that exists between the law and medicine and end of life decision making, the findings of research conducted by academics at the Queensland University of Technology in Australia have recently been published in the *Medical Journal of Australia*, and are valuable here. White et al. undertook empirical research to 'examine doctors' level of knowledge of the law on withholding and withdrawing life-sustaining treatment from adults who lack decision-making capacity'. The findings of the study are transferrable to the infant patient and end of life decisions given their similar lack of capacity and autonomy.

After conducting a postal survey with respondents including doctors 'working in emergency services, intensive care and palliative care in New South Wales (NSW), Victoria and Queensland', the authors noted several important findings. They found that there are 'critical gaps in the legal knowledge of many doctors who practise end-of-life medicine'.[220] Many doctors lack knowledge about the

217 Jane Fortin, *Children's Rights and the Developing Law* (Cambridge University Press, 3rd edn, 2009) 373.
218 Right Honourable the Lord Woolf, 'Are the Courts Excessively Deferential to the Medical Profession?' (2001) 9(1) *Medical Law Review* 1, 15.
219 Cameron Stewart, 'Legal Constructions of Life and Death in the Common Law' (2002) 2(Summer) *Oxford University Commonwealth Law Journal* 67, 89.
220 White et al., 'Doctors' Knowledge of the Law on Withholding and Withdrawing Life-sustaining Medical Treatment' (2014) 201(4) *Medical Journal of Australia*, 229, 229.

validity of advance care directives (living wills) and understanding in 'determining the legally authorised decision maker for medical treatment'.[221] The results of the study led the authors to recommend 'legal reform; improved training and resources; and a shift in doctor's attitudes to knowing the law'.[222] The authors of this study also noted the critical need for a single national legislative framework to assist medical practitioners in end of life decision making for adults lacking capacity, as argued in Chapter 3.

As Willmott et al. assert, 'medicine is no longer an autonomous professional enterprise, but a social endeavor occurring within social, cultural and legal frameworks'.[223] Given the organic relationship between law and medicine, better education and knowledge of the law should translate to more informed and considered decisions being made by doctors, and should create a platform for more objective end of life decision making.

Thus far, it has been noted that medical opinion has informed and continues to inform legal opinion and decisions to withdraw or withhold life-sustaining treatment. White et al. note that 'there is no duty [on the part of doctors] to provide futile treatment' and as such 'he or she [the doctor] is the legal-decision-maker and may decline to treat'.[224] This has been highlighted in relation to critically ill infants, with doctors often overriding parental wishes. For the rule of law to operate more effectively in this area, it is important that the determining factors in end of life decision making for critically impaired infants are clarified. This book argues that one determining objective factor that should be given greater emphasis in this area of decision making is the allocation of limited public healthcare resources. This is discussed in the following chapters.

4.4 Conclusion

In this chapter, key caregivers and decision makers have been shown to make withdrawal of treatment decisions based on a range of subjective factors. The role of parents in decision making is complicated by a range of conflicting factors and claims. Further, medical practitioners, the group typically credited with basing its decisions on objectivity and clinical expertise, were also found to make unpredictable, subjective treatment decisions.

Moreover, considering the heavy reliance the judiciary place on medical opinion, it also cannot be said to operate objectively in the decision-making process. Such approaches to end of life decision making for premature and critically impaired infants are indefensible, given that life is at stake.

The penultimate chapter of this book discusses the need for the allocation of limited healthcare resources to be a cardinal consideration in end of life decision

---

221 Ibid 231.
222 Ibid 232.
223 Willmott, White, Parker and Cartwright, 'The Legal Role of Medical Professionals in Decisions to Withhold or Withdraw Life-Sustaining Treatment: Part 3', above, n 204, 773–794.
224 Ibid 787.

making for extremely premature (born at the edge of viability) and critically impaired infants, thus allowing for some much needed objectivity in decision making. However, before turning to it, a discussion about the application of theories of distributive justice is warranted.

4.5 References

A National Health Service Trust v D [2000] 2 FLR 677.

Ahluwalia, Jag, Christoph Lees and John J Paris, 'Decisions for Life Made in the Perinatal Period: Who Decides and on Which Standards?' (2008) 93(5) *Archives of Disease in Childhood: Fetal and Neonatal* 332.

Archard, David, *Children: Rights and Childhood* (Routledge, 2nd edn, 2004).

Baby D (No 2) [2011] Fam CA 176; *TS & TD v Sydney Children's Hospital ('Mohammed's case')* [2012] NSWSC 1609.

Bagaric, Mirko and Kumar Amarasekara, 'Euthanasia: Why it Doesn't Matter (Much) What the Doctor Thinks and Why There is No Suggestion that Doctors Should Have a Duty to Kill' (2002) 10(2) *Journal of Law and Medicine* 221.

Barnes, Colin, 'Disability Activism and the Struggle for Change Disability, Policy and Politics in the UK' (2007) 2(3) *Education, Citizenship and Social Justice* 203.

Barr, Peter, 'Relationships of Neonatologists' End-of-life Decisions to their Personal Fear of Death' (2007) 92(2) *Archives of Disease in Childhood: Fetal and Neonatal* 104.

Battin, Malcolm, David Knight et al., 'Improvement in Mortality of Very Low Birth Weight Infants and the Changing Pattern of Neonatal Mortality: The 50-Year Experience of One Perinatal Centre' (2012) 48(7) *Journal of Paediatrics and Child Health* 596.

Boneh, A, S Allan, D Mendelson, M. Spriggs, L H Gillam and S H Korman, 'Clinical, Ethical and Legal Considerations in the Treatment of Newborns with Non-Ketotic Hyperglycaemia' (2008) 94(2) *Molecular Genetics and Metabolism* 143.

Bracegirdle, Karen E, 'A Time to Die: Withdrawal of Paediatric Intensive Care' (1994) 3(10) *British Journal of Nursing* 513.

Burns, Jeffrey P and Christine Mitchell, 'Is There Any Consensus About End-of-life Care in Pediatrics' (2005) 159(9) *Archives of Pediatrics and Adolescent Medicine* 889.

Carlson, G, M Taylor, J Wilson and J Griffen *Menstrual Management and Fertility Management for Women Who Have Intellectual Disability and High Support Needs: Analysis of Australian Policy* (Department of Social Work and Social Policy, University of Queensland, 2nd edn, 1994).

Cooper, Margaret, 'The Australian Disability Rights Movement Lives' (1999) 14(2) *Disability & Society* 217.

Craig, Gillian M, 'On Withholding Nutrition and Hydration in the Terminally Ill: Has Palliative Medicine Gone Too Far?' (1994) 20(3) *Journal of Medical Ethics* 139.

Crowe, Christine, '"Women Want It": In-vitro Fertilization and Women's Motivations for Participation' (1985) 8(6) *Women's Studies International Forum* 547.

Cuttini, M, M Nadai, M Kaminski, G Hansen, R de Leeuw, S Lenoir et al., 'End-of-life Decisions in Neonatal Intensive Care: Physicians' Self-Reported Practices in Seven European Countries' (2000) 355(9221) *The Lancet* 2112.

Davey, Melissa and Philip Ly, 'Over-50 Mums on the Rise', *The Age* (Online) 15 June 2013. www.theage.com.au/national/over50-mums-on-the-rise-20130614-2o9uc.html

Doyal, L and D Wilsher, 'Towards Guidelines for the Withholding and Withdrawal of Life Prolonging Treatment in Neonatal Medicine' (1994) 70(1) *Archives of Disease in Childhood: Fetal and Neonatal* 66.

Duffy, D and P Reynolds, 'Babies Born at the Threshold of Viability: Attitudes of Paediatric Consultants and Trainees in South East England' (2011) 100(1) *Acta Paediatrica* 42.

Dunn, Peter, 'Appropriate Care of the Newborn: Ethical Dilemmas' (1993) 19(2) *Journal of Medical Ethics* 82.

Eichenwald, Eric C, Frank A Chervenak and Laurence B McCullough, 'Physician and Parental Decision Making in Newborn Resuscitation' (2008) 10(6) *Virtual Mentor* 616.

Evans, Kathy, 'The Edge of Life', *The Melbourne Magazine, The Age* (Australia), Issue 90, April 2012.

Fortin, Jane, *Children's Rights and the Developing Law* (Cambridge University Press, 3rd edn, 2009).

Foster, Charles, 'Why Doctors Should Get a Life' (2009) 102(12) *Journal of Royal Society of Medicine* 518.

Gampel, Eric, 'Does Professional Autonomy Protect Medical Futility Judgments?' (2006) 20(2) *Bioethics* 92.

Ghai, Anita, 'Disability in the Indian Context: Post-colonial Perspectives' in Mairian Corker and Tom Shakespeare (eds), *Disability/Postmodernity: Embodying Disability Theory* (Continuum, 2002).

Gillam, Lynne and Jane Sullivan, 'Ethics at the End of Life: Who Should Make Decisions about Treatment Limitation for Young Children with Life-Threatening or Life-Limiting Conditions?' (2011) 47(9) *Journal of Paediatrics and Child Health* 594.

Greif, Avner, 'Cultural Beliefs and the Organization of Society: A Historical and Theoretical Reflection on Collectivist and Individualist Societies' (1994) 102(51) *Journal of Political Economy* 912.

Gunderman, Richard B and William A Engle, 'Ethics and the Limits of Neonatal Viability' (2006) 236(2) *Radiology* 427.

Guyer, Ruth Levy, *Baby at Risk* (Capital Books, 2006).

Hammerman, Cathy, Eti Kombluth, Ofer Lavie, Pnina Zadka, Yeshayahu Aboulafia and Arthur I Eidelman, 'Decision-making in the Critically Ill Neonate: Cultural Background v Individual Life Experiences' (1997) 23(3) *Journal of Medical Ethics* 164.

Health Law Research Centre, *Withholding and Withdrawing Life-Sustaining Medical Treatment from Adults Who Lack Capacity: The Role of Law in Medical Practice*, Queensland University of Technology. www.qut.edu.au/research/research-projects/withholding-and-withdrawing-life-sustaining-medical-treatment

Heimer, Carol A, 'Competing Institutions: Law, Medicine, and Family in Neonatal Intensive Care' (1999) 33(1) *Law and Society Review* 17.

Higginson, Jason D, 'Emotion, Suffering and Hope: Commentary on "How Much Emotion is Enough?"' (2007) 18(4) *Journal of Clinical Ethics* 377.

Janvier, Annie, 'Can We Improve Parental Decision Making for Perinatal and Neonatal Decisions?' (Speech delivered at the Ethical, Legal and Social Implications of Neonatal Intensive Care Units Conference, Geneva, 4–5 June 2012). www.brocher.ch/en/events/ethical-legal-and-social-implications-of-neonatal-intensive-care-units

Janvier, Annie, 'Neonates are Treated Differently from Older Children and Adults' (Speech delivered at the Ethical, Legal and Social Implications of Neonatal Intensive Care Units, Geneva, 4–5 June 2012). www.brocher.ch/en/events/ethical-legal-and-social-implications-of-neonatal-intensive-care-units

Jox, Ralph J, Andreas Schaider, Georg Marckmann and Gian Domenico Borasio, 'Medical Futility at the End of Life: The Perspectives of Intensive Care and Palliative Care Clinicians' (2012) 38(9) *Journal of Medical Ethics* 540.

Kahn, Susan Martha, *Reproducing Jews: A Cultural Account of Assisted Conception in Israel* (Duke University Press, 2000).

Kerridge, Ian, Michael Lowe and Cameron Stewart, *Ethics and Law for Health Professions* (Federation Press, 4th edn, 2013).

Khoner, Nancy and Alix Henley, *When a Baby Dies: The Experience of Late Miscarriage, Stillbirth and Neonatal Death* (Pandora Press, 1991).

Kopelman, L M and A E Kopelman 'Using a New Analysis of the Best Interests Standard to Address Cultural Disputes: Whose Data, Which Values?' (2007) 28(5) *Theoretical Medicine and Bioethics* 373.

Kuschel, Carl A and Alison Kent, 'Improved Neonatal Survival and Outcomes at Borderline Viability Brings Increasing Ethical Dilemmas' (2011) 47(9) *Journal of Paediatric and Child Health* 585.

Lantos, J D, J E Tyson, A Allen, J Frader, M Hack, S Korones et al., 'Withholding and Withdrawing Life Sustaining Treatment in Neonatal Intensive Care: Issues for the 1990s' (1994) 71(3) *Archives of Disease in Childhood: Fetal and Neonatal* 218.

McHaffie, Hazel E, *Crucial Decisions at the Beginning of Life* (Radcliffe Medical Press, 2011).

McHaffie, Hazel E, Ian A Laing, Michael Parker and John McMillan, 'Deciding for Imperilled Newborns: Medical Authority or Parental Autonomy?' (2001) 27(2) *Journal of Medical Ethics* 104.

McHaffie, Hazel E, A J Lyon and P W Fowlie, 'Lingering Death after Treatment Withdrawal in the Neonatal Intensive Care Unit' (2001) 85(1) *Archives of Disease in Childhood: Fetal and Neonatal* 8.

McHaffie, Hazel E, Andrew J Lyon and Robert Hume, 'Deciding on Treatment Limitation for Neonates: The Parents Perspective' (2001) 160 *European Journal of Pediatrics* 339.

McHaffie, Hazel E and Peter W Fowlie, *Life, Death and Decisions* (Hochland & Hochland Ltd, 1996).

McVeigh, Tracey, 'I Would Have Wanted Him to Die in My Arms', *Sunday Herald Sun Magazine, Herald Sun* (Australia) 17 April 2011.

Mazza, Danielle, Christopher Harrison, Angela Taft, Bianca Brijnath, Helena Britt, Melissa Hobbs et al., 'Current Contraceptive Management in Australian General Practice: An Analysis of BEACH Data' (2012) 197(2) *Medical Journal of Australia* 110.

Meadow, William, 'Practice Variations in the Care of Critically Ill Neonates: Good, Bad or Simply Inevitable? (Speech delivered at the Ethical, Legal and Social Implications of Neonatal Intensive Care Units, Geneva, 4–5 June 2012). www. brocher.ch/en/events/ethical-legal-and-social-implications-of-neonatal-intensive-care-units

Michalowski, Sabine, 'Reversal of Fortune – Re A (Conjoined Twins) and Beyond: Who Should Make Treatment Decisions on Behalf of Young Children?' (2001) 9 *Health Law Journal*, 149.

Miller, Barbara, '1 in 3 Doctors Would Break the Law to Euthanase Disabled Babies: Survey', *AM*, 7 February 2007 (Peter Barr). www.abc.net.au/am/content/2007/s1842041.htm

Montello, Martha and John Lantos, 'The Karamazov Complex: Dostoevsky and DNR Orders' (2002) 45(2) *Perspectives in Biology and Medicine* 190.

Moro, Teresa T, Karen Kavanaugh, Teresa A Savage, Maria R Reyes, Robert E. Kimura and Rama Bhat, 'Parent Decision Making for Life Support Decisions for Extremely Premature Infants: From the Prenatal through to End-of-Life Period' (2011) 25(1) *Journal of Perinatal and Neonatal Nursing* 52.

Morris, Anne, 'Selective Treatment of Irreversibly Impaired Infants: Decision Making at the Threshold' (2009) 17(3) *Medical Law Review* 347.

Orfali, Kristina, 'Parental Role in Medical Decision Making: Fact or Fiction? A Comparative Study of Ethical Dilemmas in French and American Neonatal Intensive Care Units' (2004) 58(10) *Social Science and Medicine* 2009, 2012.

Orfali, Kristina and Elisa J Gordon, 'Autonomy Gone Awry: A Cross Cultural Study of Parents' Experiences in Neonatal Intensive Care Units' (2004) 25(4) *Theoretical Medicines and Bioethics* 329.

Paris, John J, N Graham, M D Schreiber and M Goodwin, 'Approaches to End-of-life Decision-making in the NUCI: Insights from Dostoevsky's The Grand Inquisitor' (2006) 26(7) *Journal of Perinatology* 389.

Pfeiffer, Kimberley, 'The Ethics of Caring: Expressing Humanity towards Babies Born at the Borderline of Viability' (2008) 20(2) *Bioethics Research Notes* 21.

Pignotti, Maria S, 'Extremely Preterm Births: Recommendations for Treatment in European Countries' (2008) 93(6) *Archives of Disease in Childhood: Fetal and Neonatal* 403.

Pinter, A B, 'End-of-life Decision Before and After Birth: Changing Ethical Considerations' (2008) 43(6) *Journal of Pediatric Surgery* 430.

Porta, Nicolas and Joel Frader, 'Withholding Hydration and Nutrition in Newborns' (2007) 28(5) *Theoretical Medicine and Bioethics* 443.

Quigley, Muireann, 'Best Interests: The Power of the Medical Profession, and the Power of the Judiciary' (2008) 16(3) *Health Care Analysis* 233.

R v Arthur (1981) 12 BMLR 1.

Rebagliato, M, M Cuttini, L Broggin, I Berbik, U de Vonderweid, G Hansen et al., 'Neonatal End-of-life Decision Making: Physicians' Attitudes and Relationship with Self-reported Practices in 10 European Countries' (2000) 284(19) *Journal of the American Medical Association* 2451.

Right Honourable the Lord Woolf, 'Are the Courts Excessively Deferential to the Medical Profession?' (2001) 9(1) *Medical Law Review* 1

Ross, Lainie Freidman, *Children, Families, and Health Care Decision Making* (Oxford University Press, 1998).

Roy, R, N Aladangady, K Costeloe and V Larcher, 'Decision Making and Modes of Death in a Tertiary Neonatal Unit' (2004) 89(6) *Archives of Disease in Childhood: Fetal and Neonatal* 527.

Saigal, Saroj, 'Quality of Life of Former Premature Infants during Adolescence and Beyond' (2013) 89(4) *Early Human Development* 209.

Saigal, Saroj, B Stoskopf, J Pinelli, D Streiner et al., 'Self-perceived Health-related Quality of Life of Former Extremely Low Birth Weight Infants at Young Adulthood' (2006) 118(3) *Pediatrics* 1140.

Saigal, Saroj and Jon Tyson, 'Measurement of Quality of Life of Survivors of Neonatal Intensive Care: Critique and Implications' (2008) 32(1) *Seminars in Perinatology* 59.

Savulescu, Julian, 'Autonomy, the Good Life, and Controversial Choices' in Rosamond Rhodes, Leslie P Francis and Anita Silvers (eds), *Blackwell Guide to Medical Ethics* (Blackwell Publishing, 2007).

Savulescu, Julian, 'Conscientious Objection in Medicine' (2006) 332 *British Medical Journal* 294.

Savulescu, Julian, 'Liberal Rationalism and Medical Decision-making' (1997) 11(2) *Bioethics* 115.

Shelp, Earl E, *Born to Die? Deciding the Fate of Critically Ill Newborns* (Free Press, 1986).

Shultz, Gudrun, *One-Third of Australian Doctors Would Euthanize Sick Babies, Survey Finds* (8 February 2007) LifeSitenews.com. www.lifesitenews.com/news/archive/ldn/2007/feb/07020806

Singer, Peter, *Rethinking Life and Death* (Text Publishing, 1994).

Skene, Loane, *Law and Medical Practice: Rights, Duties, Claims and Defences* (Butterworths, 1998).

Smith, Rebecca, 'Women Finding Access to Contraception Difficult', *Telegraph* (Online) 11 May 2012. www.telegraph.co.uk/health/healthnews/9257070/Women-finding-access-to-contraception-difficult.html

Stewart, Cameron, 'A Defence of the Requirement to Seek Consent to Withhold and Withdraw Futile Treatments' (2012) 196(6) *Medical Journal of Australia* 406.

Stewart, Cameron, 'Futility Determination as a Process: Problems with Medical Sovereignty, Legal Issues and the Strengths and Weakness of the Procedural Approach' (2011) 8(2) *Journal of Bioethical Inquiry* 155.

Stewart, Cameron, 'Legal Constructions of Life and Death in the Common Law' (2002) 2 (Summer) *Oxford University Commonwealth Law Journal* 67.

Stewart, Cameron, 'Who Decides When I Can Die? Problems Concerning Proxy Decisions to Forego Medical Treatment' (1997) (4) *Journal of Law and Medicine*, 386.

Tripp, J and D McGregor, 'Withholding and Withdrawing of Life Sustaining Treatment in the Newborn' (2006) 91(1) *Archives of Disease in Childhood: Fetal and Neonatal* 67.

Truog, Robert D, 'Futility in Pediatrics: From Case to Policy' (2000) 11(2) *Journal of Clinical Ethics* 136.

Warrick, Catherine, Leonie Perera, Edile Murdoch and Richard M Nicholl, 'Guidance for Withdrawal and Withholding of Intensive Care as Part of Neonatal End-of-life Care' (2011) 98(1) *British Medical Bulletin* 99.

Weiss, A R, H J Binns, J W Collins Jr, and R-A deRegnier, 'Decision Making in the Delivery Room: A Survey of Neonatologists' (2007) 27(12) *Journal of Perinatology* 754.

White, Ben, Lindy Willmott, Colleen Cartwright, Malcolm H Parker and Gail Williams, 'Doctors' Knowledge of the Law on Withholding and Withdrawing Life-sustaining Medical Treatment' (2014) 201(4) *Medical Journal of Australia*, 229.

Wilkinson, Dominic, 'The Self-Fulfilling Prophecy in Intensive Care' (2009) 30(6) *Theoretical Medicine and Bioethics* 401.

Wilkinson, Dominic, 'Is it in the Best Interests of an Intellectually Disabled Infant to Die?' (2006) 32(8) *Journal of Medical Ethics* 454.

Wilkinson, Dominic and Robert D Truog, 'The Luck of the Draw: Physician-related Variability in End-of-life Decision Making in Intensive Care' (2013) 39(6) *Intensive Care Medicine* 1128.

Willmott, Lindy, Ben White and Jocelyn Downie, 'Withholding and Withdrawal of "Futile" Life-Sustaining Treatment: Unilateral Medical Decision-making in Australia and New Zealand', (2013) 20(4) *Journal of Law and Medicine* 907.

Willmott, Lindy, Ben White, Malcolm Parker and Colleen Cartwright, 'The Legal Role of Medical Professionals in Decisions to Withhold or Withdraw Life-Sustaining Treatment: Part 3 (Victoria)' (2011) 18(4) *Journal of Law and* Medicine 773.

Wishart, Adam, *The Price of Life* (BBC Productions, 2011).

Yee, Wendy and Sue Ross, 'Communicating with Parents of High-Risk Infants in Neonatal Intensive Care' (2006) 11(5) *Paediatric Child Health* 291.

Yu, Victor, 'Ethical and Moral Dilemmas in Neonates' (2005) 1(2) *World Journal of Pediatrics* 88.

Zutlevics, Tamara, 'Pursuing the Golden Mean – Moral Decision Making for Precarious Newborns' (2009) 27(1) *Australian Journal of Advanced Nursing* 75.

5 Theories of distributive justice: healthcare and resource allocation for extremely premature and critically impaired infants

Chapter 4 explored the variety of factors that can play a role in influencing certain outcomes in end of life decision making for premature and critically impaired infants. It identified that both parents and doctors are highly subjective in their decision making. The judiciary was also found not to be objective, instead demonstrating an over-reliance on medical opinion. It was concluded that a more objective approach is needed, particularly when making end of life decisions for infants born extremely premature or severely impaired.

The primary contention of this book is that the allocation of finite healthcare resources should be a cardinal consideration in end of life decision making for extremely premature and critically impaired infants. In light of the arbitrary and subjective factors that currently inform end of life decisions as discussed in Chapters 2–4, there is a critical need for greater objectivity and transparency in decision making – given that it is life or death at stake.

The penultimate chapter of this book argues for the allocation of limited healthcare resources to be an overarching consideration in decision making primarily for infants born extremely premature (at the edge of viability) or suffering severe impairment. However, before turning to Chapter 6, it is valuable to consider some of the major theories of justice that are most acutely applicable to the discussion of resource allocation and severely impaired infants.

5.1 Ethical considerations in medical decision making for impaired infants

Beauchamp and Childress assert that there are four central principles in medical decision making that should be considered. They are autonomy, beneficence, non-maleficence and justice. However, as will be noted below, not all of these principles are applicable to impaired infants.

Autonomy

It will be recalled from Chapter 2 that the principle of autonomy allows competent patients to make self-determinations regarding treatment decisions based on free will and choice. This principle cannot apply to infants as they cannot express their autonomy or free will. Thus, treatment decisions are made overwhelmingly by virtue of a collaborative effort between treating doctors and parents. As seen in the previous chapters, there are situations in which doctors and parents disagree on treatment decisions and legal intervention for a final determination.

Beneficence

The principle of beneficence relates to a duty or responsibility to 'do good' for the patient. In familiar medical law parlance, this relates to acting in the patient's best interests. Again, as noted in Chapter 2, acting in the best interests of premature and impaired infants is ethically challenging. In circumstances in which the infant is extremely premature or severely impaired, decisions to withdraw or withhold life-sustaining treatment may be in the best interests of the infant, yet parents may disagree with this medical advice or opinion. It has been previously highlighted in this book that the very concept of 'best interests' is nebulous and is often applied arbitrarily. Further, in Chapter 4, it was noted that decisions to withdraw or withhold life-sustaining treatment are often made on the subjective beliefs and opinions of treating doctors and parents. Given infants' lack of autonomy, coupled with uncertain medical prognosis, acting in the best interests of infants is undoubtably medically and ethically complex and can come into conflict with the following principle.

Non-maleficence

The principle of non-maleficence is a duty 'not to do harm'. In Chapter 2, this was discussed in the context of the Hippocratic Oath and the modern-day Declaration of Geneva that is taken by medical practitioners in relation to their obligations towards their patients. Further, in Chapter 2, legal judgments from the UK highlighted the principle of non-maleficence by virtue of medical practitioners and judges balancing the burdens against the benefits of withdrawal or withholding of treatment. Chapter 2 also observed that weighing the burdens and benefits of treatment so as to 'not do harm' alongside acting in the best interests of the impaired infant so as to 'do good' are often conflicting principles. Additionally, as seen in Chapter 3, providing aggressive treatment to save impaired infants from death by 'doing good' can leave infants with severe lifelong debilitating impairment and disability – causing more harm than good.[1]

Justice (distributive)

The final principle that Beauchamp and Childress highlight is that of justice in healthcare. It is this principle that this chapter focuses on. The authors posit that

---

1 See, further, Ernlé W D Young and David K Stevenson, 'Limiting Treatment for Extremely Premature Low-birth-weight Infants (500 to 750 g)' (1990) 144(5) *American Journal of Diseases of Children* 549, 549. This is discussed in greater detail in Chapter 6.

the terms 'fairness', 'desert' (what is deserved) and 'entitlement' have all been used by philosophers as a basis on which to explicate the term 'justice'. These accounts interpret justice as fair, equitable, and appropriate treatment in light of what is due or owed to persons.[2] However, in reality, it is very rare for patients to have equal access to healthcare and medical treatments on the basis of entitlement or merit.

The principle of distributive justice has a long history. Roemer asserts: 'how a society or group should allocate its scarce resources or product among individuals with competing needs or claims goes back at least two millennia. Aristotle and Plato wrote on the question.'[3] Given the ageing populations in the UK and Australia, rapid advancements in technology and limited healthcare budgets, there is an increasing ethical discourse on the application and relationship between principles of justice and the allocation and distribution of finite resources.

Theories of justice and the distribution of finite healthcare recourses are of particular importance when assessing treatment decisions for extremely premature (born at 23 weeks' gestation) and subsequently severely impaired infants.[4] Can society justify expending hundreds of thousands pounds or dollars of limited public healthcare funds on providing medical treatment and care to infants who in many cases will not survive or will suffer severe disability? Those finite health resources, as a result, are not available to other patients – in particular, not available to infants born at a later gestation and likely to both survive and flourish. In order to determine efficient strategies for the allocation of limited healthcare resources, in 'practice' it may be valuable to seek some direction against the backdrop of ethical 'theories' of distributive justice.

5.2 Theories of distributive justice: extremely premature and critically impaired infants and resource allocation

Moral theories of justice have been have been critiqued and employed for hundreds of years to assist in answering some of society's most vexing issues ranging from punishment and sentencing to education and healthcare.[5] Bagaric and Dimopolous assert: 'morality is not concerned with trivialities . . . it [moral principle] relates to situations where there is an actual or potential conflict of

---

2 Tom L Beauchamp and James F Childress, *Principles of Biomedical Ethics* (Oxford University Press, 7th edn, 2008) 250.

3 John E Roemer, *Theories of Distributive Justice* (Harvard University Press, 1996) 1.

4 Barnum refers to the term 'benevolent injustice' occurring when extremely premature infants are saved from death in the neonatal intensive care unit (NICU) by medical technologies, but are left 'both medically fragile and medically dependent, and many of them are required to live in a medical facility'. Thus, aggressive treatments to save them from death may have negative and detrimental consequences. See, further, Brenda Barnum, 'Benevolent Injustice: A Neonatal Dilemma' (2009) 9(3) *Advances in Neonatal Care* 132, 133. This is discussed in detail in Chapter 6.

5 For a discussion of moral theories of justice and punishment and sentencing, see Mirko Bagaric, *Punishment and Sentencing: A Rational Approach* (Cavendish Publishing, 2001).

interest between two or more parties – it assess and weighs the respective interests.' The authors make a compelling point, that 'in a perfect world, consisting of unlimited resources and no possibility of clashes of interests, morality would be redundant'.[6]

The two main moral theories that pull in opposite directions the most are those based on 'duties' and 'consequences'.[7] As Jackson notes, "teleological" (from the Greek *telos*: consequences) theories judge the rightness or wrongness of an action in terms of consequences'[8]. Their counterparts are 'deontological' (from the Greek *deontos*: duty) theories, which, in contrast, 'insist that the intrinsic rightness or wrongness of an action does not depend on its consequences, but rather on whether it is consistent with certain basic moral principles'.[9] This chapter now turns to consider some of these theories and their application in relation to infants.

Consequentialist theory: utilitarianism and extremely premature and critically impaired infants

The most well-recognised and discussed consequentialist (teleological) theory is utilitarianism. This theory, founded by the works of Jeremy Bentham and later John Stuart Mill in the eighteenth and nineteenth centuries, is concerned with moral behaviour that promotes the good and minimises harm.[10] In its simplest form utilitarianism concerns the 'greatest good to the greatest number'. Thus, 'a utilitarian is interested only in the consequences of an action, not whether it is intrinsically either right or wrong'.[11]

Utilitarianism is based on achieving the maximum good. This theory fits most squarely with the contention of this book that the allocation of finite public resources should be a critical consideration in end of life decisions for extremely premature and critically impaired infants. Applying utilitarianism in its crudest form – seeking to 'maximise public utility in the search for the greatest benefit to society'[12] – saving infants born at the edge of viability (23 weeks) and critically impaired infants does not produce the 'greatest benefit' to society from a resource allocation perspective at least.

---

6 Mirko Bagaric and Penny Dimopoulos 'Legal Ethics is (Just) Normal Ethics: Towards a Coherent System of Legal Ethics' (2003) 3(2) *Queensland University Technology Law and Justice Journal* 367, 374–375.

7 Consequentialism and deontology generally fall under the category of normative ethics. They concern developing rules for human conduct as 'norms'. The central questions that surround normative ethics are based on how things should or ought to be done, whether they are good or bad, right or wrong and the value that is placed on things.

8 Emily Jackson, *Medical Law: Text, Cases and Materials* (Oxford University Press, 2006) 11.

9 Ibid.

10 Utilitarianism can be traced back to the Greek philosopher Epicurus of the Hellenistic period. See, further, John Stuart Mill, *Utilitarianism* (Oxford University Press, 1998).

11 Jackson, above, n 8, 11.

12 Capp et al., 'Exploring Distributive Justice in Health Care' (2001) 24(2) *Australian Health Review* 40, 41. See, also, S R Leeder, 'All for One or One for All? The Ethics of Resource Allocation for Health Care' (1987) 147(2) *Medical Journal of Australia* 68–71.

As will be discussed in greater detail in Chapter 6, treating extremely premature and critically impaired infants in the neonatal intensive care unit (NICU) is expensive and consumes large portions of limited healthcare funds. This limits those resources from being spent on other patients. Young and Stevenson state: 'expending an amount of up to half million dollars or more on someone whose survival is moot and whose level of functioning, should he or she survive, will be questionable may have been done an injustice to others who will have been deprived of help by these expenditures.'[13]

It is important to note that this book does not argue for finite healthcare resources not be available to premature or impaired infants per se. In fact, it is posited that resources should be provided to infants born at a later gestational period who are likely to have a greater chance of survival (mortality) with a lesser chance of severe disability/impairment (morbidity).[14]

Several critics have discussed the flaws of utilitarianism.[15] Eminent professor John Harris has argued that utilitarianism in healthcare is a form of '*de facto* discrimination' against marginal groups of people who require healthcare;[16] further, it results in those who are in the most acute need of healthcare being denied.[17] In response to Harris' work published in *Bioethics*,[18] ethicist Savulescu argues against Harris' suggestion that 'Doctors should give up prioritising patients according to prognosis'.[19]

In a utopian world, in which healthcare resources were limitless, as Bagaric and Dimopolous asserted earlier, there would be no room for moral principles or theory. Each patient would be provided with optimum healthcare, regardless of prognoses or health benefits. However, we live in a world in which this ideal will unfortunately never become a reality. While utilitarian theory is not without its moral and ethical challenges, primarily due to it championing overall maximisation and social utility, it is particularly at odds with disproportionate individual rights to healthcare. Utilitarianism supports the economic tool of cost–benefit analysis and the allocation of finite healthcare resources.[20] Individual rights theory (in its simplest form) and a cost–benefit analysis in a time of resource allocation would probably fall short on the premise that each patient has a boundless right to healthcare (regardless of the benefit that it would bestow). This is unlikely to occur when applying a utilitarian theory.

---

13 Young and Stevenson, above, n 1, 549.
14 Reference would need to be made here as to the gestational age at which infants are most likely to survive and with fewer impairments. This would require clinical judgement and research such as that discussed in Chapter 3.
15 See, further, John Rawls, *A Theory of Justice* (Oxford University Press, 1972); A Sen and B Williams, *Utilitarianism and Beyond* (Cambridge University Press, 1982) 4–5.
16 John Harris, 'Justice and Equal Opportunities in Health Care' (1999) 13(5) *Bioethics* 392, 393.
17 See, further, Julian Savulescu, 'Consequentialism, Reasons, Value and Justice' (1998) 12(3) *Bioethics* 212–235.
18 John Harris, What is the Good of Health Care?' (1996) 10(4) *Bioethics* 269–291.
19 Savulescu, above, n 17, 235
20 Beauchamp and Childress, above, n 2, 255.

This book acknowledges that there are flaws in a strict utilitarian approach to healthcare. However utilitarianism – 'the greatest good for the greatest number' – lends currency to the argument that the allocation of limited resources should be an important factor in end of life decision making for extremely premature and critically impaired infants. As Traci et al. note, 'the decision to resuscitate an extremely premature infant may not only have a long-term impact on the infant and family but society as a whole'.[21] Further, it may 'devastate the financial situation of families and place a significant burden on the national health care cost'.[22] This is discussed in greater detail in Chapter 6, but, for now, the discussion turns to a deontological theory of distributive justice and its application to extremely premature and infant infants.

Deontology: rights theory and extremely premature and critically impaired infants

Ostensibly, at least, the application of utilitarian theory in healthcare suggests that limited healthcare funds would be most beneficially utilised in improving the health of patients who will enjoy the maximum benefit. Thus, rather than expending large portions of the healthcare budget on one patient such as an infant born at 23 weeks, the same resources could potentially save and improve the lives of several patients. Extending this point, limited funds could be utilised to save the lives of patients who will potentially make a significant recovery and hopefully become taxpayers and pay back into the healthcare budget.[23] While utilitarian theory focuses on the 'greatest good for the greatest number', rights theory places emphasis on the individual and personal rights.

Natural rights theory asserts that humans have absolute natural rights that are not dependent on beliefs or actions.[24] In current-day parlance, this is understood as human rights.

There has been increasing awareness and popularity of a 'rights culture' post-Second World War, with several global declarations and conventions determining which rights are to be protected and championed.[25] Fundamental human rights include the right to life, the right to liberty and security and the right to a fair

---

21 Traci et al., 'Decisions and Dilemmas Related to Resuscitation of Infants born on the Verge of Viability' (2012) 12(1) *Newborn and Infant Nursing Reviews* 27, 28.
22 Ibid.
23 This touches on social utilitarianism and is discussed in Chapter 6.
24 See works by influential philosopher and founding father of classical liberalism, John Locke. Locke rejected the notion of the divine rights of kings, and supported the idea of natural rights. John Locke's two treatises of government supported the claim that 'men are by nature free and equal against claims that God had made all people naturally subject to a monarch'. See John Locke, *Works*, 10 vols. London, 1823 reprinted (Scientia Verlag, 1963). See, also, *Stanford Encyclopedia of Philosophy*. http://plato.stanford.edu/entries/locke-political
25 Some examples include the *Universal Declaration of Human Rights* (1948), *European Convention on Human Rights* (1953) and *Human Rights Act* (1998) (UK).
26 *European Convention on Human Rights* (1953), Article 2 – right to life, Article 5 – right to liberty and security and Article 6 – right to fair trial.

trial.[26] Over time and with the evolution of social mores and values, claims have been advanced by individuals to extend the scope of basic human rights to include opposing rights. As was highlighted in Chapter 2, advocates for voluntary euthanasia actively campaign for the right to die in many countries in which it remains illegal.[27]

Article 2 of the Human Rights Act in the UK provides that 'everyone's right to life shall be protected by law'. However, does that 'right to life' also afford a right to unlimited healthcare resources to preserve life? This question has also been given some academic thought by Daniels, as he points out in his influential book *Just Health Care*: 'faced with significant inequalities in the distribution of health-care services, many start by invoking the notion of individual rights and assert that a violation of basic rights is involved.'[28] If distributive justice were strictly applied through a 'rights' lens, then all infants should be treated equally. Each infant, regardless of extreme prematurity or impairment, should be afforded a right to life and a right to resources. Despite Article 2 of the Human Rights Act (UK) and other international declarations protecting the 'right to life', the right is not absolute and does not extend to encompass *any* means of protecting it, such as a claim to unlimited healthcare resources.

Charles Foster provides some compelling insight from a case judgment in which the judge asserted that the right to life under Article 2 'must be inter-preted in a way which does not impose an impossible or disproportionate burden on the authorities'.[29] Further, Foster highlights that the House of Lords candidly articulated that the allocation of healthcare resources is not an absolute right, stating:

> Human rights are the rights essential to the life and dignity of the individual in a democratic society . . . however, they [human rights] do not include the right to a fair distribution of resources or fair treatment in economic terms – in other words, distributive justice. Of course distributive justice is a good thing, but it is not a fundamental human right.[30]

27 More recently, a landmark ruling in Belgium has allowed a man convicted of rape and murder, and sentenced to life imprisonment without ever being released, the right to die. This is the first case in which a prisoner has been granted the right to end his life due to 'unbearable psychological suffering' in prison. See, further, Charlotte McDonald-Gibson 'Murderer and Rapist Frank Van Den Bleeken granted Right to Euthanasia rather the "Unbearable Suffering" of Life in Prison', *Independent* (Online), Tuesday 16 September 2014. www.independent.co.uk/news/world/europe/murderer-granted-right-to-euthanasia-rather-than-rot-in-belgian-prison-9736508.html. See, also, the case of Nathan Verheist who was granted the right to die after several failed sex change operations on similar grounds of 'unbearable psychological suffering'. See Tom Mendelsohn, 'Belgian Man dies by Euthanasia after Failed Sex Change Operation' *Independent* (Online), Tuesday 1 September 2013. www.independent.co.uk/news/world/europe/belgian-man-dies-by-euthanasia-after-failed-sex-change-operation-8851872.html
28 Norman Daniels, *Just Health Care* (Cambridge University Press, 1985) 4.
29 Charles Foster, 'Simple Rationality? The Law of Healthcare Resource Allocation in England' (2007) 33(7) *Journal of Medical Ethics* 404, 405. Case quoted: *Osman v United Kingdom* [1998] 29 EHRR 245 [116].
30 Ibid. Case quoted: *Matthews v Ministry of Defence* [2003] 1 AC 1163, Per Lord Hoffman at [26].

In contrast to utilitarianism, rights-based theories generally do not have an aspect of distributive justice. Rights theories take the view that rights are individualistic and one's person's interests should not be diminished for the good of others or for the whole. However, as discussed earlier in this chapter, the world in which we live does not enjoy limitless healthcare funds. As Foster states, 'an individual patient does not have an enforceable right to put their own hand into the public purse and take out what they happen to need'.[31] While 'rights' theories place paramount importance on individual rights, egalitarian theory promotes equality in services and goods.

Egalitarian theory and extremely premature and critically impaired infants

The discussion earlier has surrounded individual rights; egalitarianism in its simplest form, by way of contrast, asserts that 'every person should have an equal share of services and goods'. Further, it contends that 'people are morally equal and that equality in material goods and services is the best way to give effect to this moral ideal'.[32] Egalitarian theorist Rawls argued that 'each person be permitted the maximum amount of basic liberty compatible with a similar measure of liberty for others'.[33] Thus, 'all humans must be treated as equals because they are created as equals and have equal moral status'.[34] While strict egalitarianism avoids some of the problems associated with a strict utilitarian approach, it comes into conflict with other moral theories that propose that justice should be distributed on the basis of what individuals deserve.[35]

Moreover, this moral theory of distributive justice is significantly problematic in its application to resource allocation. Capp et al. support this view, stating that 'the objective of seeking a fair opportunity to access health care implies an ability of the system to provide such a service and this will not always be possible'.[36] This is virtually impossible in current-day access to healthcare services.

Arguably, at present extremely premature and critically impaired infants are consuming a disproportionate amount of finite resources. This deprives other patients (including other infants) of a fair share of services and opportunity.[37] The

---

31 Foster, above, n 29, 406.
32 Stanford Encyclopedia of philosophy. See, further, plato.stanford.edu/entries/justice-distributive/#Scope
33 Rawls, *A Theory of Justice* (Harvard University Press, 1971)
34 Beauchamp and Childress, above, n 2, 256.
35 This is known as 'desert-based' principles. Locke was an advocator of this theory in that 'those who labour most (or hardest, or most thoughtfully etc.) deserve the most return.' See, further, A John Simmons, *The Lockean Theory of Rights* (Princeton University Press, 1992) 247.
36 Capp et al., 'Exploring Distributive Justice in Health Care' (2001) 24(1) *Australian Health Review* 40, 43.
37 Influential Harvard philosopher and theorist Norman Daniels has extended Rawls's theory to healthcare, asserting that 'health care needs are special and that fair opportunity is central to any acceptable theory of justice'. In his most influential work with James Sabin, Daniels developed a procedural theory of 'reasonableness of accountability'. Daniels' theory rests on a fair process in

needs of extremely premature and critically impaired infants seemingly trump the needs of other patients. This is of particular significance in that, overwhelmingly, infants born at 23 weeks are provided with extensive and costly healthcare in spite of their poor medical prognosis – ranking very low in terms of mortality and morbidity. This does not sit comfortably within a distributive justice setting.

5.3 Three theories, one conclusion: resource allocation should be a cardinal consideration in end of life decision making for extremely premature and critically impaired infants

Major theories of justice are generally consistent with a distributive justice approach to the allocation of important and finite resources. However, distributive justice itself is an imprecise concept. As this chapter has illustrated, each theory of justice (this chapter has only considered three out of several subgroups of theories within a theory) is based on the interpretation of each moral theorist/ theory and the ideals that underpin that theory. No single theory is sufficient or constructive for the purposes of healthcare.

Each theory has its limitations and impracticalities in its application to the distribution of justice in healthcare today. In light of this, 'if it is uncertain or indeterminate how a particular distributive principle might in practice apply to the ordering of real societies, then this principle is not yet a serious candidate for our consideration'.[38] For example, simple utilitarianism proposes distributive justice based on its founding principles of the greatest good for the greatest number. However, its strict application in real societies would be confronted with significant opposition from minority groups. Further, it would come into direct conflict with notions of individualistic rights and equal access to services and opportunities.

While rights concepts and egalitarian theory is probably conceptually conceivable as a means of distribution of justice, in reality it is implausible in relation to the allocation of finite resources such as healthcare. Ultimately, the finite number of resources commands that it is untenable to totally observe one person's rights if there is not enough to go around for others. Thus, pragmatically, even rights theorists must at some point accept that the rights of others command some degree of sharing resources.

Ultimately, distributive justice theories have to be practical and workable to be effectively and efficiently incorporated into government policy and wider society. As such, 'principles [of justice] are to be implemented in real societies with the problems and constraints inherent in such application'.[39]

---

meeting health needs by means of transparency and appeals processes in healthcare rationing decisions. See, especially, Norman Daniels and James E Sabine, *Setting Limits Fairly: Can we Learn to Share Medical Resources?* (Oxford University Press, 2002) 43–66.

38 Above, n 34.
39 Ibid.

That being said, in any version, distributive justice does minimally entail that decisions regarding the allocation of cardinal benefits and burdens in the form of medical resources should be driven at least largely by treating all people equally (recognising that allocating medical resources to one person means the reduced capacity to do so to another person) and ensuring the maximum benefit from such allocations. In the following chapter, this is discussed at greater length.

In reality, none of the theories of justice or morality applied exclusively provides clear and concrete answers to the dilemmas raised in this book. However, it is evident that, at a broad level of generality, the theories converge to the conclusion that the allocation of finite healthcare resources must be an important factor to be taken into account for treatment decisions for extremely premature and critically impaired infants.

5.4 Conclusion

Questions about how limited healthcare resources are distributed is an ever-increasing area of discourse. Perhaps discussing the allocation of limited healthcare resources behind a shield of distributive justice theories is less confronting or controversial than seeking to implement real procedures or drive political discussion on this issue.

Ageing populations in the UK and Australia mean that there is a greater demand on healthcare resources. Additionally, with rapid advancements of technology and medical science, infants born extremely premature who once would have died or be considered a miscarriage are now surviving. However, as noted in Chapter 3 and will be noted again in Chapter 6, although infants at this precarious stage of life can potentially be saved from death, very often they cannot be saved from a life with severe disability. This raises concerns about the short-term and long-term cost of care and medical treatment required by these infants to their families and to wider society.

This chapter has explored selected theories of distributive justice and their application to the issue of resource allocation in healthcare. It was concluded that no single theory is plausible given the constraints of society today. However, the commonality in the discussion of the selected theories of justice is that they all lead to the conclusion that resource allocation is an important factor that should inform discussion in end of life decision making for extremely premature and critically impaired infants. The following chapter discusses this at greater length.

5.5 References

Bagaric, Mirko, *Punishment and Sentencing: A Rational Approach* (Cavendish Publishing, 2001).

Bagaric, Mirko and Penny Dimopoulos, 'Legal Ethics is (Just) Normal Ethics: Towards a Coherent System of Legal Ethics' (2003) 3(2) *Queensland University Technology Law and Justice Journal* 367.

Barnum, Brenda, 'Benevolent Injustice: A Neonatal Dilemma' (2009) 9(3) *Advances in Neonatal Care* 132.

Beauchamp, Tom L and James F Childress, *Principles of Biomedical Ethics* (Oxford University Press, 7th edn, 2008).

Capp, S, S Savage and V Clarke, 'Exploring Distributive Justice in Health Care' (2001) 24(1) *Australian Health Review* 40.

Daniels, Norman, *Just Health Care* (Cambridge University Press, 1985).

Daniels, Norman and James E Sabine, *Setting Limits Fairly: Can We Learn to Share Medical Resources?* (Oxford University Press, 2002).

European Convention on Human Rights (1953).

Foster, Charles, 'Simple Rationality? The Law of Healthcare Resource Allocation in England' (2007) 33(7) *Journal of Medical Ethics* 404.

Harris, John, 'Justice and Equal Opportunities in Health Care' (1999) 13(5) *Bioethics* 392.

Harris, John, What is the Good of Health Care?' (1996) 10(4) *Bioethics* 269.

Human Rights Act (1998) (UK).

Jackson, Emily, *Medical Law: Text, Cases and Materials* (Oxford University Press, 2006).

Leeder, S R, 'All for One or One for All? The Ethics of Resource Allocation for Health Care' (1987) 147(2) *Medical Journal of Australia* 68.

Locke John, *Works*, 10 vols. London, 1823 reprinted (Scientia Verlag, 1963). Stanford Encyclopedia of Philosophy. http://plato.stanford.edu/entries/locke-political

Matthews v Ministry of Defence [2003] 1 AC 1163.

McDonald-Gibson, Charlotte, 'Murderer and Rapist Frank Van Den Bleeken granted Right to Euthanasia rather the 'Unbearable Suffering' of Life in Prison', *Independent* (Online), Tuesday 16 September 2014. www.independent.co.uk/news/world/europe/murderer-granted-right-to-euthanasia-rather-than-rot-in-belgian-prison-9736508.html

Mendelsohn, Tom, 'Belgian Man dies by Euthanasia after failed Sex Change Operation' *Independent* (Online), Tuesday 1 September 2013. www.independent.co.uk/news/world/europe/belgian-man-dies-by-euthanasia-after-failed-sex-change-operation-8851872.html

Mill, John Stuart, *Utilitarianism* (Oxford University Press, 1998).

Osman v United Kingdom [1998] 29 EHRR 245.

Powell, Traci L, Leslie Parker, Cynthia F Dedrick, Christina M Barrera, Dawn Di Salvo, Felicia Erdman et al., 'Decisions and Dilemmas related to Resuscitation of Infants born on the Verge of Viability' (2012) 12(1) *Newborn and Infant Nursing Reviews* 27.

Rawls, John, *A Theory of Justice* (Oxford University Press, 1972).

Roemer, John E, *Theories of Distributive Justice* (Harvard University Press, 1996).

Savulescu, Julian, 'Consequentialism, Reasons, Value and Justice' (1998) 12(3) *Bioethics* 212.

Sen, A and B Williams, *Utilitarianism and Beyond* (Cambridge University Press, 1982).

Simmons, A John, *The Lockean Theory of Rights* (Princeton University Press, 1992).

Universal Declaration of Human Rights (1948).

Young, Ernlé W D and David K Stevenson, 'Limiting Treatment for Extremely Premature Low-birth-weight Infants (500 to 750 g)' (1990) 144(5) *American Journal of Diseases of Children* 549.

6 Resource allocation: an objective approach in end of life decision making for extremely premature and critically impaired infants

The previous chapter examined the application of theories of distributive justice to critically impaired and extremely premature infants. Chapter 5 concluded that while none of the theories of distributive justice discussed was independently plausible, they all lead to the same conclusion: that resource allocation should be a cardinal consideration in end of life decision making for extremely premature and critically impaired infants, thus injecting greater objectivity and a more rational approach to decision making.

As the previous chapters of this book have established, end of life decision making for premature and impaired infants is subjective and decisions are made arbitrarily. Key determinations in decisions to withdraw or withhold life-sustaining treatment have been found to be nebulous and often subject to the decision makers beliefs or opinions.

This penultimate chapter focuses on the costs associated with keeping extremely premature and consequently severely disabled or critically impaired infants alive. What is the cost to society and to families of keeping this group of infants alive? Are desirable outcomes being achieved by keeping them alive – especially in those cases in which the infant's life is likely to be very limited and of poor quality?

This book contends that, given the considerable amount of subjectivity, the allocation of limited healthcare resources should be a cardinal consideration in decisions to withdraw or withhold life-sustaining treatment from extremely premature and critically impaired infants, thus injecting objectivity to the decision-making process.

Additionally, the main focus of this book is end of life decision making and resource allocation in the UK and Australia. However, although the US model of healthcare is a more privatised healthcare system, there is much literature and focus on how healthcare dollars are spent most efficiently. Given this scrutiny and critique, for the purposes of this chapter in particular, some insights from the United States are valuable.

Any discussion of the healthcare required to sustain extremely premature and critically impaired infants would be incomplete without a full discussion of the associated resource costs. Resource allocation might be considered as the true objective standard in this area, the consideration of which would reduce much of the subjectivity and emotion that currently informs decision making, allowing for a more pragmatic approach. This chapter begins by discussing some of the key concepts that underpin current approaches to health economics.

The allocation of finite healthcare resources has been a topical issue in academic and professional spheres for several decades.[1] It is unsurprising that discussions that centre on the cost of treatment versus the benefit conferred to a patient are thorny in nature and are treated with a considerable degree of sensitivity. This is understandable, as such discussions are ostensibly of paramount human interest – of life and death.

Advances in technology and medical science have contributed to an ageing population, which, in developed nations at least, has placed a significant strain on limited healthcare resources.[2] However, no country, regardless of its economic position, has an infinite healthcare budget, with the result that, inevitably, increasing demands for health resources cannot be met.

Additionally, ageing populations contribute to a shrinking tax base, where a greater reliance on welfare and healthcare budgets exacerbates the issue of limited supply. Rapid advancements in healthcare and associated technologies, together with an ageing population, have engendered a renewed interest in health economics, from academic and administrative viewpoints. Ironically, in developed economies, these same advancements in technology have enabled the ageing of the population. When considered in terms of current and projected demographics, ageing populations over time will have greater demand for and also make more frequent use of health services.

6.1 Cost versus benefit

With increasing demands for, and limited supply of, health resources, it is unsurprising that health economics is a rapidly growing field.[3] Culyer has defined health economics as follows:

> [T]he application of the discipline and tools of economics to the subject matter of health, accordingly encompasses the full range of two-way causal relationships between the health status of individuals and groups and their economic activities – production, distribution and exchange.[4]

---

1 Professor Gavin H Mooney is considered to be one of the founding fathers of health economics. Professor Mooney's research provides seminal work in this area. For an introduction to economics from a UK healthcare perspective, see, further, Gavin Mooney, *Economics, Medicine and Health Care* (Humanities Press, 1986). See, also, the influential text by Gavin H Mooney, *The Valuation of Human Life* (Macmillan, 1977).

2 Christensen et al., 'Ageing Populations: The Challenges Ahead' (2009) 374(9696) *The Lancet* 1196–1208. For discussion on an ageing population, see Clark et al., *The Economics of an Ageing Society* (Blackwell Malden, 2004).

3 For a discussion on the theory of supply and demand in relation to health economics, see, generally, Gavin Mooney, 'Health Economics and Health Policy' in Gavin Mooney and Richard Scotton (eds), *Economics and Australian Health Policy* (Allen & Unwin, 1998) 1–13.

4 Quoted in Robert Evans, *Strained Mercy: The Economics of Canadian Health Care* (Butterworths, 1984) 3.

More than two decades ago Klein discussed health economics with reference to the National Health Service in the UK:

> As more emphasis is placed on market transactions so the demand for economic analysis will grow . . . hence the importance of looking critically at the discipline and its claim to use rational techniques of analysis to resolve complex problems of decision making in the NHS.[5]

The foremost applied methods of measuring the economic value of healthcare can be principally distilled to cost-effectiveness or cost-utility.[6] Broadly, this is a cost–benefit equation, where the costs of health treatments are measured against the benefits they are likely to confer on the patient.

Commentators have used this methodology in their critical analysis of the cost of resourcing the neonatal intensive care unit (NICU). By way of example, Zupancic et al. found that 'the incremental direct medical cost of low birth weight in the first year of life in the United States exceeded $4 billion in 1988'.[7] Other commentators estimated the direct cost of NICUs in the United States in 2004 to be closer to $21 billion.[8]

In Australia, Campbell noted:

> The typical (only initial hospitalisation after birth) costs for early birth weight babies in intensive care units are around $A 1,000 per day, and average hospitalisation costs around $A 50,000–$A 80,000 per baby. The earlier the gestation, the higher the cost. To achieve a survivor at 24 weeks in our region costs around $A 300,000.[9]

When critically evaluating the 'cost versus benefit' of treatment in terms of survival and chances to thrive, the returns are relatively diminutive in comparison with the substantial sums spent on keeping extremely premature and critically impaired infants alive. Campbell further indicated:

> Care is nowadays offered at 23 weeks' gestation, when the chances of survival are less than 10%, the chances of serious handicap in survivors around 30% and the cost for each survivor between $300,000–$400,000 . . . do caregivers

5 Rudolf Klein, 'The Role of Health Economics' (1989) 299(6694) *British Medical Journal* 275, 275.
6 This is often referred to as cost-utility analysis (CUA). Erik Nord et al., 'Maximizing Health Benefits vs Egalitarianism: An Australian Survey of Health Issues' (1995) 41(10) *Social Science & Medicine* 1429, 1429.
7 Zupancic et al., 'Economics of Prematurity in the Era of Managed Care' (2000) 27(2) *Clinics in Perinatology* 483, 483.
8 John D Lantos and William L Meadow, *Neonatal Bioethics: The Moral Challenges of Medical Innovation* (Johns Hopkins University Press, 2006) 124.
9 Neil Campbell, 'When Care Cannot Cure: Medical Problems in Seriously Ill Babies' in Helga Kuhse and Peter Singer (eds), *Bioethics: An Anthology* (Blackwell Publishing, 2nd edn, 2006) 303, 307.

really have a mandate from their society to use such large resources when returns are so poor?[10]

In his book *Too Expensive to Treat? Finitude, Tragedy and the Neonatal ICU*, Charles Camosy provides a novel and insightful Catholic social theory perspective on resource allocation and impaired infants in the US. Camosy argues that it should be illegal to use limited resources on severely impaired infants who will not benefit from treatment.[11] He asserts: 'Millions of dollars are spent each year in the NICU on babies who cannot possibly benefit from the treatment.'[12] He goes on to state: 'The fact that we send these kinds of resources right down the drain, especially in light of our health care crisis, is totally unacceptable and ought to be prohibited regardless of the source: Medicaid, private insurance and even cash.'[13]

More than 20 years ago, in a study conducted at Flinders Medical Centre in Adelaide, Australia, Marshall et al. highlighted the expense involved in keeping infants alive. Concluding in September 1984, the study illustrated the specific costs incurred, including the largest cost to any hospital – that of staffing.[14] While medical staff represented a significant cost, many other elements also required consideration. These included 'consumable, recyclable and ancillary services', such as sterile linen, hospital porters and radiology, all of which are required daily or several times a week.[15] In 1984 the figure arrived at by Marshall et al. was $A690 per day, including all services required for a high-dependency infant.

Presumably, to arrive at a present-day estimate, these costs would have to be doubled or tripled, simply to adjust for inflation. This is without any consideration of capital expenditure costs and the increased costs of modern-day technology, which would far outstrip any technology expenditure in 1984.[16] Bennett advances this argument, stating: 'Advances in medical technology have also placed

---

10　Ibid 303.
11　In his book, Camosy lists conditions such as anencephaly/acrania, kidney disease and inoperable heart anomalies among others as those being conditions for which an infant cannot receive any benefit. See, especially, Charles C Camosy, *Too Expensive to Treat? Finitude, Tragedy, and the Neonatal ICU* (Wm. Beerdmans Publishing Co., 2010).
12　Ibid 176.
13　Ibid.
14　Marshall et al., 'The Cost of Intensive and Special Care of the Newborn' (1989) 150(10) *Medical Journal of Australia*, 568, 569. For a general discussion about the healthcare system in Australia, see Michelle Foster and Jennifer Fleming, 'The Health Care System in Australia', in Sandra Taylor, Michelle Foster and Jennifer Fleming (eds), *Health Care Practice in Australia: Policy, Context and Innovations* (Oxford University Press, 2008) 46–73.
15　Marshall et al., above, n 14, 572.
16　The New South Wales Australia Legislative Assembly noted that in 2004 the average daily cost of NICU per 23 week gestation infant was, on average, $A1,200. In today's dollars with adjustments for inflation, the figure is approximately $A1,537, an increase of 28%. See, especially, www.parliament.nsw.gov.au/prod/parlment/hansart.nsf/V3Key/LA20040914022. Muraskas noted in 2008 that in the United States the daily cost for neonatal intensive care was in excess of $3,500 per infant. In today's dollars with adjustments for inflation, the figure is approximately $3,853. See, further, Jonathan Muraskas and Kayhan Parsi, 'The Cost of Saving the Tiniest Lives: NICUs versus Prevention' (2008) 10(10) *Virtual Mentor* 655–658.

additional burdens on health care resources, with the development of more expensive items of medical equipment or forms of medical treatment.'[17]

It is important to note that the figures discussed thus far relate only to staffing, accommodation, medicine and equipment costs within an NICU. They do not include the follow-up healthcare and services required post-discharge from NICU.[18] Calculating direct running costs of a NICU provides an overview of the expenditure that hospitals incur. However, this will vary by hospital and country. Further, such calculations are invariably under-estimations and contingent on other fluctuating factors. These other costs and expenditures will be examined later in this chapter. For now, the discussion turns to explore a popular tool used to measure cost utilisation in healthcare – the quality adjusted life years (QALY) measure.

6.2 Quality adjusted life years (QALY)

A prevalent tool applied in health economics to measure cost-utilisation in healthcare is quality adjusted life years, commonly referred to as QALY. This yardstick combines economics and philosophy in measuring the cost of healthcare against the benefits of such healthcare.[19] Williams' seminal work provides a definition of a QALY as:

> The essence of a QALY is that it takes a year of healthy life expectancy to be worth 1, but regards a year of unhealthy life expectancy as worth less than 1. Its precise value is lower, the worse the quality of life of the unhealthy person.[20]

Therefore, the general premise of QALY is that each year that can be lived in good health is of a higher value than each year that is lived in poor health. Adjustments to the measure are made accordingly. In economic terms, the lower the cost of obtaining positive full health years, the more cost-efficient the treatment is and the greater the priority to provide healthcare. The main objective of health

---

17 Belinda Bennett, 'Resource Allocation and the Beginning of Life' (1993) 9(Spring) *Journal of Contemporary Health Law & Policy* 77, 78.
18 Staffing is the highest cost, including nurses, doctors, social workers and therapists. See, also, Zupancic et al., above, n 7, 483–497.
19 Another leading professor in the field of health economics is Professor George Torrance, of McMaster University. His extensive research in the economics of healthcare includes the application of health economics to the area of neonatal intensive care. See. especially, Boyle et al., 'Economic Evaluation of Neonatal Intensive Care of Very-Low-Birth-Weight Infants' (1983) 308(22) *New England Journal of Medicine* 1330–1337. For a discussion and evaluation of quality adjusted life years, see, e.g., George W Torrance and David Feeny, 'Utilities and Quality-adjusted Life Years' (1989) 5(4) *International Journal of Technology Assessment in Health Care* 559–575; George Torrance, 'Measuring Utilities for Health States', in Sean McHugh and Michael T Vallis (eds), *Illness Behavior* (Springer, 1987) 365–376.
20 Tony Hope, Julian Savulescu and Judith Hendrick, *Medical Ethics and Law: The Core Curriculum* (Churchill Livingstone Elsevier, 2nd edn, 2008) 202.

economics is to 'get the best possible value for each dollar spent'.[21] Lockwood provides a more frank definition of a QALY, asserting that it is essentially about 'trading off length of life against quality of life'.[22]

The QALY measure is not without its critics. QALYs have been condemned as being an unfit measure for calculating welfare and quality of life.[23] Arguably, calculated, measured economics is incongruent with the determination of the worth or quality of a life.[24] Ethical concerns arise, especially since life quality is a subjective question; a disability or lifestyle may be intolerable to one who has acquired it mid-life, yet may be entirely reasonable and comfortable to another who has known nothing else since birth.

Perceptions of disability and quality of life vary between abled and disabled individuals. Bennett suggests that judgments by able-bodied persons about living with a disability are due chiefly to a 'lack of understanding about the realities involved'.[25] It would be grossly incorrect to assume that those living with a disability do not lead and are not capable of leading happy and fruitful lives. This may be because they fundamentally value life in any form, or have never experienced life without disability and therefore cannot draw any type of comparison.[26] The reverse is also true, and will be explored later in this chapter. The next section of this chapter, considers the application of the QALY measure to infants.

6.3 QALY and impaired infants

At both ends of the human lifecycle, the utilisation of QALYs is subject to increased scrutiny and controversy. In measuring cost-utility for premature infants, particularly those born extremely premature, at 23 weeks, the use of QALYs becomes difficult. Extremely premature infants born at the edge of viability have a significantly higher likelihood of suffering severe disability. Thus, applying the methodology of a QALY, extremely premature infants never start life with a QALY value of 1 and are unlikely to ever reach that value. Infants born at 23 weeks are likely to have a poor quality of life, both physically and economically.

Kuhse and Singer provide a rational application of the QALY and cost–benefit analysis. They highlight that, where the chances of disability to a premature infant are low, the benefit should outweigh the cost. However, where the risk of

21 Helga Kuhse and Peter Singer, 'Age and the Allocation of Medical Resources' (1988) 13(1) *Journal of Medicine and Philosophy* 101, 102.
22 Michael Lockwood, 'Quality of Life and Resource Allocation', in Helga Kuhse and Peter Singer (eds), *Bioethics: An Anthology* (Blackwell Publishing, 2nd edn, 2006) 451, 453.
23 See, further, John Rawles, 'Castigating QALYs' (1989) 15(3) *Journal of Medical Ethics* 143–147. See, also, Gavin Mooney, 'QALYs: Are They Enough? A Health Economist's Perspective' (1989) 15(3) *Journal of Medical Ethics* 148–152.
24 See George P Smith, 'Death Be Not Proud: Medical, Ethical and Legal Dilemmas in Resource Allocation' (1987) 3 *Journal of Contemporary Health Law and Policy* 47–63. See, also, John Harris, 'QALYfying the Value of Life' (1987) 13(3) *Journal of Medical Ethics* 117–123.
25 Bennett, above, n 17, 88.
26 Norman Daniels, 'Justice, Health and Healthcare' (2001) 1(2) *American Journal of Bioethics* 2, 4.

severe disability is high and there is the chance of a second pregnancy producing a healthy and able-bodied child, then the high cost of a neonatal intensive care unit (NICU) to save the premature infant 'produces a loss rather than a gain'.[27]

The authors note that western society tends to assume that 'it is better to save the lives of the young than the old, and the younger those saved are, the better it is'.[28] Presumably, those who advocate for scarce resources to be used to save the young rather than the old apply the notion that the young have their entire lives ahead of them, that they are the future and should have the opportunity to experience life and all it has to offer. Kuhse and Singer argue against this idea that saving the very young is better than saving an adult:

> The lives of people can be seen as journeys on which they have embarked. Although people know that the final destination must be death, there are goals along the way that they are hoping to achieve before the trip is over. Adding life-years extends the journey.[29]

The authors go on to argue that foetuses and newborn infants are yet to gain the capacity to embark on life's journey:

> There is no sharp, morally significant boundary between the foetus and newborn infant. If the foetus lacks the capacity to see itself as being with a future, so presumably does the newborn infant ... being capable of seeing itself as a traveller, and capable of wanting to reach some goal, however simple that goal might be, then the journey does not begin at birth.[30]

Extending this argument, severely premature infants are unlikely to ever gain the capacity required to travel life's journey independently or to see many goals or aspirations come to fruition. The authors make a compelling point that, when having to decide whether scarce resources should be given to a newborn in an NICU or to an adult, they should go to the adult, as any improvement in health could allow that person a few more years on the long-travelled journey on which they have already embarked. This outcome is not as assured in the case of an infant in NICU. The argument put forward by Kuhse and Singer is supported by a social study conducted in Melbourne, Australia, by Nord et al. and published in the *Social Science and Medicine Journal* in 1995.[31]

In this study, a questionnaire was distributed to individuals from varying socioeconomic groups, asking respondents to consider the prioritisation of treatment and patients, taking into account factors such as age, lifestyle and

27 Kuhse and Singer, above, n 21, 112.
28 Ibid 102.
29 Ibid 106.
30 Ibid 107.
31 Nord et al., above, n 6, 1429–1437.

dependants. The third scenario posed in the questionnaire is of interest to this book.

When asked to consider which patient should receive one available organ transplant, 44.2% of respondents stated the organ should be given to 'the young child' as opposed to the 'newborn infant'.[32] The authors of the study noted that 'the common reason for opting for the young child was that the respondents assumed that the young child had a better chance of successful operation'.[33] In addition, 'the loss of a young child was thought to be more acutely felt by parents and others than that of the newborn who has not had the opportunity to touch as many lives'.[34]

This book contends that it is becoming increasingly necessary to exercise a greater level of scrutiny and to engage in a public, open and honest dialogue regarding to which patients limited financial resources should be allocated. While parents of critically impaired infants do not consider the cost of treatment for their children, as noted in Chapter 4, often demanding futile treatments based on hope, it is important for all caregivers and treatment providers to recognise and discuss these costs. Treatment for incapacitated persons, whether adults, children or infants, is costly, and the issue of resource management cannot be ignored.

Any form of medical intervention or treatment, however minor, incurs a monetary cost. The cost of different types of treatment varies and other factors must also be considered – for instance, length of hospital stay, medication, surgery and rehabilitation.[35] Each patient also differs by age, gender, ethnicity, access to healthcare and socioeconomic status.[36] Savings in healthcare mean that finite resources can be distributed to other social needs, such as education and housing, that are also subject to funding constraints.[37] In developed nations at least, discussions surrounding the value of life in monetary terms, especially that of an

---

32 Ibid 1433.
33 Ibid 1434.
34 Ibid.
35 In an Australian report in June 2009, it was estimated that the costs associated with acute coronary syndrome, including hospitalisation, in Australia would be approximately $15.5 billion. See, especially, Access Economics, 'The Economic Costs of Heart Attack and Chest Pain' (Acute Coronary Syndrome) (Report, June 2009) 5. The cost of treating influenza in Australia, including time away from employment, in 2007 was between $828 and $884 million per year. See, especially, Anthony T Newall, Paul A Scuffham and Brent Hodgkinson, 'Economic Report into the Cost of Influenza to the Australian Health System' (Report, Research and Practice Development Centre, University of Queensland and Blue Care, March 2007) 6. Another example of healthcare costs is the rising cost of treatment for mental illness. In Australia, treatment for mental illness was recently reported to be in the region of $190 billion per year. See Matt Wade, 'Income Up, But Mental Illness Costing $190b a Year' *Sydney Morning Herald* (Online) 8 June 2013. www.smh.com.au/data-point/income-up-but-mental-illness-costing-190b-a-year-20130607-2nvjy.html
36 In 2007, in the UK, it was found that ethnic minority patients generally have poorer health outcomes than do white Caucasian patients. See, especially, Parliamentary Office of Science and Technology, 'Ethnicity and Health' (Postnote, No 276, January 2007) 1–4. See, also, Memon et al., 'Health Issues in Ethnic Minorities: Awareness and Action' (2002) 95(6) *Journal of the Royal Society of Medicine* 293–925.
37 Lockwood, above, n 22, 451.

infant, are, presumably, considered distasteful. Public opinion on this issue would broadly be driven by questions that McKie et al. highlight:

> How could we possibly arrive at any figure that would represent the value of human life? And even if we could, would that not be a crass attempt to convert to money values something that is, quite literally, beyond any price?[38]

However, with an ageing population, increasing costs and limited budgets, clinical decisions have to be made regarding how and to whom health resources are allocated.[39] Questions need to be asked about the cost of keeping severely premature infants alive. Further, what health benefits will be gained by investing scarce fiscal resources into NICUs? More than 20 years ago, Lyon made this observation:

> In the end, the issue of whether to let defective babies die may be solved, not by the elegant arguments of ethicists or by rhetoric in a court of law, but by the grim realities of the marketplace. The rising cost of medical treatment is placing a tremendous burden on society.[40]

The issue remains as topical today as it was in 1985. Importantly, Lyon's assertion about the allocation and cost of healthcare is beginning to be discussed more openly. However, as highlighted later in this chapter, discussion about the allocation of limited resources is still not as candid as it should be. Having explored some of the ways in which the cost of healthcare and the benefits it confers are measured and accounted for, the next section considers cost-efficiency in the NICU.

6.4 The efficacy of the neonatal intensive care unit (NICU)

Insights from the United States

There is an abundance of literature and academic discussion on resource allocation and health economics from the United States. This is unsurprising given the limited government healthcare funding and the role played by the private sector in the provision of health services in that country. Buchh et al. documented the length of stay and survival of infants in a Chicago NICU between 1978 and 2003. They found that, although there had been a significant rise in the

---

38 John McKie et al., *The Allocation of Health Resources: An Ethical Evaluation of the 'QALY' Approach* (Dartmouth Publishing Company Limited, 1998) 1.
39 Bennett, above, n 17, 77.
40 Jeff Lyon, *Playing God in the Nursery* (W W Norton, 1985) 280.

number of admissions and bed-days in the NICU,[41] the NICU was a 'very cost-efficient mode of ICU care'.[42]

This is in comparison with adult intensive care units, where 'over 50 per cent of [adult intensive care unit] bed-days are devoted to non-survivors as opposed to patients who will be discharged'.[43] The authors noted that the NICU was 'impressively efficient'.[44] The authors placed emphasis on health dollars spent on surviving infants:

> Even when we were not very good at saving ELBW (extremely low birth weight) babies' lives, neonatology was still remarkably efficient in directing NICU bed-days/dollars/resources toward surviving infants as opposed to their doomed confreres.[45]

Further, the authors reported that, 'in 1978, when 82% of our ELBW babies died, only 24% of our ELBW dollars were devoted to these non-survivors'. In addition, since 1978, birth-weight-specific (450–750 grams) mortality rates have decreased, with a higher number of survivors. These data are encouraging, although advancements in technology allowing premature infants to be saved from death at least may be attributable to this decrease.

Compared with 30 years ago, recent technological advancements mean that infants born severely premature can now be saved. Second, where Buchh et al. discuss the cost-efficiency of the NICU based on fewer health dollars being devoted to 'non-survivors', this could be attributed to weaker, smaller 'non-survivors' dying sooner, requiring little or no medical treatment or bed-days.

This is supported by research conducted by Meadow et al. The authors noted changes in mortality rates and low birth weight infants during the 1990s. They found that some 20 years ago, infants born pre-term with little chance of survival died more quickly. As a consequence, parents were able to determine the 'life or death' outcome of their child sooner: '[I]f parents could "hold their breaths" for a few days, the outcome for their infants was much clearer.'[46] In its crudest form, NICU beds were occupied for the shortest period of time, making a NICU a financially viable and economical unit to manage.

With improvements in neonatal medicine and care by the 1990s, Meadow and his colleagues illustrated that although non-surviving infants still tended to die, they took longer to do so. Therefore, to have a better understanding of prognosis, parents had to 'hold their breath' for much longer, sometimes a 'week and a

---

41 This rise was fourfold, from 25 to 100 per year and tenfold for bed-days from 700 to 7,000 per year.
42 Buchh et al., 'Neonatology Has Always Been a Bargain – Even When We Weren't Very Good At It!' (2007) 96(5) *Acta Paediatrica* 659, 661.
43 Ibid 662.
44 Ibid.
45 Ibid.
46 Meadow et al., 'Changes in Mortality for Extremely Low Birth Weight Infants in the 1990s: Implications for Treatment Decisions and Resource Use' (2004) 113(5) *Pediatrics* 1223, 1223.

half'.[47] One consequence of this 'prolongation' of death is that NICU beds are occupied for longer, even as expensive treatments continue to result in the inevitable death of infants.

However, the authors did not consider the devotion of NICU beds for 'doomed' infants as economically unviable. They stipulate that, for the weakest, smallest infants, the 'median day of death is 3'.[48] Therefore, those who survive to see day four are likely to have a 'more than 50% chance' of survival.[49] Of those born at under 25 weeks, Meadow et al. assert:

> Of every 100 such infants, 75 will die, but half will be dead in 3 days. The 25 survivors, by contrast, will remain in the NICU for an average of 100 days. Consequently, even for a majority of NICU bed-days (< 90% in our NICU) will be devoted to survivors. [. . .] NICU dollars are remarkably well targeted to survivors as opposed to non survivors, independently of the absolute risk of death.[50]

Lantos, Mokalla and Meadow advocate that scarce resources are better spent in the NICU than in intensive care for the elderly, which involves 'a far greater proportional expenditure of money towards those who will not survive'.[51] Buchh et al. support the view that 'ICU dollars spent on patients who will die before leaving the hospital seem less well directed than ICU dollars spent on patients who will survive to be discharged'.[52]

Taking a similar view to their colleagues, Lantos et al. argue that premature infants present with serious medical complications early in life (often the first few days after birth). This makes the NICU a cost-efficient area of medicine because pre-term infants 'declare themselves' by means of either early rapid decline or surviving medical complications early in life.[53] All three authors emphasise NICUs as cost-efficient hospital departments that produce 'survivors'.

It is necessary to consider whether the economic value of NICUs in producing 'survivors' is isolated to the United States or whether other global studies or literature illustrate a similar trend. Professor Lex Doyle in Victoria, Australia, has provided seminal work that contributes to the discussion of economics and resource allocation in the NICU.

---

47 Ibid 1226.
48 William Meadow, 'Epidemiology, Economics, and Ethics in the NICU: Reflections from 30 Years of Neonatology Practice' (2007) 45 *Journal of Pediatric Gastroenterology and Nutrition* 215, 216.
49 Ibid.
50 Ibid.
51 John D Lantos, Mani Mokalla and William Meadow, 'Resource Allocation in Neonatal and Medical ICUs: Epidemiology and Rationing at the Extremes of Life' (1997) 156(1) *American Journal of Respiratory and Critical Care Medicine* 185, 189. See, generally, Kenneth Kipnis, 'Harm and Uncertainty in Newborn Intensive Care' (2007) 28(5) *Theoretical Medicine and Bioethics* 393–412.
52 Buchh et al., above, n 42, 659.
53 Lantos, Mokalla and Meadow, above, n 51, 188.

Australian and UK NICUs

Doyle conducted long-term studies over four epochs (1979–1980, 1985–1987, 1991–1992 and 1997) to evaluate the effectiveness of NICUs for infants born premature and weighing between 500 and 999 grams.[54] The studies followed the infant's survival and development up to at least two years of age. The author placed emphasis on effectiveness and efficiency as factors of importance when evaluating the NICU.[55]

Comparably, the NICUs in Victoria, Australia, are also producing more 'survivors'. Survival rates increased from 25.4% in 1979–1980 to 73% in 1997.[56] Doyle found that 'survival rate has increased three-fold from 1 in 4 in the late 1970s to 3 in 4 by the late 1990s.'[57]

The studies conducted by Doyle are commendable. The author explicitly states that 'neonatal intensive care is expensive, especially in developed countries'.[58] He also provides a balanced view of the realities of the NICU and low birth weight infants. Although the statistics highlight an increase in survivors of low birth weight in the NICU, the studies also recognise that, although mortality has decreased, the degree of morbidity for premature infants remains unchanged.

Further, a recent study conducted over a six-year period in one Australian hospital found that infants born earlier than 24 weeks and weighing less than 500g did not survive without disability. The study is commendable, in that it has highlighted that infants born extremely premature do not survive without disability. Discussing the reality of mortality and morbidity is leading discussion in this area in the right direction – to more open and transparent dialogue. However, this book argues that the findings from this study could be an opportunity to extend this discussion further, and to begin to consider the significant amount of financial resources that are utilised to save infants from death, but not from a life with severe disability. Tudehope highlights this point further, asserting that 'it is generally accepted that investment in neonatal intensive care reduces mortality but the costs of services are high especially if morbidity is not reduced'.[59]

54 Another study conducted in Victoria, Australia, examined the cost-efficiency of NICU for babies born weighing 500–999 grams during 1979–1980 and 1985–1987. See also, W H Kitchen et al., 'The Cost of Improving the Outcome for Infants of Birthweight 500–999g in Victoria: The Victorian Infant Collaborative Study Group' (1993) 29(1) *Journal of Paediatrics and Child Health* 56.

55 Lex W Doyle, 'Evaluation of Neonatal Intensive Care for Extremely Low Birth Weight Infants in Victoria over Two Decades: I Effectiveness' (2004) 113(3) *Pediatrics* 505, 505; Lex W Doyle, 'Evaluation of Neonatal Intensive Care for Extremely Low Birth Weight Infants in Victoria over Two Decades: II Efficiency' (2004) 113(3) *Pediatrics* 510, 510.

56 Doyle, 'Evaluation of Neonatal Intensive Care for Extremely Low Birth Weight Infants in Victoria over Two Decades: I Effectiveness', (2004) 113(3) *Pediatrics* 505, 507.

57 Doyle, 'Evaluation of Neonatal Intensive Care for Extremely Low Birth Weight Infants in Victoria over Two Decades: II Efficiency' (2004) 113(3) *Pediatrics* 510, 510.

58 Lex W Doyle, 'Evaluation of Neonatal Intensive Care for Extremely Low Birth Weight Infants' (2006) 11(2) *Seminars in Fetal and Neonatal Medicine* 139, 139.

59 Susie O'Brien, 'Leading Doctors Claim Smallest Premature Babies Should Not Be Resuscitated', *Herald Sun* (Online) 13 October 2013. www.heraldsun.com.au/news/victoria/leading-doctors-

Infants born at extremely low birth weight (500–999 grams) continue to suffer severe disability and poor life outcomes. The studies found that even over a 20-year period the decrease in cerebral palsy was marginal, from 13.5% in 1979 to 10.7% in 1997. In addition, 'deafness, developmental delay, and overall neurosensory disability rates were not significantly different over time in survivors in our cohorts'.[60] In sum, Doyle highlighted that the NICUs in Victoria, Australia are both efficient and effective at improving survival rates. However, he qualified his statement as follows:

> The dramatically improving survival and quality-adjusted survival rates for ELBW infants in Victoria over two decades argue strongly the case for an increasing need for neonatal services in the state. Moreover, such care can be provided relatively efficiently.

He went on to state: 'Neonatal intensive care is approaching 100% availability for ELBW infants in Victoria. As most ELBW infants now survive, the remaining major challenge is to improve the quality of their survival.'[61]

Severe disability and/or long-term health problems associated with premature birth, especially infants born at 23 weeks, remain as challenging today as 30 years ago. This is reflected in the findings of the UK EPICure studies, which were considered in Chapter 3. In these studies, it was found that, although the survival rates of severely premature infants have increased, the pattern of major neonatal morbidity, and the proportion of survivors affected, are unchanged. These observations reflect an 'important increase in the number of preterm survivors at risk of later health problems'.[62]

Petrou et al. have reported similar findings in the UK to those in Australia. Although there have been improvements in survival rates for premature infants, 'these infants remain at risk of developing a broad range of short-term and long-term complications'.[63] Further, 'infants born at the lower limit of viability have the highest morbidity and disability rates'.[64]

A structured literature review conducted by Petrou et al. found that initial hospital costs incurred for premature birth in the UK were often linked to surgical intervention and the need for assisted ventilation. In their paper, the authors noted that the overall number of days of ventilation and/or length of stay in

claim-smallest-premature-babies-should-not-be-resuscitated/story-fni0fit3-1226738907028. See, also, D I Tudehope, 'Economic Evaluation in Medicine' (1997) 33(3) *Journal of Paediatrics and Child Health* 185, 185.

60 Doyle, 'Evaluation of Neonatal Intensive Care for Extremely Low Birth Weight Infants in Victoria over Two Decades: I Effectiveness' above, n 56, 508.

61 Doyle, above, n 58, 144.

62 K L Costeloe et al., 'Short Term Outcomes after Extreme Preterm Birth in England: Comparison of Two Birth Cohorts in 1995 and 2006 (The Epicure Studies)' (2012) 345(8 December) *British Medical Journal* 1, 14.

63 Petrou et al., 'A Structured Review of the Recent Literature on the Economic Consequences of preterm Birth' (2011) 96(3) *Archives of Disease in Childhood: Fetal and Neonatal* 225.

64 Ibid.

hospital varied between '1.8 days for term born survivors and 128 days for infants born at 23 gestational weeks'.[65]

Studies from the UK show that the cost of both short-term neonatal care and long-term care required by survivors of the NICU is significant. Mangham et al. conducted a study on a hypothetical cohort of 669,601 children based on live births and pre-term birth from 2006.[66] The study considered the cost of pre-term birth throughout childhood in England and Wales. Its findings were published in 2009. The study found that, over childhood, the cost of pre-term birth to the public sector was an estimated at £2.946 billion. Further, '34% is attributable to those born very preterm (born before 33 weeks gestation) and 8% to those born extremely preterm (born before 28 weeks gestation)'.[67] Additionally, the 'incremental cost per preterm child surviving to 18 years compared with a term survivor (37 + weeks' gestation) was estimated at £22,885. The corresponding estimates for very and extremely preterm were substantially higher at £61,781 and £94,740 respectively.'[68]

6.5 The profitability of the NICU

Understandably, many neonatologists are optimistic advocates of the NICU. To most neonatologists (and to pro-life activists), any development or progress in saving infants from death is likely to be considered positive. This also sits comfortably with the principle of sanctity of life, as discussed in Chapter 2. However, as noted earlier, this principle is not necessarily the most important and other factors must also be considered in making treatment decisions.

A critical view may suggest that the drive for the allocation of limited resources to the NICU has less than benevolent intentions. The NICU may be considered a 'safe haven', with regular financial growth and profit for hospitals, where fiscal cuts are made in other departments. This point is illustrated in an article published in the *Bloomberg* magazine, which stated that 'when you add up the million-dollar imagining machines, the incubators, the expensive drugs, diagnostics, nutritional products, and physician services, neonatology is a multibillion-dollar market'.[69]

Doctors who claim that treating premature infants is not expensive cannot claim to be disinterested observers of the practice. While they may not govern the budgets they look after on behalf of the taxpayer, they do have a vested interest in maintaining the notion that treating premature infants is not a costly task. Ultimately, such medical practitioners primarily manage staffing and clinics in this area. Arguably, such doctors have established themselves, their fields of study

65 Ibid 226.
66 Mangham et al., 'The Cost of Preterm Birth throughout Childhood in England and Wales' (2009) 123(2) *Pediatrics* 312–327.
67 Ibid 316.
68 Ibid 312.
69 Bloomberg Business Week Magazine, 'Million Dollar Babies'. www.businessweek.com/stories/ 2008-06-11/million-dollar-babies

and practice in this niche area, and have created their own self-propagating industry.

Lantos candidly discussed the 'profitability' of the NICU: 'Over the past three years, the NICU has had the highest revenue-to-expense ratio of any unit in the entire hospital including both adult and paediatric units.'[70] Further: 'most new children's hospitals will have more NICU beds than the current one but will not have room left over for a new emergency department, new outpatient clinics, or an auditorium for public gatherings.'[71]

As noted earlier, the largely private American healthcare system is structured differently from that of the systems in Australia or the UK, making the issue of limited allocation of public healthcare funds particularly important. Public sector hospitals are essentially 'not for profit' organisations and are, to a greater degree, controlled by government funding and allocations.

In Australia, the government is primarily responsible for deciding the amount of public funds that will be distributed to public hospitals. To achieve this, various methodologies are applied, including 'activity-based funding', 'diagnostic-related groups' (DRG codes)[72] to classify hospital services and 'weighted inlier equivalent separation', based on specific allocations made to hospitals, reflecting historical workloads and population changes.[73] The systems that are applied are complex in nature and often do not reflect the 'true cost' of healthcare or particular treatments.

There is no universal approach to healthcare systems or government-funding models. The Nordic welfare model of healthcare, for example, places an emphasis on delivering premium health services to the maximum number of individuals. This model extends to Finland, Norway, Denmark, Iceland and Sweden and has the fundamental goal of 'equal access to social and health services, education and culture'.[74] However, such equality and universal access to welfare and healthcare for all members of society, regardless of socioeconomic background or privilege, comes at a price. The Nordic model of welfare places high demands on the taxpayer, with these countries having some of the highest taxation rates in the world.[75]

---

70 John D Lantos, 'Hooked on Neonatology' (2001) 20(5) *Health Affairs* 233, 239.
71 Ibid.
72 For further discussion about health economics in the hospital, including payment for services and DRGs, see Australian Institute of Health and Welfare, *Australian Refined Diagnosis-related Groups (AR-DRG) Data Cubes*, Australian Government. www.aihw.gov.au/ar-drg-data-cubes/#ARDRGs. For a discussion on the theory of supply and demand in relation to health economics, see S J Duckett, 'Economics and Hospital Care', in Gavin Mooney and Richard Scotton (eds), *Economics and Australian Health Policy* (Allen & Unwin, 1998) 93–114.
73 Department of Health, Victoria, Australia, *Activity Based Funding*. www.health.vic.gov.au/abf/definitions.htm
74 Christiansen, Niels Finn, Klaus Petersen, Nils Edling and Per Haave, *The Nordic Welfare Model* (Narayana Press, 2005). www.norden.org/en/about-nordic-co-operation/areas-of-co-operation/the-nordic-welfare-model/about-the-nordic-welfare-model
75 In 2012, Sweden ranked second highest in the world for tax rates at 56.6%; the highest taxation rate was 59% in Aruba. See Global Finance, *Personal Income Tax Rates*. www.gfmag.com/tools/global-database/economic-data/12151-personal-income-tax-rates.html#axzz2TcOLWXqW

Studies and literature on the costs, efficiency, effectiveness and efficacy of NICUs are limited. This is probably because only a small proportion of extremely premature infants' lives are spent inside the NICU. The relative cost of preventing impaired infants from dying discussed thus far does not take into account the long-term cost incurred by society and the families of extremely premature infants. These costs reach far beyond the NICU.

As Chapter 1 highlighted, significant development has been seen, and is ongoing, in technological advancement and medical science. Infants, among other groups, have tested the limits of technology. As little as 20 to 30 years ago, premature infants, particularly those born at 23 weeks, would have died. Today, this group of infants, born at the very edge of viability, survive. Every day in the developed world, technology and cutting-edge innovation save some of society's most vulnerable citizens from death.[76]

Many individuals applaud the thriving research in medical science, engineering and other industries that have made it possible for humans to increasingly defy nature. The media praise technological progress, highlighting stories of 'miracle babies', who, with the assistance of an army of medical professionals and aggressive and revolutionary technologies in the form of incubators and ventilators, combat death.[77]

However, as noted in previous chapters, these miracle babies rarely live happily ever after. Although infants born at 23 weeks' gestation may survive, they often fail to thrive, and their long-term health prognoses remain bleak.

Most spend several months in the NICU, where medical teams attempt to stabilise them until, with the aid of machinery and medicine, their vital organs have adequately developed. However, even with round-the-clock care and supervision, many die after days or even months of intensive care. Others may survive, but they are typically left with severe disabilities, affecting both them and their families for the rest of their lives.[78]

Health economists apply a micro view when considering costs and benefits incurred through a health industry lens. While this is important, it is also necessary to consider the broader costs involved for the family and society. The following section of this chapter considers other costs from a societal perspective, such as the costs incurred post-NICU, and both the short-term direct financial costs and longer-term costs including loss of opportunity.

6.6 Health economics beyond the NICU

Extremely premature infants often spend months in the NICU being mechanically supported and cared for in a controlled environment with constant supervision.

76　Ann Johnson, 'Disability and Perinatal Care' (1995) 95(2) *Pediatrics* 272, 272.
77　Kathy Evans, 'The Edge of Life', *The Melbourne Magazine*, *The Age* (Australia), Issue 90 April 2012, 40.
78　Pharoah et al., 'Costs and Benefits of Neonatal Intensive Care' (1988) 63(7) *Archives of Disease in Childhood: Fetal and Neonatal* 715.

The aim is to allow their organs and bodies to fully develop before they are discharged.

Time in the NICU may come as a shock to families who just want to take their newborns home.[79] However, they must quickly adapt to the reality before them: the infants may have to spend months in the NICU. In the NICU, the other parents, the doctors and nurses often become an extension of the family unit.

Eventually, medical teams of doctors and nurses cease caring for these impaired infants and reassure new parents that 'they will be fine' looking after their newborn in an uncontrolled, non-clinical environment. Once discharged, the constant support comes to an abrupt end, and parents find themselves at home with their infant, who will often be severely disabled.[80]

Evans points out that often doctors' 'egos push boundaries to produce "miracle babies" which are not going to be raised by super-parents, only ordinary ones with limited resources'.[81] Indeed, Evan's comment does not extend far enough: the needs of a survivor of the NICU will typically stretch far beyond those of a non-severely premature child.

Quality of life arguments tend to focus on physical conditions. However, such considerations should extend to the 'mass of side-effects both on those closely involved and on the wider society'.[82] These include socioeconomic factors that affect the quality of life of both infant and family.[83] Severely disabled individuals require significantly more care, time and financial resources.

Society and medical practitioners consider saving infants from the brink of death to be both an ethical and a legal duty.[84] Thus far, it has been noted that, from a health economics perspective, it is generally considered to be both cost-efficient and effective to use finite resources to save infants from death. However, Johnson provides a differing view:

> When considering the benefits of such care, it is not enough to measure these in terms of survival, without considering the later health status of the surviving children and the impact of their survival of their families, and ultimately on society.

79 Evans, above, n 77, 42.
80 Carol A Heimer and Lisa R Staffen, *For the Sake of the Children* (University of Chicago Press, 1998) 281. Charles C Camosy discusses the cost of treating critically ill infants and considers general reforms from a Catholic perspective. See, especially, Charles C Camosy, *Too Expensive to Treat? Finitude, Tragedy and the Neonatal ICU* (Wm. B. Eerdsmans, 2010).
81 Evans, above, n 77, 42.
82 Jonathan Glover, *Causing Death and Saving Lives* (Pelican Books, 1977) 168.
83 Linda D Urden, 'Ethical Analysis of Scarce Resources in Pediatric Home Care' (1987) 15(4) *Children's Health Care* 253, 256.
84 See, generally, Deborah E Campbell and Alan R Fleischman, 'Limits of Viability: Dilemmas, Decisions, and Decision Makers' (2001) 18(3) *American Journal of Perinatology* 117–128.

Additionally: 'It is clear that extremely preterm survivors are at higher risk of later motor sensory or cognitive disorders than neonates born at a later gestational age and the costs of their care are likely to be greater.'[85]

Global empirical studies highlight that, although medical advancements have reduced mortality rates for extremely low birth weight infants, morbidity in survivors remains prevalent. This point was highlighted again recently by Evans, who stated:

> Fifty per cent of babies born at his age [Joshua born at 24 weeks and 5 days] get to go home, though up to 20 per cent will be severely disabled; the rest will be either fine or affected by conditions such as milder forms of intellectual delay and cerebral palsy.[86]

Moster, Lie and Markestad detail the types of disability suffered by infants born at 23 weeks. The authors stipulate that this group of infants have a greater likelihood of 'major disabilities such as blindness or low vision, hearing loss and epilepsy'.[87] Most infants born at 23 weeks require several follow-up consultations. In addition to later surgeries and post-operative care, some infants may need medical equipment such as assisted ventilation at home. Auxiliary services, such as physiotherapy and rehabilitation, may also be required. Lantos and Meadow found:

> [F]ormer premmies have five times the rate of hospitalisation of full-term babies during the first year of life. Many former premmies require ongoing outpatient care from a variety of specialists. Some require complex home health care.[88]

The points above briefly illustrate some of the ongoing health conditions that affect extremely low birth weight infants. Caring for a healthy newborn can be challenging in itself, yet the care and attention required by a severely premature infant suffering significant disabilities is far greater.

The cost of post-NICU care far exceeds that of the NICU in terms of money, time and emotion. Some examples of the costs that begin to accumulate are the cost of travelling to and from hospital appointments and lost earnings due to one or both parents requiring time off work. This point is supported by empirical research conducted by Zupancic et al., which found that, while still in the NICU, of 109 low birth weight babies in Great Britain, '36% of mothers travelled more than 21 miles to the NICU and 88% of families visited daily'[89] with a cost

---

85 Johnson, above, n 76, 272.
86 Evans, above, n 77, 38.
87 Dag Moster, Rolv Terje Lie and Trond Markestad, 'Long-term Medical and Social Consequences of Preterm Birth' (2008) 359(3) *New England Journal of Medicine* 262, 265.
88 Lantos and Meadow, above, n 8, 123.
89 Zupancic et al., above, n 7, 486.

expenditure of £100–200 at 1990 prices.[90] The resulting financial strain, constant time pressures and burdens of caring for a severely disabled infant often affect the wider family circle.[91]

Impact on the wider family

Caring for a severely disabled infant brings significant challenges for new parents and the wider family. It may affect the existing family dynamic, and partners and other children may be adversely affected by the continuous needs of, and attention required by, the disabled infant. Wilkinson notes that 'siblings of impaired children report to work around the home more than siblings of unimpaired children, and this has been suggested to affect the development of their self-identity'.[92] Further, overall costs within the household have been noted to be 'ten times higher for parents with low-birth-weight babies when compared with those with term infants'.[93]

Wilkinson supports this view, highlighting that the 'burden of care for severely impaired infants overwhelmingly falls upon immediate family, often involving physical, financial and emotional burdens'.[94] This is very rarely spoken about or documented by the media, which prefer to portray the idyllic, resilient family.

An example of the media portrayal of the idyllic family unit comes from the UK, where a newspaper interviewed four families about their experiences of caring for their premature infants.[95] Predictably, all of the families discussed their 'miracle' infants and the joy that each of them brought to their lives. Of course, regardless of disability, parents talk about their children with great passion, pride and unconditional love. However, the article failed to highlight the realities of the financial hardship and family tensions that often arise when caring for a severely disabled infant.

Recently, one mother did openly discuss the pressure of raising a premature infant suffering severe disability. This mother had also made the decision to place her child in care, for the greater good of the rest of the family. In the article, Jane spoke about her son James, born at 25 weeks and consequently suffering with

---

90 Petrou et al., above, n 63, 227.

91 Warrick et al., 'Guidance for Withdrawal and Withholding of Intensive Care as Part of Neonatal End-of-life Care' (2011) 98(1) *British Medical Bulletin* 99, 110.

92 Dominic Wilkinson, *Death or Disability? The 'Carmentis Machine' and Decision Making for Critically Ill Children* (Oxford University Press, 2013) 119.

93 Alan T Gibson and Cath M Harrison, 'The Consequences for Society of Intensive Care for Babies Born at Less Than 30 Weeks' Gestation' (2010) 20(4) *Paediatrics and Child Health* 167, 170.

94 Dominic Wilkinson, 'A Life Worth Giving? The Threshold for Permissible Withdrawal of Life Support from Disabled Newborn Infants' (2011) 11(2) *American Journal of Bioethics* 20, 24.

95 Samantha Brick, 'Born at the Very Brink of Life: Over Half of Babies Now Survive at 24 Weeks, The Legal Abortion Limit. But at What Cost to Their Health and Families? Four Mothers Tell Us Their Stories', *Daily Mail* (Online), 2 January 2013. www.dailymail.co.uk/femail/article-2256242/ Over-half-babies-survive-birth-24-weeks-legal-abortion-limit-cost-health-families-Four-mothers-tell-stories.html

quadriplegia, severe autism and epilepsy.[96] Jane spoke about the challenges of caring for him while also raising two older, healthy children, to whom she could no longer provide adequate attention. Regarding the constant physical and mental strain placed on her and her husband, she stated: 'looking after him [James] was a round-the-clock job, and we became zombies. I would muddle through my day in a fog of exhaustion while my husband, Andrew, struggled through his working week on minimal sleep.'[97]

She also commented on the detrimental effects on her other children: 'As a family we had no social life, and Andrew and I had no time for our other two children. We knew this was having a devastating effect on them, but there was nothing we could do.'[98] In addition, 'my doctor prescribed me antidepressants and my marriage to Andrew limped along. What had become of us?'[99] Arguably, it is this type of story that the media should publicise, to allow for much-needed discussion about some of the long-term and far-reaching effects of saving infants at 23 weeks.

The long-term impacts of caring for extremely premature, severely disabled infants are profound, including broken marriages, financial hardship and, as considered earlier, detrimental impact on the other children within the family.[100] The long-term impact on a family may be far greater when the severely disabled infant is the couple's first child, potentially costing them the opportunity of having a healthy child in the future. This is considered next.

Opportunity cost

Individuals invest significant time, money, effort and emotion in raising children; this investment is all the greater, and the sacrifices more magnified, when caring for infants born at 23 weeks' gestation. Where an infant is born extremely prematurely, and as a result suffers severe disability, the likelihood of parents having another child is reduced. This could be due to the time or financial constraints associated with the care of the disabled child, or the concern that a second pregnancy may also result in a premature birth. Kuhse and Singer support this view:

> It seems reasonable to suppose that families are more likely to have subsequent child if a premature infant dies than if the infant lives; many couples have an

---

96 Jane Raca, 'Would you Give Up Your Disabled Son to Allow Your Other Children a Chance of Happiness? Despite Agonies of Guilt, Jane Says it's the Best Decision She Ever Made', *Daily Mail* (Online), 14 March 2013. www.dailymail.co.uk/femail/article-2293579/Would-disabled-son-allow-children-chance-happiness.html

97 Ibid.
98 Ibid.
99 Ibid.
100 Neil Campbell, 'When Care Cannot Cure: Medical Problems in Seriously Ill Babies' in Helga Kuhse and Peter Singer (eds), *Bioethics: An Anthology* (Blackwell, 2nd edn, 2006) 307–308.

idea of how many children they would like to have, and will 'replace' an infant who dies in order to reach that number.[101]

The authors goes on to state that 'this assumption is also consistent with data that show that a family with a disabled child is less likely than other families to have further children'.[102]

In this regard, the NICU enables premature infants to survive, but also potentially prevents couples from having other healthy children in the future.

Taking Kuhse and Singer's argument further, the opportunity cost of raising a severely disabled infant could mean that families never reach their economic potential due to having to give up careers or promotions, which then has a detrimental effect on all children within the family. These children may be deprived of better clothing, social outings or holidays, or even lose access to better education and subsequent career opportunities and experiences. This argument is particularly broad and may not affect all families. However, it is worth noting.

More broadly, there is also a concomitant lost opportunity for society when parents have severely premature and disabled children. Unlike a healthy child born at full term, a severely disabled infant is unlikely to be able to contribute to the economic work force later in life.

This does not mean that the disabled infant who survives into adult years will not contribute to and be an integral part of society in other ways. However, he or she is unlikely to be able to contribute economically.

It is both necessary and timely for developed nations such as the UK and Australia to revisit the methodology and reasons for saving infants born extremely premature. New advanced technologies are used to save these infants. However, this often yields poor outcomes and leaves these infants with severe disabilities, consequently affecting the nation's productivity and future.[103]

From an economic perspective, the question becomes whether society is doing itself a disservice by reducing the chances of families having a healthy child later in life. Several commentators have reflected on this question. For example, Lyon considered the billions of dollars that are required to care for severely impaired children by institutions paid for by the taxpayer:

> None of these figures appear to make note of the loss to society of the child's productivity as a potential wage earner. Nor do they tabulate the associated costs that the government must bear, including the provisions of special education, disability payments and public accommodations for the handicapped.[104]

---

101 Kuhse and Singer, above, n 21, 109.
102 Kuhse and Singer, above, n 21, 109.
103 Lockwood, above, n 22, 457.
104 Lyon, above, n 40, 285–286. Also see Wilkinson, above, n 92, 24.

Any discussion about opportunity cost in this regard would be incomplete without considering the loss of opportunity and life experiences that may affect the severely disabled infant throughout his or her life.

Moster, Lie and Markestad have explored this issue and state that those born extremely premature with disabilities begin, and continue, life with poor outcomes. Their study of pre-term infants born between 1967 and 1983 conducted in Norway found that 'a lower gestational age at birth was associated with a reduced likelihood of completing high school, of receiving a bachelor's degree, or receiving a post graduate degree and of having a high income'.[105] The findings also indicate that those born with medical disabilities are less likely to be able to fulfil personal goals such as 'finding a life partner or having children'.[106]

Further, a study conducted by Pharoah et al. in Liverpool supports the view that low birth weight infants have lower educational success. During 1979–1981, the authors examined low birth weight infants (under 150 grams). They classified disability into a four-point scale measure, from 1 (no disability) to 4 (severe disability), including conditions such as blindness, quadriplegia and epilepsy. The surviving infants were followed through to the age of four, and a projection was made that those infants that fell within scale 4 of the measure (severe disability) were 'assumed to require special education from the age of 4 to 19 years and institutional care from the age of 19 until death'.[107]

Zupancic et al. contribute to this discussion, asserting the 'need for special education for children suffering disability as a result of pre-term birth in the United States was approximately $360 million dollars per year'. Petrou et al. in the UK have noted the figure for educational cost for infants born extremely premature were '£4,150 greater than for the control group born at term'.[108] With increasing survival rates and no significant changes in morbidity, there is also a 'greater burden on early intervention and educational institutions'.[109]

The allocation of limited public health resources generally remains an 'unspoken issue', but cannot be neglected any longer.[110] The limited resources available to healthcare are increasingly under scrutiny, and it is timely to discuss and seriously consider the allocation of such resources as an objective standard when making end of life decisions for extremely premature and critically impaired infants.

Gunderman and Engle provide some insight, asserting that often decisions to withdraw or withhold life-sustaining treatment focus on the best interests of the child, the likelihood of that child having a poor quality of life and whether

105 Moster, Terje Lie and Markestad, above, n 87, 266.
106 Ibid.
107 Pharoah et al., above, n 78, 716.
108 Petrou et al., above, n 63, 229.
109 Zupancic et al., above, n 7, 493.
110 Rob Heywood, 'Parents and Medical Professionals: Conflict, Co-Operation, and Best Interests' (2012) 20(4) *Medical Law Review* 29, 31.

treatment is futile. The authors also suggest that some commentators may find it appropriate to:

> argue that the community as a whole cannot afford to spend hundreds of thousands of dollars saving the life of a premature neonate whose subsequent disabilities will only impose additional hundreds of thousands of dollars in medical costs of a lifetime.[111]

In addition, empirical studies show that carers are the least happy group in the wider community, with the highest rate of depression. Although these studies are not sensitive enough to be broken down into the type of people being cared for, there is no reason to suggest that the experiences of carers of impaired infants are any different to those of carers in general.[112]

Morris asserts that 'paying lip service to the value of every life while failing to give adequate support to children and their careers is hypocritical'.[113] Thus, the question can be asked: Is society fulfilling its social contract by keeping severely disabled infants alive, considering that they are not then provided with the care, facilities and support they need for the rest of their lives?[114]

6.7 Australian and UK economic budget pressures

Governments, particularly in developed countries, allocate a substantial portion of their fiscal budget to healthcare, education and welfare. Projected government spending and the annual budget announcement is becoming one of the most anticipated events of the year. This is understandable, given that it impacts all members of society in some way. Public funds are not infinite, and expenditure in the area of healthcare is increasing as a result of a growing ageing population. A recent report by the Grattan Institute entitled *Budget Pressures on Australian Governments* revealed that 19% of the 2012–2013 budget was allocated to

111 Richard B Gunderman and William A Engle, 'Ethics and the Limits of Neonatal Viability' (2006) 236(2) *Radiology* 427 430.

112 Australian Institute of Family Services, *Half of Australia's Carers are Depressed – Making a Hard Job Even Harder*, Australian Government. http://aifs.govspace.gov.au/2012/10/18/half-of-australia%E2%80%99s-carers-are-depressed-%E2%80%93-making-a-hard-job-even-harder/; National Health and Medical Research Council, *New Research Tackles Depression Among Older Australian and their Carers*, Australian Government. www.nhmrc.gov.au/media/releases/2011/new-research-tackles-depression-among-older-australians-and-their-carers. See, also, Dominic Wilkinson, *Death or Disability? The 'Carmentis Machine' and Decision Making for Critically Ill Children* (Oxford University Press, 2013)116–117.

113 Anne Morris, 'Selective Treatment of Irreversibly Impaired Infants: Decision-making at the Threshold' (2009) 17(3) *Medical Law Review* 347, 376.

114 See, e.g., Amir Paz-Fuchs, 'The Social Contract Revisited: The Modern Welfare State' (Report, The Foundation for Law, Justice and Society, University of Oxford, 2011).

healthcare.[115] It was noted that, in real terms over the past ten years, government expenditure in healthcare has risen by 75%.[116] The report found that 'the ageing and aged care services are the highest, and the fastest growing spending category'.[117] Further, 'the expense that did most to increase government spending above GDP [gross domestic product] was hospital spending'.[118]

The most recent Australian budget for 2013–2014 proposed two significant fiscal reforms: an investment in education of '$9.8 billion over six years, to enhance Australia's future productivity and wellbeing'[119] and '$19.3 billion over seven years to disability care'.[120] This latter proposal represents the most significant reform in social policy in Australia since the introduction of public-funded healthcare.

In the UK, the King's Fund report titled *Spending on Health and Social Care over the Next 50 Years: Why Think Long Term?*[121] provides an insightful understanding of public spending in the UK. The report notes that over a 50-year period public spending on the National Health Service (NHS) has increased from approximately 3.4% of GDP to 8.2%.[122] In 2014 18% of public spending was on healthcare in excess of £129 billion, the second largest expenditure after pensions at 20% at £143 billion.[123] The increase has been attributed to population growth, national wealth, costs associated with providing care and developments in medical technology.[124] Predictions state that by the year 2061 the spending per head of population could rise to £9,914.[125]

There is increasing discussion in both the UK and Australia concerning public spending and forecasts for future public spending. In the UK, the toll that public spending could potentially have on the NHS is of increasing concern, with recent discussions on additional taxes to assist funding the NHS.[126] The King's Fund report estimates that 'if health spending increased by 1 per cent of GDP (around £15 billion) and all of this were funded through additional tax revenues, this would add around £570 a year to the tax bill of every household in the United Kingdom'.[127]

---

115 The Grattan Institute is an independent body in Australia that aims to examine, critique and present unbiased reportage and 'practical solutions to some of the country's most pressing problems'. See Grattan Institute, *About Us*. grattan.edu.au/about-us

116 John Daley, *Budget Pressures on Australian Governments* (Grattan Institute, 2013) 16.

117 Ibid 14.

118 Ibid 15.

119 Australian Government, *Key Initiatives of the 2013–14 Budget*. www.budget.gov.au/201314/content/overview/html/overview_key_initiatives.htm

120 Ibid.

121 John Appleby, *Spending on Health and Social Care over the Next 50 Years: Why Think Long Term?* (King's Fund, 2013).

122 Ibid ix.

123 UK Public Spending. www.ukpublicspending.co.uk/year_spending_2014UKbt_14bc1n#ukgs302

124 Ibid.

125 Ibid.

126 David Nicholson, 'We Need a New Tax to Fund the NHS' *Guardian* (Online) 19 September 2014. www.theguardian.com/healthcare-network/2014/sep/19/david-nicholson-need-new-tax-fund-nhs

127 Appleby, above, n 122, x.

With a general election in 2015 in the UK, improvements to the NHS and fiscal spending are of increasing public and political discourse.[128] John Appleby, in the King's Fund report, correctly asserts that 'important political and social choices are to be made, not only about the aggregate of spending from the public purse, but also the types and volumes of services that should be provided and how they should be funded'.[129]

6.8 The National Disability Insurance Scheme (NDIS) Act in Australia

The new National Disability Insurance Scheme (NDIS), now governed under legislation, is admirable.[130] Some of the core values of the NDIS are based on providing independence and opportunities to those with significant disability. In addition, the scheme aims to provide care and support to their families and carers, assisting the disabled to have greater access to facilities and to reach their full potential.[131]

Section 22 (1) of the National Disability Insurance Scheme Act 2013[132] stipulates that the age requirement for eligibility to the scheme:

> A person meets the age requirements if:
>
> a   the person was aged under 65 when the access request in relation to the person was made; and
> b   if the National Disability Insurance Scheme rules for the purposes of this paragraph prescribe that on a prescribed date or a date in a prescribed period the person must be a prescribed age – the person is that age on that date.

Section 23 states that persons wishing to participate in the scheme must be a citizen of Australia or hold permanent residency. Eligibility to the scheme based on disability is defined under s. 24:

> a   the person has a disability that is attributable to one or more intellectual, cognitive, neurological, sensory or physical impairments or to one or more impairments attributable to a psychiatric condition; and
> b   the impairment or impairments are, or are likely to be, permanent; and

---

128 Chris Ham, 'The NHS in England and the 2015 General Election' (2014) 349 *British Medical Journal* 6129.
129 Ibid 50.
130 National Disability Insurance Scheme Act 2013 (No 20) (Cth). See, also, Harold Luntz, 'Compensation Recovery and the National Disability Insurance Scheme' (2013) 20 *Torts Law Journal* 153, 155–157.
131 National Disability Insurance Scheme, *About Us*. www.ndis.gov.au/about-an-ndis/what-is-an-ndis/
132 National Disability Insurance Scheme Act 2013 (No 20) (Cth) s 22(1).

   c   the impairment or impairments result in substantially reduced functional capacity to undertake, or psychosocial functioning in undertaking, one or more of the following activities:

      (i) communication;
     (ii) social interaction;
    (iii) learning;
    (iv) mobility;
     (v) self-care;
    (vi) self-management; and

   d   the impairment or impairments affect the person's capacity for social and economic participation; and

   e   the person is likely to require support under the National Disability Insurance Scheme for the person's lifetime.

(2) For the purposes of subsection (1), an impairment or impairments that vary in intensity may be permanent, and the person is likely to require support under the National Disability Insurance Scheme for the person's lifetime, despite the variation.[133]

The scheme, due to be gradually rolled out, beginning in Tasmania, South Australia and areas of Victoria and NSW (New South Wales) aims to 'recognise that disability is for a lifetime, and so it will take a lifelong approach to providing care and support. This means that assessment will look beyond the immediate need, and across the course of the person's life.'[134] In addition, it provides that:

> Individual support will also be given to people for whom there is good evidence that early intervention would substantially improve functioning (for example, autism, acquired brain injury, cerebral palsy or sensory impairments), and those for whom early intervention will delay or lessen a decline in functioning (for example, multiple sclerosis and Parkinson's disease).[135]

The financial support provided to those suffering disability will no longer be subject to fluctuating budget allocations, but come from a funding pool on a needs assessment basis. In light of this recent reform, it is appropriate to consider its merits in relation to the subject matter of this chapter and the overall book.

The intent of the scheme is noble, and the impact it will have on the lives of those living with disability and/or carers will be profound. It is accepted that dialogue about life and death, disability and the costs associated with such are uncomfortable for many. However, to have an objective and rational discussion

---

133 National Disability Insurance Scheme Act 2013 (No 20) (Cth) s. 24.
134 National Disability Insurance Scheme, *What is an NDIS?* www.ndis.gov.au/about-an-ndis/what-is-an-ndis
135 National Disability Insurance Scheme, *FAQs*. www.ndis.gov.au/about-an-ndis/frequently-asked-questions/#eligible

about resource allocation, it is necessary to look beyond the benevolence of the NDIS and consider the longer-term impacts on society and public spending.

Although remarkable in theory, the far-reaching ramifications of the scheme on the public purse are likely to be significant. Funded by increasing the compulsory Medicare levy by half of one per cent, there will be a section of society that is resistant to any additional taxation and who may thus consider that schemes or models for disability care should be provided for out of the existing fiscal budget.

As noted earlier, the cost of allowing infants to survive at 23 weeks, often with profound disabilities, is significant both in the NICU and beyond. Indeed, scarce resources may be better spent on saving the lives of infants born even a few weeks later in the gestation period, as they are less likely to suffer disability.

One of the unintended consequences of the NDIS may be to encourage a culture that is reliant on government financial assistance. Where parents may once have considered financial and personal support as factors in deciding to opt for palliative care rather than aggressive treatment, they may now be swayed towards deciding to raise a profoundly disabled child due to the safety net and the added financial security that the scheme provides.

The burden on the Australian taxpayer is thus now twofold. First, there are compulsory tax contributions to the general healthcare budget, allowing infants to be saved in the NICU. Second, the increase in the Medicare levy will fund the NDIS, to provide lifelong care post-NICU.

The introduction of the NDIS scheme in Australia, funded by public tax revenue, calls for a critical rethink on the correlation of resources and patient outcomes. Despite projections made by the treasury, the $19.8 billion investment over seven years runs at a risk. It is ultimately dependent on continued population growth or, at the very least, on a stable number of working taxpayers, able to pay the required levy to fund the scheme.

Macro factors may also pose a risk to the funds available to the NDIS. For example, if the economy contracts and unemployment rises, the available pool of taxpayers available to pay the levy would shrink. Moreover, if the real cost of living declines and wages fall, the amount of tax the government collects would also diminish. An example of drastically fluctuating fiscal environments can be found in the current economic status of Europe.

If any of these risks are realised, there may simply not be enough in the public purse to satisfy need, potentially leaving all scheme participants with insufficient funding. Public funds and the resulting benefits (healthcare, education and welfare) to members of society all depend on a healthy and productive workforce, employed and paying taxes. To maintain a balance between economically productive members of society and those who need to be supported, there needs to be serious parliamentary consideration for a framework or model to determine the minimum gestational age at which medical assistance and treatment should be provided for those born extremely premature.

In light of this, some ethical theories support the premise that the allocation of limited public resources should be guided by those who will benefit the most from treatment, and consequently cost less for society. Utilitarian and consequentialist theories, based largely on the notion of 'the greatest good for the greatest number',[136] suggest that focusing limited resources on infants born even a few weeks later in the gestational calendar would be for the greater good of society and the public purse.[137]

Gibson and Harrison support this view, noting that if treatment and care were not provided to infants unless born at 25 weeks or above, this would 'reduce costs from £2.945 billion to £2.903 billon'.[138] This is because those starting life on a reasonably healthy footing, with no significant disabilities, are less likely to be frequent users of the limited public health dollar over the course of their lives.

Several consequential benefits flow from targeting limited resources to those most likely to make a substantial or full health recovery. For example, such recipients are more likely to be able to pay back the investment via a meaningful contribution to the economy and taxation base, although, of course, this is not guaranteed.[139] As noted in Chapter 5, when applying a utilitarian theory to resource allocation, maximising the greater good of the community is preferable. Arguably, applying this theory 'medical institutions and [personnel] are trustees of society and must consider the probable future contributions of patients'.[140] Of course, a literal application of this theory to infants would potentially be controversial and would not be readily accepted by all members of society, particularly the families of impaired infants.

If choices have to be made regarding priority, it is reasonable for public money to be spent in a way that maximises public good.[141] In his well-received book *Too Expensive to Treat? Finitude, Tragedy and the Neonatal ICU*, Charles Camosy provides a novel and insightful Catholic social theory about resource allocation and impaired infants. Camosy argues that it is problematic to consider the best interest of an individual separate to those of the community. He states: 'Jesus' command to Christians is to love our neighbour as we love ourselves – an idea which is also present in many secular understandings of solidarity.'[142] Thus, 'each and every newborn baby counts just as much as a mature human person – but no *more*. Care must be taken to ration resources justly and in due proportion with the common good.'[143]

It is too soon to measure the success of the recent enactment of the National Disability Scheme Act 2013 in Australia, given that it is still in the early stages of

---

136 Julian Savulescu, 'Consequentialism, Reasons, Value and Justice' (1998) 12(3) *Bioethics* 212, 213.
137 Pharoah et al., above, n 78, 718. See, also, John McKie et al., above, n 38, 536.
138 Gibson and Harrison, above, n 93, 172.
139 There will always be a portion of society that may later acquire chronic disease, commit crimes or suffer harmful addictions.
140 Tom L Beauchamp and James F Childress, *Principles of Biomedical Ethics* (Oxford University Press, 7th edn, 2013) 291.
141 Hope, Savulescu and Hendrick, above, n 20, 210.
142 Charles Camosy, 'Which Newborns are Too Expensive to Treat? A Response to Dominic Wilkinson' (2013) 39(8) *Journal of Medical Ethics* 507, 507.
143 Camosy, above, n 11

its implementation. Further, the NDIS is not relevant to all healthcare allocations; thus, the issue of limited healthcare resources remains contentious.

Having considered the role of health economics and the social implications of the allocation of limited health resources, this leads to the question as to whether it is just and appropriate that the wishes of parents to have life-sustaining treatment continued for their extremely premature and critically ill infant should prevail and have greater claim over community resources.

This book argues that there is a need for an open public debate as to whether wider society is truly willing and prepared to expend limited public health funds to keep severely premature infants alive.[144] Considerations such as the cost to society at large ought to feature prominently in such debates.

The relationship between sophisticated medical technology and disability is paradoxical: high-tech equipment now allows medical teams to save the lives of infants who, as recently as 20 years ago, would probably have died. Some individuals may consider this to be an enormous achievement for mankind, defeating nature and pushing the limits of human biology. However, others may question whether saving critically impaired infants born extremely premature is appropriate and the best use of public funds. The next section explores this question.

6.9 Technology: doing more harm than good?

There is a need for a critical re-evaluation of the intersection between what health outcomes *can* be achieved using advanced medical technology and what outcomes *should* be achieved. Western societies are seemingly fixated on the preservation of life. This is reflected in attitudes towards suicide, the unlawfulness of euthanasia and the disregard by some medical practitioners of advance directive end of life wishes.[145]

A recent opinion piece by an anonymous Victorian physician in Melbourne takes this idea further, asserting that doctors are not only 'trained to treat' in almost all circumstances, but also find it difficult to let patients, particularly the elderly, die of 'natural causes'. The author stated:

> As a GP with 25 years' experience, I am increasingly disturbed by this trend in modern medical care. It is ironic that we are debating euthanasia when we can currently be denied the opportunity to die of natural causes at a point when it would be appropriate and the kindest thing for the individual.[146]

144 See, e.g., Carol Nader, 'Premature Baby Debate Needed: Pike', *The Age* (Online), 7 June 2005. www.theage.com.au/news/National/Premature-baby-debate-needed-Pike/2005/06/06/1117910240693.html

145 See, further, L Willmott, Ben White and Michelle Howard, 'Overriding Advance Refusals of Life-Sustaining Treatment' (2006) 25(4) *Medicine and Law* 647–661. The authors argue that the current legislation in Queensland under the Powers of Attorney Act 1998 (Qld) s. 103, whereby a doctor may override a patient's refusal of treatment under an advance directive based on 'good medical practice', should be repealed.

146 Anonymous, 'Why is it So Hard to Grant the Wish to Die in Peace?' *The Age* (Online), 16 May 2013. www.theage.com.au/comment/why-is-it-so-hard-to-grant-the-wish-to-die-in-peace-20130515-

This preference to save all lives disregards the principles of personal autonomy and dignity, particularly at the end of life, and fails to consider the increasing expense of hospital care. Australian intensive care specialist, Dr Peter Saul, comments:

> The simple solution is to be guided more by what people want, particularly at the end of their lives. What we know is that the default setting in acute care is that people receive an enormous amount of, probably not in the end life saving treatment which carries a huge burden financially and in other ways.[147]

Although Dr Saul's assertions are in relation to decision making for the aged, his comments are persuasive. Similar arguments can be made about treatment decisions for extremely premature infants. Expensive treatments in the NICU for extremely premature infants generally result in either prolonging an inevitable death or sustaining life with subsequent severe disabilities.

Of course, when the patient is an infant, it is not possible to ascertain their treatment wishes. This is further exacerbated by parents pushing for expensive life-sustaining treatment, and doctors overwhelmingly taking the standpoint of the need to 'save life at all costs', whether these costs be to the infant, the family or to society.

Protecting and saving the lives of the very sick, the very young and the vulnerable are considered perhaps to be some of the core values and moral obligations placed on western developed societies.[148] Severely impaired infants meet all of these criteria, making their treatment morally fraught. Some commentators have referred to the over-use of technology and medicine to treat extremely premature infants as a 'form of extremism'. The phrase seems relevant here.[149]

Thus far, it has been argued in this chapter that NICUs are expensive to manage, and that, even with cutting-edge technology, infants born extremely premature rarely escape severe lifelong disability. Even in an austerity-driven environment in which the cost of treatment and care far outweighs the benefits to the individual and society, governments continue to provide significant resources to NICUs.

Where governments allocate large portions of the healthcare budget to save impaired infants in the NICU, the argument can be made that there is a corresponding moral duty to extend this to a commitment to allocate monies to

2jmnt.html. See, also, Will Cairns, 'A Natural End', 2 September 2013, *Medical Journal of Australia: Insight*. www.mja.com.au/insight/2013/33/will-cairns-natural-end

147 Eleanor Hall, 'To Cut Hospital Costs, Talk to the Patients', *The World Today*, 29 April 2013 (Dr Peter Saul). www.abc.net.au/worldtoday/content/2013/s3747260.htm

148 See, generally, David Thomasma, 'The Vulnerability of the Sick' (2000) 16(2) *Bioethics Forum* 5–12.

149 Brenda Barnum, 'Benevolent Injustice: A Neonatal Dilemma' (2009) 9(3) *Advances in Neonatal Care* 132, 135. See, also, William A Silverman, 'Overtreatment of Neonates? A Personal Retrospective' (1992) 90(6) *Pediatrics* 971–976.

provide all necessary support to these individuals for the rest of their lives. Therein lies the problem: public funds do not, and cannot, stretch to this extent. Several other competing claims can be made for the same pool of resources.[150]

Kuhse and Singer argue that:

> There is a limit to the burden of dependence which any community can carry. If we attempt to keep all handicapped infants alive, irrespective of their future prospects, we will have to give up other things which we may well regard as at least equally important.[151]

There are two schools of thought on disability: that life is valuable and any existence is better than none and that a life lived under the constraints of a severe disability is no life at all. An example of this latter point can be found in popular support for euthanasia among a wide section of society, who champion the right to die with respect and dignity.

A further illustration of the view of a life of mere existence being no real life at all is provided by Henner and Kluge. The authors stipulate that severely disabled infants may, in some cases, be 'better off dead':

> [T]he very fact of living constitutes a continuous injury to the newborn who is being kept alive. To keep the newborn alive is to impose on the child a life that most other persons would not want to live and which, given the chance, they would want to leave.[152]

This statement clearly relates to those who are extremely disabled at birth. Many people living with disability are a valuable part of society. Further, individuals living with a disability are distinct from those who merely exist or survive with disability. It is the latter group to which Henner and Kluge are referring. Unfortunately, due to limited resources, premium care cannot be provided to all who require it.[153]

Chapter 4 introduced Heather, who, in a BBC documentary, spoke candidly about her life, her struggles with depression and her fears of losing her parents. The first-hand experiences and thoughts of 21-year-old Heather, born extremely premature and living with severe disabilities, are valuable here.

Born at 26 weeks, her parents and doctors made the decision to keep her alive. However, she is provided with little or no financial support from the government. Heather advocated the need for lifelong care and financial support for services, stating, 'it's very selfish to keep a baby alive, we've done our bit for society

---

150 Renée R Anspach, *Deciding Who Lives* (University of California Press, 1993) 170.
151 Helga Kuhse and Peter Singer, *Should the Baby Live?* (Oxford University Press, 1985) 170.
152 Eike-Henner and W Kluge, 'Severely Disabled Newborns', in Helga Kuhse and Peter Singer (eds), *A Companion to Bioethics* (Blackwell Publishers, 1998) 242, 245.
153 For a discussion about the cost of care for disabled individuals in the UK, see Smith et al., *Disabled People's Costs of Living: More Than You Think* (Joseph Rowntree Foundation, 2004).

(hospital/government) it's not true or right, the baby thinks I'm alive, but what do I do now?'[154] She went on to say:

> What's my purpose now – we kept you alive (hospital/government) but now you cost us too much money, so we are not going to bother . . . if you are willing to support someone at the beginning of life, you should be willing to support them to the end.[155]

Heather's position is understandable, given that it is her life that is constrained by lack of public funds, affecting her quality of life. Moreover, her position is supported by some doctors, who also find the high levels of government funding to the NICU spurious.

Dr Anne Orkit, a paediatrician consultant from Birmingham, UK, discussed the lack of public funds allocated to post-NICU care:

> Money from the NHS (National Health Service) has gone into NICU, but not much into community care or disabled care. As a society we don't look at lower profile things – saving a miracle baby grabs the public and NHS commissioner's imagination. The need for physio for a cerebral palsy kid does not sound sexy, and you don't get money in the same way.[156]

Some Australian doctors offer similar sentiments. For example, neonatologist, Dr Andrew Watkins, stated: 'Australia has a poor track record in providing good-quality care for people with disabilities. Is it ethical to bring children into a world that offers so little in terms of support?'[157]

Governments in both the UK and Australia are in a difficult position, being the source of both the problem and the solution. A rational solution could be to allocate finite resources to saving infants born at a later gestational age, or focusing on prevention of prematurity to encourage the birth of healthy, abled and productive future members of the economic workforce. However, this does not align with the current situation of large portions of the healthcare budget being absorbed by saving infants that are so premature they could legally be aborted. Dr Orkit advocates a critical re-evaluation of healthcare funds and their prioritisation:

> We should change in terms of looking at what we do at the very early twenty-three week gestation period and have a hard look at the out-comes from that group and make a decision on that. Just as the same way we've made hard decisions around things like cancer drugs and seeing the outcome are not good enough to use, therefore we won't spend that money.

---

154 Adam Wishart, *The Price of Life* (BBC Productions, 2011) 00.40.30–00.40.35.
155 Ibid 00.40.41–00.40.48.
156 Ibid 00.38.51–00.39.30.
157 Evans, above, n 77, 42.

With the financial situation as it is, we simply can't go on giving people what they want.[158]

Daphne Austin, from the West Midlands NHS specialised commissioning department, also supports a more cautious use of public funds: 'I can't think of very many interventions that have such poor outcomes as resuscitating 23 week babies, we're spending an awful lot of money on treatment with very marginal benefit.'[159] She goes on to state: 'If I came out and said I'm going to stop resuscitating babies at below 24 weeks there would be a witch hunt.'[160]

Discussions about the allocation of finite public funds in regards to life and death decisions for severely premature infants are uncomfortable for many individuals, due in large part to their taboo nature. However, despite not being openly discussed, placing a financial value on life is an active practice, as discussed in the next section.

6.10 Determining the price and value of life: a common practice?

Many facets of everyday life have an impact, both positive and negative, on health and life outcomes. The consequential effect of some of these practices is reflected in public expenditure. Taxpayer monies are often spent on items or developments from which not all individuals may receive a specific benefit. For example, taxation revenue is often used for the maintenance or construction of new buildings or roads that will not be accessed or used by all taxpayers. This is also true of healthcare funds, which may be utilised for specific initiatives or programmes that an individual may never participate in or benefit from. As Savulescu et al. note, the contrary is also true, with some public initiatives and regulations, such as speed limits, contributing to all individuals' health and wellbeing.[161] There are some current practices in which a value is placed on life and where the utilisation of public funds is of significant consideration.

Road death tolls

Enforcing speed limits to protect drivers and pedestrians does not provide absolute protection from danger. Road death tolls provide an indication of the number of lives that could be saved if cars were banned from certain areas, or particular drivers were stopped from driving.

Statistics from the Transport Accident Commission (TAC) in Australia highlight that, in 2011–2012, there were 276 fatalities on Victorian roads, across Melbourne and rural areas. Of those, 200 were male and 121 were the driver of the vehicle.

158 *The Price of Life*, above, n 155, 00.53.35.
159 Ibid 00.57.28.
160 Ibid 00.57.32.
161 Hope, Savulescu and Hendrick, above, n 20, 211.

Further, the age groups most affected were between 30 and 39 and over 70 years of age.[162] The TAC statistics also indicate that drivers and motorcyclists killed in drink driving accidents accounted for 25% of all road deaths; of those, 79% were male.[163]

If all life is measured equally, it could be argued that the most effective way of 'saving' 276 or more lives each year would be to ban from driving those drivers most likely to cause or be involved in road traffic accidents. However, despite the indication that banning men from driving would statistically considerably reduce the road toll, such a move would be absurd.[164] Extending this argument further, in its strictest form, if all life is to be considered sacred and worthy of preservation at all costs, perhaps it would be appropriate to ban all vehicles from the road. Ostensibly, this is an illustration of the price or value placed on life where the use of road transport and the benefits to society are measured by the cost of lives in the road toll.

Triage/emergency room categories

Triage facilities in emergency departments of hospitals provide a sharp illustration of the value of life and healthcare being separated and rationed. If an equal value were placed on all life, there would not be a system of prioritisation of treatment for patients based on the urgency or severity of their needs.[165]

Historically, deriving from the French verb 'to separate, sift or select' (*trier*), triage was a practice developed by the military services more than a century ago: '[T]he military were looking at cost-effective medicine, and were selecting those patients for whom the medical services could offer something useful.'[166] The practice of prioritising medical treatment originated on the battlefield, initiated by the medical fraternity itself, based on the status of the patient on whom limited funds should be conferred.[167] The same principle applies in public hospitals today, to target 'limited resources to the patients with the best chance of survival'.[168]

In Australia, rationing healthcare and targeting emergency treatment based on need is neatly ranked and categorised from 1 to 5: resuscitation, emergency,

---

162 Transport Accident Commission, *Rolling 12 Month Road Toll*. http://reporting.tacsafety.com. au/s/search.html?collection=tac-xml-meta&form=tac-report-safety-rolling

163 Transport Accident Commission, *Drink Driving Statistics*. www.tacsafety.com.au/statistics/drink-driving-statistics

164 Interestingly, Asquith LJ commented on the social utility of a defendant's negligent conduct in the English case of *Daborn v Bath Tramways Motor Co Ltd and Smithey* [1946] 2 All ER 333, in which he stated [at 449]: If all the trains in this country were restricted to a speed of five miles an hour, there would be fewer accidents, but our national life would be intolerably slowed down. The purpose to be served if sufficiently important, justifies the assumption of abnormal risk.'

165 Deborah Cook and Mita Giacomini, 'The Sound of Silence: Rationing Resources for Critically Ill Patients' (1999) 3(1) *Critical Care* 1, 2–3.

166 Edward W Brentnall, 'A History of Triage in Civilian Hospitals in Australia' (1997) 9(1) *Emergency Medicine* 50, 50. Also see Bennett, above, n 17, 80.

167 Kenneth V Iserson and John C Moskop, 'Triage in Medicine, Part I: Concept, History, and Types' (2007) 49(3) *Annals of Emergency Medicine* 275–281.

168 Lantos, Mokalla and Meadow, above, n 51, 187.

urgent, semi-urgent and non-urgent.[169] Based on these categories, assessments are made by medical teams as to the approximate timeframe within which they see each patient, ranging from immediately to within 120 minutes.[170] Many patients will be treated effectively and discharged, while others will require a hospital stay, and some will be referred to their general practitioners for follow-up treatment.

When patients being treated by their general practitioners require elective surgeries, they are placed on 'waiting lists' for treatment. In Victoria, the number of patients waiting for elective surgery as of March 2014 was 45,851,[171] with limited public healthcare resources making it necessary to ration treatment by need and chance of improvement. By the time a patient reaches the top of the waiting list, there is the possibility that, during the course of the wait, they may have died, or their condition may have increased in severity, requiring the deployment of even greater healthcare resources to restore them to full health. Indeed, an Australian hospital statistics report for 2013–2014 found that of those waiting for elective surgery, 2,400 were 'removed from waiting lists because they had died or could not contacted before their schedule date'.[172] While the discussion above provides an implicit example of determinations made on the basis of cost-efficiency, Camosy proposes an explicit list of four triage categories for the treatment of impaired infants. The author suggests 'must treat', 'unclear – emergent', 'unclear – non-emergent' and 'must not treat' categories, whereby the most severely imperilled should be provided with palliative care only.[173]

The Australian Pharmaceutical Benefits Scheme (PBS)

The Australian Pharmaceutical Benefits Scheme (PBS) provides another example of the value of life being accounted for by dollars. If all life were measured with the same worth, all medicine and treatments would be covered under the scheme to save or control as many diseases as possible. Yet medicines that are considered too expensive to be funded under public health are not covered under the scheme, even where those medicines might be effective in treating a particular category of illness.

169 Referred to as Australasian Triage Scale Categories (ATS). See, further, Australasian College for Emergency Medicine, 'Policy on the Australasian Triage Scale' Revised in July 2011. www.acem. org.au/getattachment/693998d7-94be-4ca7-a0e7-3d74cc9b733f/Policy-on-the-Australasian-Triage-Scale.aspx

170 Our Emergency Departments, *The State of Our Public Hospital June 2008 Report (Part 4)*, Australian Government. www.health.gov.au/internet/main/publishing.nsf/Content/E6CAF670D550F646 CA25747700074A51/$File/Our%20emergency%20departments.pdf

171 Department of Health, Victoria, Australia, *Victorian Health Services Performances*. http:// performance.health.vic.gov.au/Home/Report.aspx?ReportKey=44. See, also, Kate Hagan, 'Hospitals Waiting List to Ensnare 55,000', *The Age* (Online), 20 March 2013. www.theage.com. au/victoria/hospitals-waiting-list-to-ensnare-55000-20130319-2gdns.html

172 Brigid O'Connell, 'Elective Surgery, Operation Problems Rise in Victoria Hospitals' *Herald Sun* (Online), 20 October 2014. www.heraldsun.com.au/news/victoria/elective-surgery-operation-problems-rise-in-victorian-hospitals/story-fni0fit3-1227096503471?nk=473f120404dbefb34cc 76ae98cd7e903

173 Camosy, above, n 11, 197.

The schemes and practices described here reveal that western society does, certainly in some contexts, place a monetary value on life, albeit indirectly. Difficult decisions in the current tough financial climate are made daily as to which patients should receive an allocation of finite public resources.

Gampel's coining of the term 'noble lies' for the subtle practice of rationing healthcare provides a unique interpretation. His first application of the 'lie' is in situations in which medical practitioners consider palliative care to be the best option, as further treatment would be futile. This 'noble lie' is advantageous in two ways: it allows doctors to avoid being seen as emotionless; and it preserves parents from the guilt of expressing their wishes for treatment to be discontinued.[174]

Perhaps Gampel's most acute observation of the application of the 'noble lie' is that it is simply 'necessary in order that health care providers perform the function of rationing in a society that is not facing up to the task'.[175] He further asserts: 'Families are less likely to take such actions when they are told the treatments are futile, than if told the treatments are "potentially effective", but that the odds of providing a meaningful improvement were too low given the financial costs involved.'[176]

6.11 The role of the judiciary in resource allocation discussion

Chapter 2 considered the role of the judiciary in end of life decisions for premature and impaired infants, where futility of treatment, the best interests principle and quality of life are key considerations of the court.

These decisions, which are of paramount human interest, are not taken lightly. It is appropriate and necessary that parliament and its legislative powers provide societal reforms based on the changing attitudes and social mores of the day. This is reflected in present-day activism in the UK and Australia for the legalisation of gay marriage and voluntary euthanasia. However, judges have the freedom to guide law making outside the democratic process, a freedom that an elected parliament does not have. Although judges are inherently conservative, they do possess the autonomy to be robust, which can influence parliament.

The courts can suggest and influence the creation of law, but changes to law remain the prerogative of parliament. Courts have been influential as activists and instigators for change, reflected in pivotal moments in Australian and English legislative history, with changes later confirmed in statute.[177] However, regarding resource allocation and the withdrawal or withholding of life-sustaining treatment, the courts have been guarded in their response, avoiding the core issues. Heywood

---

174 Eric Gampel, 'Does Professional Autonomy Protect Medical Futility Judgments?' (2006) 20(2) *Bioethics* 92, 102.

175 Ibid 103.

176 Ibid.

177 An example of this can be found in the landmark case of Mabo in Australia, which recognised native title. *Mabo* (1992) 175 CLR *v Queensland (No 2)* [1992] HCA 23.

contends that members of the legal fraternity 'tread carefully around this issue, but it is undoubtedly considered, even if not overtly, by the courts in their decision making'.[178]

Unlike in Australia, the issue of resource allocation and medical treatment has been briefly discussed by courts in the UK – the operative word here being 'briefly'. However, the courts have been quick to separate themselves from questions of healthcare rationing and consider that allocation of finite resources is not a matter that is within the courts' remit. Further, as Jackson notes, 'the courts have proved extremely reluctant to criticize funding decisions'.[179] There have been a number of cases in the UK concerning both adult patients and children in which parties have applied to the courts under judicial review in that the health authority in question has acted outside its statutory powers or acted unreasonably or unlawfully in depriving the patient of treatment.[180]

Perhaps the most publicised case concerning resource allocation and medical treatment for a child is *R v Cambridge Health Authority, ex parte B*.[181] In this case, a young girl, later identified as Jaymee Bowen (Child B for anonymity purposes), was diagnosed with acute lymphoblastic leukaemia (non-Hodgkin's lymphoma) at the age of five. She was successfully treated; however, at the age of ten, she developed acute myeloid leukaemia. The treating doctors were of the medical opinion that the only possible treatment of intensive chemotherapy and a second bone marrow transplant was not in her best interests. After seeking secondary opinions from other doctors in the UK and the US, her father found a doctor in the UK who was willing to provide her with the treatment, which was prohibitively expensive at £75,000. Jaymee's father sought the funds for the treatment from the Cambridge and Huntingdon Health authority. When his request was denied, he applied for judicial review.

Although, at first instance, Justice Laws had requested that the health authority substantiate the grounds for refusal of treatment, later the same day the Court of Appeal overturned the judgment and did not consider that the health authority had acted unreasonably. Before turning to discuss the reasoning for quashing the decision made at first instance, Sir Thomas Bingham MR emphasised the sanctity of life principle, stating:

> [I]t is important that I should state very clearly as the judge did, that this is a case involving the life of a young patient and that that is a fact which must dominate all consideration of all aspects of the case. Our society is one in which a very high value is put on human life. No decision affecting

---

178 Heywood, above, n 111, 31.
179 Emily Jackson, *Medical Law: Texts, Cases and Materials* (Oxford University Press, 2006) 83.
180 Often referred to as Wednesbury unreasonableness. See, especially, *R v Central Birmingham Health Authority, ex parte Walker* (1987) 3 BMLR 32 concerning an application for judicial review made by a mother for a non-urgent operation on her premature infant. See, also, *R v Central Birmingham Health Authority, ex parte Collier* (Unreported, 6 January 1988).
181 *R v Cambridge Health Authority, Ex parte B* [1995] 1 WLR 898.

human life is one that can be regarded with other than the greatest seriousness.[182]

He later went on in his judgment to assert:

> I have no doubt that in a perfect world any treatment which a patient, or a patient's family, sought would be provided if doctors were willing to give it, no matter how much it cost, particularly when a life was potentially at stake. It would however, in my view, be shutting one's eyes to the real world if the court were to proceed on the basis that we do live in such a world. It is common knowledge that health authorities of all kinds are constantly pressed to make ends meet. They cannot pay their nurses as much as they would like; they cannot provide all the treatments they would like; they cannot purchase all the extremely expensive medical equipment they would like; they cannot carry out all the research they would like; they cannot build all the hospitals and specialist units they would like. Difficult and agonising judgments have to be made as to how a limited budget is best allocated to the maximum advantage of the maximum number of patients. That is not a judgment which the court can make. In my judgment, it is not something that a health authority such as this authority can be fairly criticised for not advancing before the court.[183]

Arguably, by overwhelmingly deferring to medical opinion, which takes resourcing into account, the judiciary also do make decisions based on limited resource allocation, albeit indirectly.[184] Further, the courts' decisions are couched in the least offensive language as possible. For example, as considered in Chapter 2, judges apply nebulous terms such as futility, best interests and quality of life when treatment is unlikely to yield any improvement or significant results.[185]

In *Re J (a minor) (wardship: medical treatment)*, Lord Donaldson touched on limited resources, before quickly moving on, being careful to avoid commencing any real dialogue about allocation as it applies to healthcare and infants. He stated:

> In an imperfect world resources will always be limited and on occasion agonising choices will have to be made in allocating those resources to particular patients. It is outwith the scope of this judgment to give any guidance as to the considerations which should determine such an allocation,

---

182 Ibid 904–905.
183 Ibid 906.
184 Wilkinson asserts that 'resources may play a subliminal role in decisions made by doctors to provide intensive care treatments'. See, further, Dominic Wilkinson, *Death or Disability? The 'Carmentis Machine' and Decision Making for Critically Ill Children* (Oxford University Press, 2013) 31.
185 Tara Rayne Shewchuk, 'The Uncertain "Best Interests" of Neonates: Decision Making in the Neonatal Intensive Care Unit' (1995) 14(5–6) *Medicine and Law* 331, 348.

save to say that the fact that the child is or not a ward of court is a total irrelevance.[186]

The seminal English case *Airedale NHS Trust v Bland*, considered previously, also illustrates the court's discomfort in discussing resource allocation. Hoffman LJ betrayed the political sensitivity surrounding this issue with a carefully worded judgment, avoiding any suggestion of better resource allocation:

> The resources of the National Health Service are not limitless and choices have to be made. This qualification on the moral duty to provide care did not enter into the argument in this case at all. The Airedale NHS Trust invited us to decide the case on the assumption that its resources were unlimited and we have done so. But one is bound to observe that the cost of keeping a patient like Anthony Bland alive is very considerable and that in another case the health authority might conclude that its resources were better devoted to other patients. We do not have to consider such a case, but in principle the allocation of resources between patients is a matter for the health authority and not for the courts.[187]

Lord Browne-Wilkinson also raised questions about resource allocation, but failed to provide any guidance or direction about future discussion on this. He asserted:

> In addition to these ethical questions, the new technology raises practical problems. Given that there are limited resources available for medical care, is it right to devote money to sustaining the lives of those who are, and always will be, unaware of their own existence rather than to treating those who, in a real sense, can be benefited, e.g. those deprived of dialysis for want of resources.[188]

As discussed in Chapter 2, while resource allocation is not an overtly important consideration in infant treatment cases, the trend of cases and judicial decisions indicates that, in reality, it is probably a forceful driving consideration.

6.12 Conclusion

Advances in technology and medical science have entrenched the expectation that 'everything that can be done, should be done' to save lives. Resource realities are a controversial but real consideration, relating to the question of which individuals are more cost-efficient to keep alive and the likely benefits to society of doing so. On both of these criteria, extremely premature and critically impaired infants rank low.

---

186 *Re J (a minor) (wardship: medical treatment)* [1990] 3 All ER 930, 934
187 *Airedale NHS Trust v Bland* [1993] AC 789, 883.
188 Ibid 879.

This chapter has explored the contentious issue of balancing treatment decisions with limited public healthcare resources. Further, this chapter has highlighted that decisions to preserve the lives of extremely premature and impaired infants should not be limited to the immediate financial costs of medical treatment. More specifically, there should be a full appreciation of the cost of disability to the family, requirements for long-term care, and the benefits and associated costs of life, not only to the patient, but also to society. Additionally, in this chapter, it has been illustrated that considerations of cost and value of life are common practice in certain situations, and that discussions surrounding health care rationing are perhaps not as taboo as first suspected.

As noted in Chapters 2 to 4 of this book, much of the end of life decision making for extremely premature and critically impaired infants is driven by subjective considerations.

This book posits that discussions about resource allocation for this group of infants is one means by which decision making in this area can be informed by greater objectivity and rationality.

Substantial public funds are consumed in keeping extremely premature and impaired infants alive, with the typical outcome being that they live with severe disability or endure a painful and prolonged death. This calls into question whether as a society we are doing the right thing by keeping these infants alive. Are we actually causing these groups of infants and society more harm by keeping them alive?

The next and final chapter of this book provides some other piecemeal observations in end of life decision making for impaired infants. It also draws together the central themes of this book and presents concluding remarks.

6.13 References

Access Economics, 'The Economic Costs of Heart Attack and Chest Pain' (Acute Coronary Syndrome) (Report, June 2009).

Airedale NHS Trust v Bland [1993] AC 789.

Anonymous, 'Why is it So Hard to Grant the Wish to Die in Peace?' *The Age* (Online), 16 May 2013. www.theage.com.au/comment/why-is-it-so-hard-to-grant-the-wish-to-die-in-peace-20130515-2jmnt.html

Anspach, Renée R, *Deciding Who Lives* (University of California Press, 1993).

Appleby, John, *Spending on Health and Social Care over the Next 50 Years: Why Think Long Term?* (King's Fund, 2013).

Australasian College for Emergency Medicine, 'Policy on the Australasian Triage Scale'. www.acem.org.au/getattachment/693998d7-94be-4ca7-a0e7-3d74cc9b733f/Policy-on-the-Australasian-Triage-Scale.aspx

Australian Government, *Key Initiatives of the 2013–14 Budget*. www.budget.gov.au/201314/content/overview/html/overview_key_initiatives.htm

Australian Institute of Family Services, *Half of Australia's Carers are Depressed – Making a Hard Job Even Harder*, Australian Government. aifs.govspace.gov.au/2012/10/18/half-of-australia%E2%80%99s-carers-are-depressed-%E2%80%93-making-a-hard-job-even-harder

Australian Institute of Health and Welfare, *Australian Refined Diagnosis-related Groups (AR-DRG) Data Cubes*, Australian Government. www.aihw.gov.au/ar-drg-data-cubes/#ARDRGs

Barnum, Brenda, 'Benevolent Injustice: A Neonatal Dilemma' (2009) 9(3) *Advances in Neonatal Care* 132.

Beauchamp, Tom L and James F Childress, *Principles of Biomedical Ethics* (Oxford University Press, 7th edn, 2013).

Bennett, Belinda, 'Resource Allocation and the Beginning of Life' (1993) 9(Spring) *Journal of Contemporary Health Law & Policy* 77.

Bloomberg Business Week Magazine, 'Million Dollar Babies'. www.businessweek.com/stories/2008-06-11/million-dollar-babies

Boyle, M H, G W Torrance, J C Sinclair and S P Harwood, 'Economic Evaluation of Neonatal Intensive Care of Very-Low-Birth-Weight Infants' (1983) 308(22) *New England Journal of Medicine* 1330.

Brentnall, Edward W, 'A History of Triage in Civilian Hospitals in Australia' (1997) 9(1) *Emergency Medicine* 50.

Brick, Samantha, 'Born at the Very Brink of Life: Over Half of Babies Now Survive at 24 Weeks, The Legal Abortion Limit. But at What Cost to Their Health and Families? Four Mothers Tell Us Their Stories', *Daily Mail* (Online), 2 January 2013. www.dailymail.co.uk/femail/article-2256242/Over-half-babies-survive-birth-24-weeks-legal-abortion-limit—-cost-health-families-Four-mothers-tell-stories.html

Buchh, B, N Graham, B Harris et al., 'Neonatology Has Always Been a Bargain – Even When We Weren't Very Good At It!' (2007) 96(5) *Acta Paediatrica* 659.

Cairns,Will, 'A Natural End' (2 September 2013) *Medical Journal of Australia: Insight*. www.mja.com.au/insight/2013/33/will-cairns-natural-end

Camosy, Charles, 'Which Newborns are Too Expensive to Treat? A Response to Dominic Wilkinson' (2013) 39(8) *Journal of Medical Ethics* 507.

Camosy, Charles C, *Too Expensive to Treat? Finitude, Tragedy and the Neonatal ICU* (Wm. B. Eerdsmans, 2010).

Campbell, Deborah E and Alan R Fleischman, 'Limits of Viability: Dilemmas, Decisions, and Decision Makers' (2001) 18(3) *American Journal of Perinatology* 117.

Campbell, Neil, 'When Care Cannot Cure: Medical Problems in Seriously Ill Babies' in Helga Kuhse and Peter Singer (eds), *Bioethics: An Anthology* (Blackwell, 2nd edn, 2006).

Christensen, Kaare, Gabriele Doblhammer, Roland Rau and James W Vaupel, 'Ageing Populations: The Challenges Ahead' (2009) 374(9696) *The Lancet* 1196.

Christiansen, Niels Finn, Klaus Petersen, Nils Edling and Per Haave, *The Nordic Welfare Model* (Narayana Press, 2005). www.norden.org/en/about-nordic-co-operation/areas-of-co-operation/the-nordic-welfare-model/about-the-nordic-welfare-model

Clark, Robert Louis, Richard V Burkhauser, Marilyn Moon, Joseph F Quinn and Timothy M Smeeding, *The Economics of an Ageing Society* (Blackwell Malden, 2004).

Cook, Deborah and Mita Giacomini, 'The Sound of Silence: Rationing Resources for Critically Ill Patients' (1999) 3(1) *Critical Care* 1.

Costeloe, Kate L, Enid M Hennessy, Sadia Haider, Fiona Stacey, Neil Marlow and Elizabeth S Draper, 'Short Term Outcomes after Extreme Preterm Birth in England: Comparison of Two Birth Cohorts in 1995 and 2006 (The Epicure Studies)' (2012) 345(8 December) *British Medical Journal* 1.

Daborn v Bath Tramways Motor Co Ltd and Smithey [1946] 2 All ER 333.

Daley, John, *Budget Pressures on Australian Governments* (Grattan Institute, 2013).

Daniels, Norman, 'Justice, Health and Healthcare' (2001) 1(2) *American Journal of Bioethics* 2.

Department of Health, Victoria, Australia, *Activity Based Funding*. www.health.vic.gov.au/abf/definitions.htm

Department of Health, Victoria, Australia, *Victorian Health Services Performances*. http://performance.health.vic.gov.au/Home/Report.aspx?ReportKey=4

Doyle, Lex W, 'Evaluation of Neonatal Intensive Care for Extremely Low Birth Weight Infants' (2006) 11(2) *Seminars in Fetal and Neonatal Medicine* 139.

Doyle, Lex W, 'Evaluation of Neonatal Intensive Care for Extremely Low Birth Weight Infants in Victoria over Two Decades: I Effectiveness' (2004) 113(3) *Pediatrics* 505.

Doyle, Lex W, 'Evaluation of Neonatal Intensive Care for Extremely Low Birth Weight Infants in Victoria over Two Decades: II Efficiency' (2004) 113(3) *Pediatrics* 510.

Duckett, S J, 'Economics and Hospital Care', in Gavin Mooney and Richard Scotton (eds), *Economics and Australian Health Policy* (Allen & Unwin, 1998).

Evans, Kathy, 'The Edge of Life', *The Melbourne Magazine, The Age* (Australia), Issue 90 April 2012.

Evans, Robert, *Strained Mercy: The Economics of Canadian Health Care* (Butterworths, 1984).

Foster, Michelle and Jennifer Fleming, 'The Health Care System in Australia', in Sandra Taylor, Michelle Foster and Jennifer Fleming (eds), *Health Care Practice in Australia: Policy, Context and Innovations* (Oxford University Press, 2008).

Gampel, Eric, 'Does Professional Autonomy Protect Medical Futility Judgments?' (2006) 20(2) *Bioethics* 92.

Gibson, Alan T and Cath M Harrison, 'The Consequences for Society of Intensive Care for Babies Born at Less Than 30 Weeks' Gestation' (2010) 20(4) *Paediatrics and Child Health* 167.

Global Finance, *Personal Income Tax Rates*. www.gfmag.com/tools/global-database/economic-data/12151-personal-income-tax-rates.html#axzz2Tc0LWXqW

Glover, Jonathan, *Causing Death and Saving Lives* (Pelican Books, 1977).

Grattan Institute, *About Us*. http://grattan.edu.au/about-us

Gunderman, Richard B and William A Engle, 'Ethics and the Limits of Neonatal Viability' (2006) 236(2) *Radiology* 427.

Hagan, Kate, 'Hospitals Waiting List to Ensnare 55,000' *The Age* (Online), 20 March 2013. www.theage.com.au/victoria/hospitals-waiting-list-to-ensnare-55000-20130319-2gdns.html

Hall, Eleanor, 'To Cut Hospital Costs, Talk to the Patients', *The World Today*, 29 April 2013 (Dr Peter Saul). www.abc.net.au/worldtoday/content/2013/s3747260.htm

Ham, Chris, 'The NHS in England and the 2015 General Election' (2014) 349 *British Medical Journal* 6129.

Harris, John, 'QALYfying the Value of Life' (1987) 13(3) *Journal of Medical Ethics* 117–123.

Heimer, Carol A and Lisa R Staffen, *For the Sake of the Children* (University of Chicago Press, 1998).

Henner, Eike and W Kluge, 'Severely Disabled Newborns' in Helga Kuhse and Peter Singer (eds), *A Companion to Bioethics* (Blackwell Publishers, 1998) 242.

Heywood, Rob, 'Parents and Medical Professionals: Conflict, Co-Operation, and Best Interests' (2012) 20(4) *Medical Law Review* 29.

Hope, Tony, Julian Savulescu and Judith Hendrick, *Medical Ethics and Law: The Core Curriculum* (Churchill Livingstone Elsevier, 2nd edn, 2008).

Iserson, Kenneth V and John C Moskop, 'Triage in Medicine, Part I: Concept, History, and Types' (2007) 49(3) *Annals of Emergency Medicine*, 275.

Jackson, Emily, *Medical Law: Texts, Cases and Materials* (Oxford University Press, 2006).

Johnson, Ann, 'Disability and Perinatal Care' (1995) 95(2) *Pediatrics* 272.

Kipnis, Kenneth, 'Harm and Uncertainty in Newborn Intensive Care' (2007) 28(5) *Theoretical Medicine and Bioethics* 393.

Kitchen, W H, E Bowman, C Callanan, N T Campbell, E A Carse, M Charlton et al., 'The Cost of Improving the Outcome for Infants of Birthweight 500–999g in Victoria: The Victorian Infant Collaborative Study Group' (1993) 29(1) *Journal of Paediatrics and Child Health* 56.

Klein, Rudolf, 'The Role of Health Economics' (1989) 299(6694) *British Medical Journal* 275.

Kuhse, Helga and Peter Singer, 'Age and the Allocation of Medical Resources' (1988) 13(1) *Journal of Medicine and Philosophy* 101.

Kuhse, Helga and Peter Singer, *Should the Baby Live?* (Oxford University Press, 1985).

Lantos, John D and William L Meadow, *Neonatal Bioethics: The Moral Challenges of Medical Innovation* (Johns Hopkins University Press, 2006).

Lantos, John D, 'Hooked on Neonatology' (2001) 20(5) *Health Affairs* 233.

Lantos, John D, Mani Mokalla and William Meadow, 'Resource Allocation in Neonatal and Medical ICUs: Epidemiology and Rationing at the Extremes of Life' (1997) 156(1) *American Journal of Respiratory and Critical Care Medicine* 185.

Lockwood, Michael, 'Quality of Life and Resource Allocation', in Helga Kuhse and Peter Singer (eds), *Bioethics: An Anthology* (Blackwell Publishing, 2nd edn, 2006).

Luntz, Harold, 'Compensation Recovery and the National Disability Insurance Scheme' (2013) 20 *Torts Law Journal* 153.

Lyon, Jeff, *Playing God in the Nursery* (W W Norton & Company, 1985).

Mabo v Queensland (No 2) (1992) 175 CLR.

McKie, John, Peter Singer, Helga Kuhse and Jeff Richardson, *The Allocation of Health Resources: An Ethical Evaluation of the 'QALY' Approach* (Dartmouth Publishing Company Limited, 1998).

Mangham, Lindsay J, Stavros Petrou, Lex W. Doyle, Elizabeth S. Draper, Neil Marlow et al., 'The Cost of Preterm Birth throughout Childhood in England and Wales' (2009) 123(2) *Pediatrics* 312.

Marshall, P B, H J Halls, S L James, A R Grivell, A Goldstein and M N Berry, 'The Cost of Intensive and Special Care of the Newborn' (1989) 150(10) *Medical Journal of Australia,* 568.

Meadow, William, 'Epidemiology, Economics, and Ethics in the NICU: Reflections from 30 Years of Neonatology Practice' (2007) 45 *Journal of Pediatric Gastroenterology and Nutrition* 215.

Meadow, William, Grace Lee, Kathy Lin and John Lantos, 'Changes in Mortality for Extremely Low Birth Weight Infants in the 1990s: Implications for Treatment Decisions and Resource Use' (2004) 113(5) *Pediatrics* 1223.

Memon, M, F Abbas, M Khaonolakar, J Dixon and I Singh, 'Health Issues in Ethnic Minorities: Awareness and Action' (2002) 95(6) *Journal of the Royal Society of Medicine* 293.

Mooney, Gavin, 'Health Economics and Health Policy' in Gavin Mooney and Richard Scotton (eds), *Economics and Australian Health Policy* (Allen & Unwin, 1998).

Mooney, Gavin, 'QALYs: Are They Enough? A Health Economist's Perspective' (1989) 15(3) *Journal of Medical Ethics* 148.

Mooney, Gavin, *Economics, Medicine and Health Care* (Humanities Press, 1986).

Mooney, Gavin H, *The Valuation of Human Life* (Macmillan, 1977).

Morris, Anne, 'Selective Treatment of Irreversibly Impaired Infants: Decision-making at the Threshold' (2009) 17(3) *Medical Law Review* 347.

Moster, Dag, Rolv Terje Lie and Trond Markestad, 'Long-term Medical and Social Consequences of Preterm Birth' (2008) 359(3) *New England Journal of Medicine* 262.

Muraskas, Jonathan and Kayhan Parsi, 'The Cost of Saving the Tiniest Lives: NICUs versus Prevention' (2008) 10(10) *Virtual Mentor* 655.

Nader, Carol, 'Premature Baby Debate Needed: Pike', *The Age* (Online), 7 June 2005. www.theage.com.au/news/National/Premature-baby-debate-needed-Pike/2005/06/06/1117910240693.html

National Disability Insurance Scheme, *About Us*. www.ndis.gov.au/about-an-ndis/what-is-an-ndis/

National Disability Insurance Scheme, *FAQs*. www.ndis.gov.au/about-an-ndis/frequently-asked-questions/#eligible

National Disability Insurance Scheme, *What is an NDIS?* www.ndis.gov.au/about-an-ndis/what-is-an-ndis/

National Disability Insurance Scheme Act 2013 (No 20) (Cth).

National Health and Medical Research Council, *New Research Tackles Depression Among Older Australian and their Carers*, Australian Government. www.nhmrc.gov.au/ media/releases/2011/new-research-tackles-depression-among-older-australians-and-their-carers

Newall, Anthony T, Paul A Scuffham and Brent Hodgkinson, 'Economic Report into the Cost of Influenza to the Australian Health System' (Report, Research and Practice Development Centre, University of Queensland and Blue Care, March 2007).

Nicholson, David, 'We Need a New Tax to Fund the NHS' *The Guardian* (Online) 19 September 2014. www.theguardian.com/healthcare-network/2014/sep/19/david-nicholson-need-new-tax-fund-nhs

Nord, Erik, Jeff Ralph Richardson, Andrew David Street, Helga Kuhse and Peter Singer, 'Maximizing Health Benefits vs Egalitarianism: An Australian Survey of Health Issues' (1995) 41(10) *Social Science & Medicine* 1429.

O'Brien, Susie, 'Leading Doctors Claim Smallest Premature Babies Should Not Be Resuscitated', *Herald Sun* (Online) 13 October 2013. www.heraldsun.com.au/news/victoria/leading-doctors-claim-smallest-premature-babies-should-not-be-resuscitated/story-fni0fit3-1226738907028

O'Connell, Brigid, 'Elective Surgery, Operation Problems Rise in Victoria Hospitals' *Herald Sun* (Online), 20 October 2014. www.heraldsun.com.au/news/victoria/elective-surgery-operation-problems-rise-in-victorian-hospitals/story-fni0fit3-1227096503471?nk=473f120404dbefb34cc76ae98cd7e903

Our Emergency Departments, *The State of Our Public Hospital June 2008 Report (Part 4)*, Australian Government. www.health.gov.au/internet/main/publishing.nsf/Content/E6CAF670D550F646CA25747700074A51/$File/Our%20emergency%20departments.pdf

Parliamentary Office of Science and Technology, 'Ethnicity and Health' (Postnote, No 276, January 2007).

Paz-Fuchs, Amir, 'The Social Contract Revisited: The Modern Welfare State' (Report, The Foundation for Law, Justice and Society, University of Oxford, 2011).

Petrou, Stavros, Oya Eddama and Lindsay Mangham, 'A Structured Review of the Recent Literature on the Economic Consequences of Preterm Birth' (2011) 96(3) *Archives of Disease in Childhood: Fetal and Neonatal* 225.

Pharoah, P O D, R C Stevenson, R W I Cooke and B Sandu, 'Costs and Benefits of Neonatal Intensive Care' (1988) 63(7) *Archives of Disease in Childhood: Fetal and Neonatal* 715.

Powers of Attorney Act 1998 (Qld).

R v Cambridge Health Authority, ex parte B [1995] WLR 898.

R v Central Birmingham Health Authority, ex parte Collier (Unreported, 6 Jan 1988).

R v Central Birmingham Health Authority, ex parte Walker (1987) 3 BMLR 32.

Raca, Jane, 'Would you Give Up Your Disabled Son to Allow Your Other Children a Chance of Happiness? Despite Agonies of Guilt, Jane Says it's the Best Decision She Ever Made', *Daily Mail* (Online), 14 March 2013. www.dailymail.co.uk/femail/article-2293579/Would-disabled-son-allow-children-chance-happiness.html

Rawles, John, 'Castigating QALYs' (1989) 15 (3) *Journal of Medical Ethics* 143.

Re J (a minor) (wardship: medical treatment) [1990] 3 All ER 930.

Savulescu, Julian, 'Consequentialism, Reasons, Value and Justice' (1998) 12(3) *Bioethics* 212.

Shewchuk, Tara Rayne, 'The Uncertain "Best Interests" of Neonates: Decision Making in the Neonatal Intensive Care Unit' (1995) 14(5–6) *Medicine and Law* 331.

Silverman, William A, 'Overtreatment of Neonates? A Personal Retrospective' (1992) 90(6) *Pediatrics* 971.

Smith, George P, 'Death Be Not Proud: Medical, Ethical and Legal Dilemmas in Resource Allocation' (1987) 3 *Journal of Contemporary Health Law and Policy* 47–63.

Smith Noel, Sue Middleton, Kate Ashton-Brooks, Lynne Cox and Barbara Dobson with Lorna Reith, *Disabled People's Costs of Living: More Than You Think* (Joseph Rowntree Foundation, 2004).

Thomasma, David, 'The Vulnerability of the Sick' (2000) 16(2) *Bioethics Forum* 5.

Torrance, George, 'Measuring Utilities for Health States', in Sean McHugh and Michael T Vallis (eds), *Illness Behavior* (Springer, 1987).

Torrance, George W and David Feeny, 'Utilities and Quality-adjusted Life Years' (1989) 5(4) *International Journal of Technology Assessment in Health Care* 559.

Transport Accident Commission, *Drink Driving Statistics*. www.tacsafety.com.au/statistics/drink-driving-statistics.

Transport Accident Commission, *Rolling 12 Month Road Toll*. http://reporting.tacsafety.com.au/s/search.html?collection=tac-xml-meta&form=tac-report-safety-rolling

Tudehope, D I, 'Economic Evaluation in Medicine' (1997) 33(3) *Journal of Paediatrics and Child Health* 185.

UK Public Spending. www.ukpublicspending.co.uk/year_spending_2014UKbt_ 14bc1n# ukgs302

Urden, Linda D, 'Ethical Analysis of Scarce Resources in Pediatric Home Care' (1987) 15(4) *Children's Health Care* 253.

Wade, Matt, 'Income Up, But Mental Illness Costing $190b a Year' *Sydney Morning Herald* (Online) 8 June 2013. www.smh.com.au/data-point/income-up-but-mental-illness-costing-190b-a-year-20130607-2nvjy.html

Warrick Catherine, Leonie Perera, Edile Murdoch and Richard M Nicholl, 'Guidance for Withdrawal and Withholding of Intensive Care as Part of Neonatal End-of-life Care' (2011) 98(1) *British Medical Bulletin* 99.

Wilkinson, Dominic, *Death or Disability? The 'Carmentis Machine' and Decision Making for Critically Ill Children* (Oxford University Press, 2013).

Wilkinson, Dominic, 'A Life Worth Giving? The Threshold for Permissible Withdrawal of Life Support from Disabled Newborn Infants' (2011) 11(2) *American Journal of Bioethics* 20.

Willmott, L, Ben White and Michelle Howard, 'Overriding Advance Refusals of Life-Sustaining Treatment' (2006) 25(4) *Medicine and Law* 647.

Wishart, Adam, *The Price of Life* (BBC Productions, 2011).

Zupancic, J A F, D K Richardson, K Lee and M C McCormick, 'Economics of Prematurity in the Era of Managed Care' (2000) 27(2) *Clinics in Perinatology* 483.

7 Other observations and concluding remarks

Chapter 6 of this book explored the topical issue of resource allocation and its application to extremely premature and critically impaired infants, concluding that the allocation of finite public resources should be an important consideration in end of life decision making for this group of infants. This final chapter explores other observations that can improve consistency and outcomes in end of life decision-making processes for premature and critically impaired infants.

7.1 An insight from the Netherlands and Belgium: Groningen Protocol: permissible neonatal euthanasia and beyond

The Netherlands is well known for its progressive ideologies relating to health and personal autonomy at the end of life. For example, adult euthanasia has been legalised[1] and individuals over the age of 12 with a 'limited life expectancy and [who] experience severe and persistent suffering' are permitted to die.[2]

The Groningen Protocol, formulated by a number of medical practitioners based at the University Medical Centre in Groningen in the Netherlands, provides criteria to guide doctors in end of life decision making concerning critically ill infants. The protocol and its objectives have been the subject of public debate and controversy.

Jotkowitz et al. strongly oppose the protocol, stating 'any effort to actively euthanize infants is morally unacceptable and violates the traditional ethical codes of physicians and the moral values of the overwhelming majority of citizens of the world'.[3] However, such criticism reflects the degree of misunderstanding surrounding the protocol.

---

1 A A Eduard Verhagen, 'The Groningen Protocol for Newborn Euthanasia; Which Way Did the Slippery Slope Tilt?' (2013) 39(5) *Journal of Medical Ethics* 293, 293. See, also, Alex K Huibers, 'Beyond the Threshold of Life: Treating and Non-Treating of Critically Ill Newborns in the Netherlands' (1995) 16(2) *Journal of Legal Medicine* 227.
2 A A E Verhagen and P J J Sauer, 'End-of-life Decisions in Newborns: An Approach from the Netherlands' (2005) 116(3) *Pediatrics* 736, 736.
3 Alan Jotkowitz, S Glick and B Gesundheit, 'A Case against Justified Non-voluntary Active Euthanasia (The Groningen Protocol)' (2008) 8(11) *American Journal of Bioethics* 23, 23.

The authors' emphasis on the violation of 'ethical and moral codes' fails to consider that one of the core motivations of the protocol is to alleviate 'hopeless and unbearable suffering', which, to many people, is a *moral responsibility*. This is particularly so for very young individuals who are unlikely to be able to tolerate the same amount of pain or suffering as an adult, and who, unlike adults, have no comprehension of the reason for their pain and suffering.

One of the chief contributors to the protocol, eminent physician Dr Eduard Verhagen, points out that end of life decisions for infants generally fall within three categories:

1 there is no chance of survival
2 the child has a very poor prognosis and is dependent on intensive care and their future condition is grim
3 those with a hopeless prognosis who experience what parents and medical experts deem to be unbearable suffering; their quality of life will be very poor and for whom there is no hope of improvement.[4]

As noted in Chapters 2 and 3 of this book, English and Australian courts are conceivably already applying these criteria, permitting the withdrawal or withholding of treatment when doctors and parents are in agreement. However, the judgments that record these decisions are careful only to apply time-honoured legal principles of quality of life, futility and best interests.[5] Thus, where the Dutch have succeeded, English and Australian jurisdictions have not been able to codify the approach identified, nor have they called on parliament for such.

Another contentious issue considered throughout this book – the over-reliance on medical technology that yields poor results – is also addressed by Verhagen and Sauer, who state that 'even modern technology cannot produce adequate solutions as regards treatment or adequate relief of the suffering caused by disease'.[6] This is a primary focus of the protocol, whereby unbearable pain and suffering to a newborn is alleviated by active euthanasia. The Groningen Protocol expressly stipulates conditions that must be met 'before' and 'after' any active steps are taken to end the life of a severely impaired infant. These conditions are:

1 certainty of the diagnosis/prognosis
2 there must be hopeless and unbearable suffering
3 the hopeless and unbearable suffering must be confirmed by at least one independent doctor
4 both parents must give informed consent.[7]

---

4 A A Eduard Verhagen and P J J Sauer, 'The Groningen Protocol – Euthanasia in Severely Ill Newborns' (2005) 352(10) *New England Journal of Medicine* 959, 959.
5 Julian Savulescu, 'Abortion, Infanticide and Allowing Babies to Die, 40 Years On' (2013) 39(5) *Journal of Medical Ethics* 257, 258.
6 Pieter J J Sauer and A A Eduard Verhagen, 'The Groningen Protocol, Unfortunately Misunderstood' (2009) 96(1) *Neonatology* 11, 11.
7 Verhagen and Sauer, above, n 4, 960.

Further, post-infant death, the decision is subject to review by an 'outside legal body' to determine whether 'all necessary procedures have been followed'.[8] This requirement reflects the checks and balances inherent in the protocol. Decisions must be weighed and justified, and doctors are not immune from prosecution. The authors sensibly assert that 'all cases must be reported if the country is to prevent uncontrolled and unjustified euthanasia and if we are to discuss the issue publicly and thus further develop norms regarding euthanasia in newborns'.[9]

Taking the idea of the Groningen Protocol further, Belgium has extended its euthanasia laws to include lawful euthanasia to critically ill children of any age, thus including infants.[10]

Given the discomfort surrounding legal voluntary assisted euthanasia for competent and freely consenting adults in the UK and Australia, it is unlikely that a counterpart to the Groningen Protocol or Belgian position will be undertaken in either of these countries in the near future. Nevertheless, the objectivity and transparency of the Groningen Protocol should be championed by the UK and Australia.[11]

The Groningen Protocol offers doctors a comprehensive framework to 'responsibly end the lives of severely impaired newborns'.[12] Verhagen and Sauer describe the protocol as a codified process under which is it acceptable to deliver death as a means of alleviating unbearable pain and suffering in the most exceptional cases of severe impairment in infants.

7.2 Prevention rather than cure

The undercurrent to this discussion is whether it is appropriate to keep extremely premature infants – those born at 23 weeks or under – alive. While the significant financial resources that have been injected into new technologies and medicines have pushed the boundaries of medical science, this has not proved to be entirely successful.

The prioritisation of healthcare funds for extremely premature infants needs to be revisited, and prevention of premature birth rather than cure should be of central importance. Dr Imogen Morgan, clinical director of neonatology at Birmingham Children's Hospital in the UK, champions this approach, stating 'that's where we put our money in preventing premature birth if we possibly can'.[13]

---

8 Ibid.
9 Ibid.
10 Barbara Miller, 'Euthanasia Law: Belgium Passes Legislation Giving Terminally Ill Children Right to Die', *ABC News* (Online), 14 February 2014. www.abc.net.au/news/2014-02-14/belgium-child-euthanasia-law/5259314
11 Darin Achilles, 'Examining the Groningen Protocol: Comparing the Treatment of Terminally-Ill Infants in the Netherlands with Treatment Given in the United States and England' (2010) 28(4) *Wisconsin International Law Journal* 795, 797.
12 Hilde Lindemann and Marian Verkerk, 'Ending the Life of a Newborn: The Groningen Protocol' (2008) 38(1) *Hastings Center Report* 42, 42.
13 *The Price of Life*, a documentary directed by Adam Wishart for BBC Productions, 2011, 00.46.47.

Bennett also advocates that 'there is no doubt that funding of prenatal care must always be a priority in the funding of health care'.[14] Emphasis needs to be placed on initiatives and resources to reduce the number of premature births.

As considered earlier, the role of the media and government allocation of health funds reflect a priority to save extremely premature infants from death, perhaps more so than investing monies into prevention of premature birth. This is considered more appealing than dealing with long-term difficulties and poor health prognoses in any great detail. Musaskas and Parsi support this view, stating: 'In many ways the world of neonatology is a microcosm of our health care system which greatly rewards rescuing our most vulnerable patients through a panoply of technological interventions but downplays the role of prevention.'[15] To prioritise prevention of premature births requires an assessment of the causes of such births.

7.3 Increases in educational awareness and reduction of poverty

Rather than injecting finite resources into the NICU to treat 23-week-old infants, a better use may be to redirect some of those funds to improve the overall health and wellbeing of those groups in society most likely to produce premature infants. As Weightman et al. argue, government policies and priorities need to focus on 'tackling social determinants, which . . . includes health, education, and child poverty'.[16]

Poverty and social disadvantage are significant factors associated with premature birth and poor healthcare outcomes.[17] Dr Orkit contends that the 'problem is outside the hospital. You are more likely to give birth to a child with extreme prematurity if you live in poverty.'[18] In the UK, teenage pregnancy rates are the highest in western Europe and 'teenage mothers and their babies are at increased risk of poor health outcomes'.[19]

Public funds should be provided for educational initiatives targeting teenagers and school-aged children that highlight the increased chance of premature birth and the subsequent likelihood of neonatal death or survival with severe disability.

---

14 Belinda Bennett, 'Resource Allocation and the Beginning of Life' (1993) 9(Spring) *Journal of Contemporary Health Law & Policy* 77, 84.

15 Jonathan Muraskas and Kayhan Parsi, 'The Cost of Saving the Tiniest Lives: NICUs versus Prevention' (2008) 10(10) *Virtual Mentor* 655, 657.

16 Alison L Weightman et al., 'Social Inequality and Infant Health in the UK: Systematic Review and Meta-Analyses' (2012) 2(3) *BMJ Open* 1, 11.

17 R T Webb, C E Marshall and K M Abel, 'Teenage Motherhood and Risk of Premature Death: Long-Term Follow-up in the ONS Longitudinal Study' (2011) 41(9) *Psychological Medicine* 1867, 1875.

18 *The Price of Life*, above, n 13, 00.45.41–00.46.09.

19 Shantini Paranjothy et al., 'Teenage Pregnancy: Who Suffers?' (2009) 94(3) *Archives of Disease in Childhood: Fetal and Neonatal* 239, 239. See, also, Gordon C S Smith and Jill P Pell, 'Teenage Pregnancy and Risk of Adverse Perinatal Outcomes Associated with First and Second Births: Population Based Retrospective Cohort Study' (2001) 323(September) *British Medical Journal* 476.

Suburbs with the highest rates of teenage pregnancy and social disadvantage could be targeted under such a scheme. Arguably, behaviours are more likely to be mimicked in suburbs with high numbers of school leavers and teenage pregnancies. Thus, targeting these areas would have a good chance of success.

Paranjothy et al. found, in a randomised controlled study, that there was a reduction in the 'pre-term rate among females under 18 years',[20] stipulating the need for 'comprehensive social and medical care using antenatal clinics specific for teenagers'.[21]

It is encouraging that, in the UK, the compulsory legal age requirement for attendance at an educational institution was raised from 16 to 17 in 2013. High teenage pregnancy rates were an impetus for this change in law. Researcher Tanya Wilson indicated that 'incarcerating' teenagers in the schooling system until they are 17 could potentially lead to 'postponement of motherhood by one year'.[22] This educational reform is commendable, but results will have to be weighed for their efficacy once available.

7.4 Prenatal advanced directive

As discussed in Chapter 4, there is a significant amount of subjectivity within each group of caregivers when making end of life decisions for impaired infants. Parents of premature infants are the group most affected. As part of the prenatal care process, parents are informed of fetal development, and advanced technologies now allow parents not only to see their unborn child via ultrasound but also to take sophisticated three-dimensional images of their unborn child. Given the wealth of information that is being imparted to parents regarding the development of their infant, there is an opportunity for open and frank discussions with parents about the possibilities of and risks involved in premature birth.

The preparation of prenatal advance directives – that is, a 'pre-negotiated treatment plan for an imperilled newborn' – should be considered.[23] Arguably, arranging such directives would be less confronting for parents than to experience a pre-term birth and the discussions that must follow.

Catlin supports this view, stating: 'much of the education women receive about preterm delivery occurs at the bedside when preterm labour is occurring, or during or immediately after a preterm birth. At these critical periods, they are often asked to make to serious decisions.'[24] For expectant parents to be able to

---

20 Paranjothy, above, n 19, 242.
21 Ibid.
22 Jamie Doward, 'Rise in School Leaving Age is Predicted to Cut Number of Teenage Pregnancies', *Guardian* (Online), 7 April 2013. www.guardian.co.uk/society/2013/apr/07/teenage-pregnancy-school-leaving-age/
23 Ruth Levy Guyer, *Baby at Risk* (Capital Books, 2006) 76.
24 Anita Catlin, 'Thinking Outside the Box: Prenatal Care and the Call for a Prenatal Advance Directive' (2005) 19(2) *Journal of Perinatal & Neonatal Nursing* 169, 171. See, also, Helen Harrison, 'The Offer They Can't Refuse: Parents and Perinatal Treatment Decisions' (2008) 13(5) *Seminars in Fetal and Neonatal Medicine* 329, 332.

make a truly informed decision, it is important that they understand all the information provided to them and have time to make rational choices based on that information. The optimum time for this to occur is before the birth, when prospective parents can take away information and discuss it. Catlin again reinforces this point, asserting that 'for women to be able to make coherent choices about their own care and the care of their prematurely born foetuses, they must appropriately understand the actual meaning of prematurity and the possible short and long term consequences'.[25] Competent adults often prepare advance care directives about their health and wellbeing; thus, 'competent parents' should be afforded the same liberty as regards potential life-changing circumstances that will affect them.

Of course, the thought of a premature disabled infant and the reality are markedly different. Understandably, parents' attitudes may change radically after birth. However, a prenatal advanced directive is a powerful tool, creating a platform for an honest and open discussion about the realities of premature birth and possible associated disability or even death.

7.5 Parliamentary intervention

Chapter 2 of this book discussed the development of case law with regard to decisions to withdraw or withhold life-sustaining treatment from critically ill infants. Three decades on from the case of Baby Pearson in 1980 in the UK, treatment decisions for critically impaired infants remain fraught with subjectivity.

It must be questioned whether the courts should be presiding over cases concerning whether impaired infants live or die when this is unsupported by statute. A host of considerations, moral, legal and constitutional, support the view that parliament as a democratically elected institution is the correct home for such a determination, and that the courts should not play the role of moral arbiter.[26]

A policy-based approach to end of life decision making for infants born at the edge of viability – that is, at 23 weeks – is perhaps the best means of development of a legislative framework. Such a framework could stipulate a minimum threshold at which those born premature and suffering pain and ongoing debilitation should not be resuscitated.

As noted earlier in this chapter, such a debate is unlikely to occur in the current climate of either the UK or Australia. That parliament adopts an inherently conservative approach to legislative and ethical change is evident in the ongoing debate surrounding voluntary active euthanasia for competent adults, despite 85% of Australians supporting this initiative.[27] However, academic and community

---

25 Anita Catlin, 'Thinking Outside the Box: Prenatal Care and the Call for a Prenatal Advance Directive' (2005) 19(2) *Journal of Perinatal & Neonatal Nursing* 169, 172.
26 A view shared by L Willmott and Ben White, 'A Model Form of Decision Making at the End-of-life: Queensland and Beyond' (2006) 25(1) *Medicine and Law* 201, 208.
27 *Queensland Times*, 'Seven in 10 Support Voluntary Euthanasia' 19 November 2012. www.qt.com.au/news/seven-10-support-voluntary-euthanasia/1627273/

interest in the issue could, through the democratic process, compel this issue on to the parliamentary agenda.

7.6 Concluding remarks

Just over three decades ago, discussion concerning withdrawing or withholding life-sustaining treatment from critically ill infants began to receive serious public, political and legal attention in the UK and Australia. Today the area continues to be fraught with ethical, moral and legal issues and remains unresolved.

The aim of this book was twofold: to identify the deficiencies in the manner in which these decisions are currently being made; and to recommend that limited healthcare resources inform end of life decision making for extremely premature and impaired infants, and, by doing so, inject greater objectivity and transparency into the process.

To meet the objectives of this book, it was necessary to critically examine the key factors currently affecting life and death decision making with regard to critically impaired infants, and further to identify the most problematic and contentious issues hindering objectivity, transparency and uniformity.

This book has confirmed that the manner in which decisions are made to withdraw or withhold life-sustaining treatment from critically impaired infants is inconsistent, not transparent and heavily influenced by the subjective opinions, beliefs and emotions of caregivers and decision makers. The development of sophisticated technologies means that extremely premature and critically impaired infants, who 20–30 years ago would have died, now live. This includes infants born at the edge of viability at 23 weeks' gestation (a stage of development at which abortion is still legal).

Although infants can now be saved from death at 23 weeks, the current state of technology and medical science means that these infants continue to be at risk of severe disability. As one commentator candidly asserted: 'science is moving fast, but until we invent an amniotic sac, there's a big cost to these babies, and nature is against their survival.'[28]

This book has focused on decision making in the UK and Australia. While Australia only has a handful of cases on record that have required coronial or legal intervention, English case law has an abundance of cases in which medical practitioners and parents have disagreed on the withdrawal or withholding of life-sustaining treatment from premature and critically impaired infants.

Chapter 2 critically examined case judgments, highlighting the lack of consistency in the courts in attempting to reconcile the sanctity of life principle, a longstanding tenet of society, with making decisions that uphold dignity and serve a patient's best interests. Judges often apply nebulous and ill-defined principles such as futile treatment and poor quality of life, and weigh up the burdens of

---

28 Tracey McVeigh, 'I Would Have Wanted Him to Die in My Arms', *Sunday Herald Sun Magazine, The Herald Sun* (Australia), 17 April 2011, 18.

treatment against the benefits it will confer in a scoreboard-like fashion, arguably cloaking decisions that ultimately amount to the lawful withdrawal or withholding of life-sustaining treatment.

The over-reliance on medical opinion by the courts further underscores the reluctance of the courts to drive any meaningful reform of the law in this area. This has given rise to the current situation in which determinations are unpredictable, often almost arbitrary and seemingly driven by the idiosyncratic sentiments of the decision maker.

In Chapter 3, a critical evaluation of the most current clinical guidelines in the UK and Australia found that they, too, are interspersed with inconsistencies and lack any codification or uniformity. While the 2006 Nuffield Report on Bioethics was commended for attempting to provide further guidance and certainty, it was ultimately a missed opportunity to generate any robust reforms. The inter-relationship between the courts and doctors also came to the fore in the discussion of these guidelines, which advocate a holistic approach encompassing ethical, legal and clinical factors in decision making. It appears that judges rely on medical opinion and doctors rely on case decisions when developing guidelines to assist in decision making.

Overall, the one aspect of uniformity that exists between these guidelines is their variability. In a particularly stark example, guidelines within the same country, and even within the same state, all provide different gestational ages at which resuscitation is 'best practice'.

Chapter 4 examined the roles and influence of the key caregivers and decision makers – parents, doctors and judges – as an integral part of the decision-making process. Inconsistency and subjectivity in decision making was strongly evident.

Chapter 5 explored selected theories of distributive justice and resource allocation. The chapter concluded that no one theory is plausible in light of the societal constraints in which we live. However, Chapter 5 did highlight that there is a need for discussions about resource allocation and it should be an important factor in end of life decision making.

The penultimate chapter of this book then discussed resource allocation as an objective factor in decision making in greater detail. Moral, cultural and religious values and norms continue to render discussing human life in monetary terms taboo. However, in the end, (near) impossible choices appear to be driven by the thinking that finite resources should not be devoted to saving and extending all life. Framing end of life decisions relating to extremely premature and critically impaired infants in these terms would therefore be in line with that which informs most life-defining medical decisions. Moreover, doing so transparently would improve the soundness of end of life decisions for impaired infants. The suggestion made here that the allocation of finite healthcare resources should drive medical choices relating to premature infants is not novel. However, a key contribution of this book to the research and thinking in this area is in showing that, in reality, resource allocation considerations already influence medical decisions.

The brief discussion of the key points of each chapter just given serves to highlight the present inconsistent and highly subjective state of decision making as regards the withdrawing or withholding of life-sustaining treatment for critically impaired infants. This book argues that a formalised process is required at a national level, formulated on objective and pragmatic principles. This could be achieved with reference to the following points:

1   An immediate focus on resource allocation, where decisions to save and preserve damaged lives are made in consideration of the immediate costs of medical treatment, the costs of disability for the family, requirements for long-term care, and the benefits and associated costs of life, not only to the patient but also to society.
2   An immediate discussion of this topic by parliament, with the eventual aim of a legislated, mandatory and national framework for decision making.

The conservative social and political climate of Australia, and to a lesser extent in the UK, explains why the discussion continues around the issue of end of life decision making for impaired infants three decades on from the cases of the 1980s. This book has attempted to raise general consciousness of the issue, particularly against the present-day backdrop of improving medical technologies and declining healthcare monies. With improvements in technology, there will no doubt be a greater number of infants surviving at 23 weeks, despite the future prospects of these infants remaining bleak.

It is unlikely that, in the near future, resource allocation in end of life decision making for extremely premature and impaired infants will be given the serious consideration it deserves. In light of this, this book proposes the adoption of less confronting approaches (as compared with the basing of life and death decisions on resource allocation) that can be actioned now, such as a focus on prevention of premature birth.

While critically impaired and extremely premature infants *can* be kept alive, in most instances they probably *should not* be. This book recognises and acknowledges that decisions to withdraw or withhold life-sustaining treatment leading to inevitable death should not be taken lightly. Moreover, this book does not take a position that a life with disability is a worthless life. However, despite medical practitioners' best efforts and the deployment of substantial public funds to keep extremely premature and critically impaired infants alive, they are often left with lifelong debilitating disabilities.

That we are unable to provide such support, which has far greater resource implications than the act of saving them in the first instance, is a moral failing in its own right. As a society, in making the choice to actively save impaired infants and compel them to live a life of pain and disability, we are failing in not providing requisite standards of care post-NICU support. Until medical technology advances to the point that saving extremely premature infants does more good than harm, doing so remains detrimental to the infant, family and society. In choosing to preserve such lives, are we making decisions that are best for the infants, best for the parents, or best for our collective moral conscience as a society?

7.7 References

Achilles, Darin, 'Examining the Groningen Protocol: Comparing the Treatment of Terminally-Ill Infants in the Netherlands with Treatment Given in the United States and England' (2010) 28(4) *Wisconsin International Law Journal* 795.

Bennett, Belinda, 'Resource Allocation and the Beginning of Life' (1993) 9 (Spring) *Journal of Contemporary Health Law & Policy* 77.

Catlin, Anita, 'Thinking Outside the Box: Prenatal Care and the Call for a Prenatal Advance Directive' (2005) 19(2) *Journal of Perinatal & Neonatal Nursing* 169.

Doward, Jamie, 'Rise in School Leaving Age is Predicted to Cut Number of Teenage Pregnancies', *Guardian* (Online), 7 April 2013. www.guardian.co.uk/society/2013/apr/07/teenage-pregnancy-school-leaving-age

Guyer, Ruth Levy, *Baby at Risk* (Capital Books, 2006).

Harrison, Helen, 'The Offer They Can't Refuse: Parents and Perinatal Treatment Decisions' (2008) 13(5) *Seminars in Fetal and Neonatal Medicine* 329.

Huibers, Alex K, 'Beyond the Threshold of Life: Treating and Non-Treating of Critically Ill Newborns in the Netherlands' (1995) 16(2) *Journal of Legal Medicine* 227.

Jotkowitz, Alan, S Glick and B Gesundheit, 'A Case against Justified Non-voluntary Active Euthanasia (The Groningen Protocol)' (2008) 8(11) *American Journal of Bioethics* 23.

Lindemann, Hilde and Marian Verkerk, 'Ending the Life of a Newborn: The Groningen Protocol' (2008) 38(1) *Hastings Center Report* 42.

McVeigh, Tracey, 'I Would Have Wanted Him to Die in My Arms', *Sunday Herald Sun Magazine, The Herald Sun* (Australia), 17 April 2011.

Miller, Barbara, 'Euthansia Law: Belgium Passes Legislation Giving Terminally Ill Children Right to Die', *ABC News* (Online), 14 February. www.abc.net.au/news/2014-02-14/belgium-child-euthanasia-law/5259314

Muraskas, Jonathan and Kayhan Parsi, 'The Cost of Saving the Tiniest Lives: NICUs versus Prevention' (2008) 10(10) *Virtual Mentor* 655, 657.

Paranjothy, Shantini, Hannah K Broughton, Roshan Adappa and David Fone, 'Teenage Pregnancy: Who Suffers?' (2009) 94(3) *Archives of Disease in Childhood: Fetal and Neonatal* 239.

Queensland Times, 'Seven in 10 Support Voluntary Euthanasia' 19 November 2012. www.qt.com.au/news/seven-10-support-voluntary-euthanasia/1627273

Sauer, Pieter J J and A A Eduard Verhagen, 'The Groningen Protocol, Unfortunately Misunderstood' (2009) 96(1) *Neonatology* 11.

Savulescu, Julian, 'Abortion, Infanticide and Allowing Babies to Die, 40 Years On' (2013) 39(5) *Journal of Medical Ethics* 257.

Smith, Gordon C S and Jill P Pell, 'Teenage Pregnancy and Risk of Adverse Perinatal Outcomes Associated with First and Second Births: Population Based Retrospective Cohort Study' (2001) 323(September) *British Medical Journal* 476.

Verhagen, A A Eduard, 'The Groningen Protocol for Newborn Euthanasia; Which Way Did the Slippery Slope Tilt?' (2013) 39(5) *Journal of Medical Ethics* 293.

Verhagen, A A E and P J J Sauer, 'End-of-life Decisions in Newborns: An Approach from the Netherlands' (2005) 116(3) *Pediatrics* 736.

Verhagen, A A Eduard and P J J Sauer, 'The Groningen Protocol – Euthanasia in Severely Ill Newborns' (2005) 352(10) *New England Journal of Medicine* 959.

Webb, R T, C E Marshall and K M Abel, 'Teenage Motherhood and Risk of Premature Death: Long-Term Follow-up in the ONS Longitudinal Study' (2011) 41(9) *Psychological Medicine* 1867.

Weightman, Alison L, Helen E Morgan, Michael A Shepherd, Hilary Kitcher, Chris Roberts and Frank D Dunstan, 'Social Inequality and Infant Health in the UK: Systematic Review and Meta-Analyses' (2012) 2(3) *BMJ Open* 1.

Willmott, L and Ben White, 'A Model Form of Decision Making at the End-of-life: Queensland and Beyond' (2006) 25(1) *Medicine and Law* 201.

Wishart, Adam, *The Price of Life* (BBC Productions, 2011.

Index

artificial feeding, withdrawal or
  withholding of, 65–6 *see also* life-
  sustaining treatment, withdrawal or
  withholding of
Australian clinical guidelines, 73, 75,
  89–99
  individual hospital specific, 91–2
  Royal Australasian College of
    Physicians, 89–91
  uniform, need for, 97–8
autonomy, 2, 150–1
  best interests principle and, 27
  deemed, 39–40
  family, 103
  hospital, 84, 102
  individual, 3, 19, 105, 126, 190, 207
  infants, 99, 134, 142, 151
  medical practitioners, 41, 126–7,
    137
  parental, 124
  patient, 6, 21, 27

beneficence, 151
best interests principle, 9, 140–1, 196
  acts and omissions and, 32–4
  Australian case law, early, 54–7
  Australian case law, recent, 61–6
  autonomy and, 27
  Bolam test and, 29–30
  Bland and, 26–9
  courts and, 9, 20, 32, 66, 73
  doctors and, 29, 138
  effectiveness of, 40, 52, 66–7
  Family Law Rules 2004 and, 60–1
  futility and, 19–21
  life sustaining treatment and, 34–5
  proposition five and, 52–3
  Re Marion and, 57–9
  Re Marion (No 2) and, 60–1

reliance on the medical profession,
  29–32
right to life and, 21
Royal Australasian College of
  Physicians clinical guidelines, 89
sanctity of life principles and, 13–19,
  27–8
substituted judgment test and, 28–9
UK case law, early, 21–6
UK case law, impaired infants, 36–44
UK case law, recent, 45–54
vagueness of, 50, 59,
withdrawal of nutrition and hydration
  and, 34–6
Bland, 2, 25, 26–36, 43–4, 80, 98, 199
Bolam test, 29–30, 98, 141
borderline of viability, 4, 74, 94
  Consensus Statement, New South
    Wales and Australian Capital
    Territory, 92–5
British Association of Perinatal Medicine
  clinical guidelines, 85–7
British Medical Association clinical
  guidelines, 79–80
burdens and benefits of medical treatment
  balance sheet approach to, 47, 80

clinical guidelines
  academic discussion of, 95–7
  Australia *see* Australian clinical
    guidelines
  nature of, 75
  need for uniformity in, 75, 86, 92, 97–8,
    102, 141, 213, 214
  United Kingdom *see* United Kingdom
    clinical guidelines
consent, 3, 20, 58, 62, 124, 208, 209
  doctors and, 139
  jurisdictional power to determine, 104

consequentialist theory, 153–5, 187
courts *see also* judiciary
  best interests principle and, 9, 20, 32,
    66, 73
  futility and, 21
  resource allocation and, 197–9
  role in end-of-life decision making, 5–6,
    21, 25, 26, 30–1, 36–66, 97, 98,
    140–2, 212–4
critically impaired infants
  early Australian case law, 54–7
  end-of-life decision making for *see* end-
    of-life decision making
  prevention rather than cure and,
    209–211
  quality adjusted life years, 165–9
  resource allocation and *see* resource
    allocation
  survival rate, EPICure studies (UK),
    82–5
  technological and scientific
    developments and *see* medical
    technology
  treatment of, comparison to other
    patient types, 170
  withdrawal or withholding of medical
    treatment *see* life-sustaining
    treatment, withdrawal or withholding
    of; medical treatment, withdrawal or
    withholding of

Declaration of Geneva, 17–19, 151
deontology, 155–7
disability
  doctors' perceptions of, 129–132
  impact on wider family, 124, 125,
    179–180
  insurance scheme, Australia *see* National
    Disability Insurance Scheme
  opportunity cost and, 180–3
  parental perceptions and realities of,
    114–115
  perceptions of, 116–118, 131, 166
distributive justice, 151–2
  consequentialist theory, 153–5
  deontology, 155–7
  egalitarian theory, 157–8
doctors
  as functionaries, 137–9
  best interests of the patient and, 29, 138
  change in doctor-patient dynamic and,
    126–7
  conflicting interests and views of, 126–7
  consent and, 139

'framing effect' and, 134–6
  futility and, 139
  infant pain and suffering and, 130, 135
  information from parents, exclusion of,
    139
  junior, 79
  knowledge of the law, 142–3
  perceptions of death and disability,
    129–32
  personal beliefs and attitudes of, 127
  religious beliefs and cross-country
    attitudes and, 127–9
  'roster lottery' and, 136–7
  'staging' of communication with
    parents, 125
  treatment of different types of parents
    by, 132–3
doctrine of causation, 36
doctrine of necessity, 44

egalitarianism, 157–8
efficacy of NICU
  Australia, 172–3
  United Kingdom, 173–4
  United States, 169–71
end of life decision making *see also* medical
    treatment, withdrawal or withholding
    of *see also* life-sustaining treatment,
    withdrawal or withholding
    of best-interests principle and
    see best-interests principle
  Bland and, 26–35
  care givers and, 58–9
  hospital frameworks for, 76, 87, 89, 92,
    99
  intolerability and *see* intolerability
  importance of for critically impaired
    infants, 4–6
  judiciary and *see* judiciary
  lack of consistency in Australian
    hospitals and, 92
  parens patriae jurisdiction and, 20, 104
  quality of life and *see* quality of life
  religious, cultural and subjective beliefs
    and, 6, 9, 138, 151
  resource allocation and *see* resource
    allocation role of courts in, 5–6, 20,
    23, 26, 30, 32 *see also* best interests
    principle *see also* judiciary
  sanctity of life principle and *see* sanctity
    of life principle
EPICure studies (UK), 82–5, 87, 127, 173
  Study 1, 1995, 82–3
  Study 2, 2006, 83–4

ethical considerations
  autonomy *see* autonomy
  beneficence, 127, 151 *see also* best
    interests principle
  egalitarian theory, 157–8
  justice, distributive *see* distributive justice
  medical *see* medical ethics
  non-maleficence, 16, 127, 150, 151
  rights theory and, 154, 155–7
euthanasia, 17, 31–3, 36, 54, 189, 191
  active, 88
  Declaration of Geneva and, 17
  Hippocratic Oath and, 17
  Nuffield Council on Bioethics and, 86,
  permissible, Groningen protocol, 88,
    207–9
  Royal College of Obstetricians and
    Gynaecologists and, 88
  voluntary, 3, 156, 196
extremely premature infants *see* critically
    impaired infants

futility, 44, 47, 54, 66, 80, 87, 91, 196,
    198, 208
  best interests principle and, 19–21
  concept of, 21, 34–5, 77
  courts and, 21
  doctors and, 99, 138–9

General Medical Council clinical
    guidelines, 81
government economic budget pressures
  Australia, 183–4
  United Kingdom, 184–5
Groningen protocol, 88, 207–9

health economics *see also* resource
    allocation
  ageing populations and, 7, 152, 159,
    162, 169
  beyond the NICU, 176–9
  cost v benefit, 163
  definition of, 162
  government economic budget pressures
    and, 183–5
  opportunity cost and, 180–3
  quality adjusted life years, 165–9
health care resources, allocation to
    critically impaired infants *see* resource
    allocation
Hippocratic Oath, 15–17, 18, 151
hydration and nutrition, withdrawal of, 26,
    34–41, 44–5 *see also* artificial feeding,
    withdrawal or withholding of *see also*

life-sustaining treatment, withdrawal
    or withholding of

incapacitated infants *see* critically impaired
    infants
infants
  end-of-life decision making for *see* end-
    of-life decision making
  extremely premature *see* critically
    impaired infants
  impaired *see* critically impaired infants
  incapacitated *see* critically impaired
    infants pain and suffering, doctors
    and, 130, 135
  pain and suffering, parental response to,
    113, 123
  resource allocation to *see* resource
    allocation
intolerability, 9, 44, 54, 78, 80, 87, 90

judiciary *see also* courts
  medical opinion and, 140–3, 150
  role in resource allocation, 196–9
  sanctity of life and, 24, 27–8, 33, 35,
    38–40, 42–3, 66

life
  obligation to preserve, 19, 50, 131, 189
  sanctity of *see* sanctity of life
life and law, concept of, 2–3
life-sustaining treatment *see also* end-of-life
    decision making; medical treatment,
    withdrawal or withholding of
  parents and, 25, 124–5, 189–90
  requests for, 4, 80, 125
  withdrawal of withholding of, 2, 4, 5–6,
    7, 8, 19, 26, 29, 34–41, 44–5, 47, 50,
    52, 54, 61, 62–7, 73, 76–80, 90, 92,
    97, 98, 109, 111, 130, 140, 142, 143,
    151, 161, 183, 196, 212, 213 *see also*
    artificial feeding, withdrawal or
    withholding of *see also* hydration and
    nutrition, withdrawal of

media
  coverage of 'miracle babies' by, 106,
    107, 176
  lack of realistic survival rate coverage
    by, 107–8
  portrayal of idyllic, resilient family by,
    179
  push for futile treatment by, 120, 210
medical ethics, 2, 30
  Declaration of Geneva, 17–19

Greco-Roman principles and
    Hippocratic Oath, 15–17
Judeo-Christian tradition, 13–15
medical law, 1–2
medical technology, 74, 106, 162, 176,
    210
    development of incubators, 7
    doing harm or good, 189–93, 215
    overreliance on, 190
    relationship to disability, 133, 189
medical treatment
    costs of, 152 159, 169, 197–8, 200, 215
      see also resource allocation
    withdrawal or withholding of, 3, 22, 27,
      34, 36, 50, 76, 78, 79–80 *see also* end
      of life decision making; life-
      sustaining treatment, withdrawal or
      withholding of
    Bland and, 26–36
    Bolam test and, 28, 30, 98, 141
    clinical guidelines *see* clinical guidelines
    critically impaired infants *see* critically
      impaired infants
    differentiation between 'act' and
      'omission', 32–4
    early UK case law, 21–6
    'good medical practice' and, 54–5
    incapacitated patients and, 3, 19, 25
    lethal injection scenario, 33–4
    'necessary and reasonable steps' and, 55
    need for national, formalised process,
      215
    parents and *see* treatment decisions,
      parents and 'miracle babies', 106,
      107, 119, 176–7, 179, 192

National Disability Insurance Scheme,
    185–9
    consequential benefits from, 188
    legislation, 185–6
    ramifications of, 187
neonatal intensive care unit (NICU)
    cost of, 163–5, 167, 169, 187, 190–2
    efficacy of *see* efficacy of NICU
    health economics beyond, 176–9
    parent perception of, 5
    profitability of, 174–6
    survival rate of infants in, 82, 87, 107–8,
      163, 169–72
neonatology
    historical development of, 6–7
non-maleficence, 151
Nuffield Council on Bioethics report, 9,
    86–9, 103, 214

'partnership of care' and, 87
survival rates of premature infants,
    74–5, 87

opportunity cost, 180–3

palliative care
    physiological response to, 35
parents, 7
    autonomy as decision-makers, 103,
      124–6
    bias of, 112–3
    conflicting interests and views of,
      104–24
    decision-making, burden of
      responsibility in, 120–4
    different types of, treatment by doctors,
      118–20
    'dying process' and, 114–5
    ethnicity and, 110–13
    'everything done' and, 113
    guilt and, 108, 117–8, 120–4
    hope and, 96, 105–6, 108, 109–10
    life experience and, 111–12
    media influence and scientific
      developments and, 105–8
    pain and suffering of infant and, 113,
      123
    perception of NICU, 5
    perceptions and realities of disability
      and, 116–18
    prenatal advance directives and, 211–12
    religious and cultural beliefs and,
      108–9
    requests for treatment by, 4–5
    transparency in decision-making
      process and, 127
    treatment decisions and *see* treatment
      decisions, parents and
    trust and confidence in medical team
      and, 92, 98, 118–20
    wishes of, 23, 45, 73, 85, 87, 118, 122,
      125, 136, 143, 189, 196
    withdrawal of life-sustaining treatment
      and, 25, 124–5, 189–90
Pharmaceutical Benefits Scheme
    (Australia), 195–6
premature birth
    contributing factors to, UK, 74
    disability and, 138, 173
    prevention of, 210, 215
    relationship to poverty, 211
pre-natal advance directives,
    211–12

price of life, determination of
　Pharmaceutical Benefits Scheme
　　(Australia), 195–6
　road toll deaths and, 193–4
　triage/emergency room and, 194–5

quality adjusted life years, 165–9
quality of life, 7, 9, 19, 40, 44, 51–3, 54–6,
　　75, 81, 88, 97, 116–8, 128, 131, 177,
　　183, 197–8, 208, 213
　dictionary definition of, 65
　future, 39
　dismissal of concept of, 54–5
　resource allocation and, 27

Re Marion, 57–9
Re Marion (No 2), 60–1
resource allocation *see also* health
　　economics
　as cardinal consideration in treatment
　　decisions, 9, 143, 150, 158–9, 161
　critically impaired infants, 8–9, 158–9,
　　161–96
　distributive justice and *see* distributive
　　justice
　educational awareness and, 210–11
　egalitarian theory and, 157–8
　'noble lie' and, 196
　Parliamentary intervention and, 212–13
　poverty reduction and, 210–11
　prevention of premature birth and, 210,
　　215
　role of judiciary in, 196–9
　utilitarianism and, 153–5
right to life, 155–6
　best interests principle and, 21
　recognition of, 2
rights theory, 154, 155–6
　Royal Australasian College of
　　Physicians
　　best interests principle and, 89
　　clinical guidelines, 89–91
　Royal College of Obstetricians and
　　Gynaecologists, 88

Royal College of Paediatrics and Child
　　Health clinical guidelines, 76–9, 80,
　　87, 88, 89, 98
　junior doctors and, 79
　situations where ethical to consider
　　termination of life-sustaining
　　treatment, 76–7

sanctity of life, 3, 13
　Bland and, 26–9
　early UK case law and, 19, 21–7
　judiciary and, 27–8, 33, 35, 38–40,
　　42–3, 66
　shift away from, 19, 24, 31
sanctity of life perspectives, 13–19
　Declaration of Geneva, 17–19, 151
　Greco-Roman principles and the
　　Hippocratic Oath, 15–17, 151
　Judeo-Christian, 13–15
substituted judgment test, 28–9
sterilization, non-therapeutic
　Re Marion and, 57–9
　Re Marion (No 2) and, 60–1

technology *see* medical technology
treatment decisions, parents and, 6,
　　10, 19
　Family Court of Australia jurisdiction
　　and, 57
　Family Law Act 1975 (Cth) and, 62

United Kingdom clinical guidelines, 75–6
　British Association of Perinatal
　　Medicine, 85–6
　British Medical Association, 79–80
　General Medical Council, 81
　Royal College of Paediatrics and Child
　　Health, 76–9, 89
utilitarianism, 153–5, 157, 158

withdrawal or withholding of medical
　　treatment *see* medical treatment,
　　withdrawal or withholding of
worthwhileness, 47